EARLY GREEK WARFARE

EARLY GREEK WARFARE
HORSEMEN AND CHARIOTS IN THE
HOMERIC AND ARCHAIC AGES

P. A. L. GREENHALGH

CAMBRIDGE
AT THE UNIVERSITY PRESS 1973

CAMBRIDGE UNIVERSITY PRESS
Cambridge, New York, Melbourne, Madrid, Cape Town, Singapore,
São Paulo, Delhi, Dubai, Tokyo, Mexico City

Cambridge University Press
The Edinburgh Building, Cambridge CB2 8RU, UK

Published in the United States of America by Cambridge University Press, New York

www.cambridge.org
Information on this title: www.cambridge.org/9780521181280

© Cambridge University Press 1973

This publication is in copyright. Subject to statutory exception
and to the provisions of relevant collective licensing agreements,
no reproduction of any part may take place without the written
permission of Cambridge University Press.

First published 1973
First paperback edition 2010

A catalogue record for this publication is available from the British Library

Library of Congress Catalogue Card Number: 72-87437

ISBN 978-0-521-20056-1 Hardback
ISBN 978-0-521-18128-0 Paperback

Cambridge University Press has no responsibility for the persistence or
accuracy of URLs for external or third-party internet websites referred to in
this publication, and does not guarantee that any content on such websites is,
or will remain, accurate or appropriate.

TO MARY

CONTENTS

Sources of Illustrations	ix
Abbreviations	xi
Note on chronology and chronological terms	xiii
Acknowledgments	xvi
Introduction	1
I The Chariot in Homer	7
II The Chariot in Geometric Art	19
III The Homeric *Hippēes*	40
IV Dipylon Warrior, Hoplite, and Cavalryman	63
V Mounted Warriors in the Seventh Century	84
Corinth	84
Athens	88
Euboea	90
Other States	93
VI Mounted Warriors in the Sixth Century	96
Corinth	96
Athens	111
'Chalcidian'	136
East Greece	143
VII Conclusions	146
Appendix: The Historical Basis of the Homeric Background Picture	156
Notes	173
Lists of Vase-Paintings	186
Index of Collections	196
Bibliography	200
General Index	206

SOURCES OF ILLUSTRATIONS

1 After F. Studniczka, *Jdl*, 22 (1907), 149, fig. 2.
2 After W. Reichel, *Homerische Waffen* (Vienna, 1901), p. 139, fig. 88.
3 The American School of Classical Studies at Athens (Agora Excavations).
4 After G. Lippold, *Münchener Archäologische Studien* (1909), 451, fig. 21.
5 Drawing by Martin Jones after H. L. Lorimer, *Homer and the Monuments* (London, 1950), pl. 25.1.
6 Drawing by Martin Jones after W. Reichel, *Homerische Waffen*, p. 125, fig. 67.
7 Drawing by Martin Jones after W. Reichel, *Homerische Waffen*, p. 124, fig, 64.
8 The British Museum (by courtesy of the Trustees).
9 The Royal Ontario Museum, Toronto.
10 Rijksmuseum van Oudheden te Leiden.
11 Staatliche Museen, Berlin (West).
12 Dr R. C. Bronson.
13 Metropolitan Museum of Art, New York: Rogers Fund, 1910.
14 Metropolitan Museum of Art, New York: Rogers Fund, 1921.
15 Kunstsammlung der Universität Erlangen.
16 The British Museum (by courtesy of the Trustees).
17 The British Museum (by courtesy of the Trustees).
18 Archäologisches Institut der Universität des Saarlandes.
19 The American School of Classical Studies at Athens (Agora Excavations).
20 After *Eph. Arch.*, 1896, pl. 3.
21 After A. J. Evans, *The Palace of Minos* (London, 1921–36), vol. 4, p. 816, fig. 795 (by courtesy of the Trustees of Sir Arthur Evans' estate).
22 After A. J. Evans, *P of M*, vol. 4, p. 788, fig. 763a (by courtesy of the Trustees of Sir Arthur Evans' estate).
23 After A. J. Evans, *P of M*, vol. 4, p. 823, fig. 803 (by courtesy of the Trustees of Sir Arthur Evans' estate).
24 Drawing by Martin Jones after A. Furtwängler and G. Loeschcke, *Mykenische Vasen* (Berlin, 1886), pl. 41, no. 427.
25 After Curtius and Adler, *Olympia*, vol. 4 (Berlin, 1890), pl. 15, no. 253.
26 Archäologisches Institut der Universität des Saarlandes.
27 Staatliche Museen, Berlin (West).
28 Drawing after C. F. A. Schaeffer, *Ugaritica*, vol. 2, p. 158, fig. 61C (a).
29 The National Archaeological Museum, Athens.
30 Archaeologisch-Historisch Instituut der Universiteit van Amsterdam, Allard Pierson Stichting.
31 After *Eph. Arch.*, 1904, pl. 3.
32 Deutsches Archäologisches Institut, Abteilung Athen.
33 After *AM*, 18 (1893), pl. 8.2.
34 Deutsches Archäologisches Institut, Abteilung Athen.
35 Staatliche Museen zu Berlin (East).
36 Drawing after photographs supplied by the National Archaeological Museum, Athens.
37 The British Museum (by courtesy of the Trustees).
38 After *AM*, 17 (1892), 215, fig. 4.
39 The British Museum (by courtesy of the Trustees).
40 After G. Perrot and C. Chipiez, *Histoire de l'Art*, vol. 7, p. 179, fig. 63.
41 Deutsches Archäologisches Institut, Abteilung Athen.
42 Deutsches Archäologisches Institut, Abteilung Athen.
43 The American School of Classical Studies at Athens (Corinth Excavations).

SOURCES OF ILLUSTRATIONS

44 Staatliche Museen zu Berlin (East).
45 After *Perachora*, vol. 2, pl. 61, no. 1571 (by kind permission of the Managing Committee of the British School of Archaeology at Athens).
46 After *Perachora*, vol. 2, pl. 97, no. 2434 (by kind permission of the Managing Committee of the British School of Archaeology at Athens).
47 After *Perachora*, vol. 2, pl. 61, no. 1556 (by kind permission of the Managing Committee of the British School of Archaeology at Athens).
48 After *Perachora*, vol. 2, pl. 61, no. 1590 (by kind permission of the Managing Committee of the British School of Archaeology at Athens).
49 The National Archaeological Museum, Athens.
50 After A. Furtwängler, *Sammlung Somzée* (Munich, 1897), pl. 43.
51 Deutsches Archäologisches Institut, Abteilung Athen.
52 The British Museum (by courtesy of the Trustees).
53 Herzog Anton Ulrich-Museum, Braunschweig (Museumsfoto: B. P. Keiser).
54 Lowie Museum of Anthropology, University of California, Berkeley.
55 Antikenmuseum der Karl-Marx-Universität, Leipzig.
56 After *Mon. Ant.*, 22 (1913), pl. 57.
57 Soprintendenza alle Antichità della Puglia, Taranto.
58 After B. Graef, *Die antiken Vasen von der Akropolis zu Athen* (Berlin, 1909), pl. 31.
59 Antikenmuseum der Karl-Marx-Universität, Leipzig.
60 The British Museum (by courtesy of the Trustees).
61 After *Corpus Vasorum Antiquorum*, Italy 20 (Naples 1), pl. 950 (by kind permission of Instituto Poligrafico dello Stato, Libreria dello Stato, Roma).
62 The British Museum (by courtesy of the Trustees).
63 Muzeum Narodowe w Warszawie.
64 Musée du Louvre, Paris (Photo: Chuzeville).
65 Staatliche Museen, Berlin (West).
66 The British Museum (by courtesy of the Trustees).
67 Metropolitan Museum of Art, New York: Rogers Fund, 1941.
68 Acropolis Museum, Athens (by kind permission of Mr J. Miliadis and Mr George Dontas).
69 Musée du Louvre, Paris (Photo: Chuzeville).
70 Martin von Wagner-Museum der Universität Würzburg.
71 Musées Royaux d'Art et d'Histoire, Bruxelles.
72 Musée du Louvre, Paris (Photo: Chuzeville).
73 Martin von Wagner-Museum der Universität Würzburg.
74 Musée du Louvre, Paris (Photo: Chuzeville).
75 Martin von Wagner-Museum der Universität Würzburg.
76 Museum of the Hermitage, Leningrad.
77 After A. S. Murray, *Terracotta Sarcophagi in the British Museum* (London, 1898), pl. 1.
78 Staatliche Antikensammlungen und Glyptothek, München.

ABBREVIATIONS

This list excludes specific works whose abbreviations are simply the authors' names or are always preceded by the authors' names whenever they are cited. They will be found in alphabetical order of authors in the bibliography, pp. 200–205.

AA	*Archäologischer Anzeiger*
ABV	J. D. Beazley, *Attic Black-Figure Vase-Painters* (Oxford, 1956)
AE	Ἀρχαιολογικὴ Ἐφημερίς
AJA	*American Journal of Archaeology*
AM	*Mitteilungen des deutschen archäologischen Instituts, Athenische Abteilung*
Ann. dell'Inst.	*Annali dell'Instituto di Corrispondenza Archeologica*
Arch. Hom.	*Archaeologica Homerica* (Göttingen)
Argive Heraeum	C. Waldstein, *The Argive Heraeum* (Boston, 1902–5)
Artemis Orthia	'The Sanctuary of Artemis Orthia at Sparta', *JHS*, Supp. 5 (London, 1929)
ARV	J. D. Beazley, *Attic Red-Figure Vase-Painters* (Oxford, 1963)
Asine	C. Frödin and A. W. Persson, *Asine: Results of the Swedish Excavations, 1922–30*
BCH	*Bulletin de Correspondance hellénique*
Bf	Black Figure
BMQ	*British Museum Quarterly*
BSA	*Annual of the British School at Athens*
CQ	*Classical Quarterly*
CVA	*Corpus Vasorum Antiquorum*
EC	Early (Ripe) Corinthian (625–600 B.C.)

ABBREVIATIONS

EG	Early Geometric (900–850 B.C. for Attic)
EGAW	A. M. Snodgrass, *Early Greek Armour and Weapons* (Edinburgh, 1964)
EPA	Early Protoattic (*c.* 700–680 B.C.)
EPC	Early Protocorinthian (*c.* 720–700 B.C.)
EVP	J. D. Beazley, *Etruscan Vase-Painting* (Oxford, 1947)
GGP	J. N. Coldstream, *Greek Geometric Pottery* (London, 1968)
GPP	R. M. Cook, *Greek Painted Pottery* (London, 1960; 2nd edn. 1972)
HM	H. L. Lorimer, *Homer and the Monuments* (London, 1950)
JdI	*Jahrbuch des deutschen archäologischen Instituts*
JHS	*Journal of Hellenic Studies*
Kerameikos	*Kerameikos: Ergebnisse der Ausgrabungen* (6 vols., Berlin, 1939–70)
LC	Late (Ripe) Corinthian (575–550 B.C. for relevant pottery)
LG	Late Geometric (*c.* 760–700 B.C. for Attic)
LH	Late Helladic (*c.* 1600–1150 B.C.)
LM	Late Minoan (*c.* 1550–1400 B.C.)
LPC	Late Protocorinthian (650–640 B.C.)
MC	Middle (Ripe) Corinthian (600–575 B.C.)
MG	Middle Geometric (850–760 B.C. for Attic)
MMS	*Metropolitan Museum Studies*
Mon. Ant.	*Monumenti Antichi per cura della R. Accademia dei Lincei*
MPC	Middle Protocorinthian (700–650 B.C.)
Perachora	*Perachora* (2 vols., Oxford, 1931, 1962)
PG	Protogeometric (*c.* 1025–900 B.C.)
Rf	Attic Red Figure
sub-G	sub-Geometric (*c.* 700 B.C.)
Tiryns	W. Müller and F. Oelmann, *Tiryns* (1912)

NOTE ON CHRONOLOGY AND CHRONOLOGICAL TERMS

The Troy which Mycenaean Age Greeks helped to destroy, which was almost certainly Troy VIIa, fell about 1300 B.C., and the Mycenaean civilization itself did not long survive it. The last and greatest major period of Bronze Age civilization in mainland Greece, called 'Mycenaean' or 'Late Helladic' (LH), lasted from the sixteenth to the twelfth centuries, and the corresponding Late Minoan (LM) period in Crete seems to have been of shorter duration, from the sixteenth century to the fourteenth.

The collapse of the Mycenaean world in the twelfth century plunges us into the Greek Dark Ages for the next four hundred years. Throughout this period there is no evidence of the art of writing in Greece, and there are no references to Greeks in the contemporary written documents from Syria, Mesopotamia and Egypt. The communities which emerged from the period of chaos and migrations which followed the collapse were much humbler in scale and simpler in organization than the vast, bureaucratic palace-states of the Mycenaean Age, with whose passing the need for the detailed written records and catalogues of the Linear B tablets had disappeared. But the lack of written records is the only reason for speaking of the 'Dark Ages', which were certainly not a period of stagnation at a low level of culture.

Dark Age archaeology soon records technical innovations, and it was in the Dark Ages that the bulk of the Homeric epics was composed. The Age of Bronze gives way to the Iron Age in the eleventh century, and about 1025 B.C. there emerges a new style of pottery, whose characteristic geometric designs give a convenient name to the next three hundred years. Protogeometric pottery was produced from *c.* 1025 to *c.* 900 B.C., when it matured into the Geometric style

CHRONOLOGY AND CHRONOLOGICAL TERMS

proper, which spans the next two centuries (900–700 B.C.). The Geometric period itself is sub-divided into Early (EG), Middle (MG) and Late (LG), and it is the Late Geometric period of the second half of the eighth century with which I shall be particularly concerned since it provides figured vase-paintings. Most of these are Attic, and in the analysis of chariot-representations in Chapter II I follow the classification and chronology of J. N. Coldstream's *Greek Geometric Pottery*. Attic LG Ia belongs to the decade 760–750 B.C., LG Ib to the period 750–735 B.C., LG IIa to 735–720 B.C., and LG IIb to the remainder of the century.

The period from the end of the Geometric Age to the Persian Wars, from about the end of the eighth century to the early fifth, is conventionally known as the Archaic period, and it is signalled by new pottery styles. About 700 B.C. in Athens and slightly earlier in Corinth the Geometric style gives way to Protoattic and Protocorinthian, which themselves mature into the Ripe Corinthian and Attic Black Figure styles in the late seventh century. For Corinthian vase-paintings I follow the chronology given in R. M. Cook's *Greek Painted Pottery* (2nd ed., 1972) for the classifications of Payne's *Necrocorinthia*. The Protocorinthian style is subdivided into Early Protocorinthian (EPC) from 720 to 700 B.C., Middle (MPC) from 700 to 650 B.C., and Late (LPC) from 650 to 640 B.C. Between 640 and 625 B.C. there is a Transitional style, and then the Ripe Corinthian period begins, often called simply 'Corinthian'. This again has the tripartite subdivision into Early (EC), Middle (MC) and Late (LC), dated respectively 625–600 B.C., 600–575 B.C., and 575–550 B.C. For Protoattic pottery I mainly follow the dating and classification of J. M. Cook in his article 'Protoattic Pottery': Early Protoattic (EPA) lasts from about 700 to 680 B.C., Middle (MPA) from 680 to 630 B.C., and Late (LPA) from 630 B.C. to a little before the end of the seventh century. The Attic Black Figure vases of the sixth century were dated for me by Professor R. M. Cook, and I am deeply indebted to him.

This very brief chronological outline will help the reader who is not familiar with the conventional terms derived mainly from the history of vase-painting, but it is important not to be misled by them. It cannot be taken for granted that uniformity of pottery style in a particular period meant uniformity in other material culture, let alone non-material culture, and conversely a change in pottery style need not have historical significance outside the history of art. Or in the case of the terms 'Mycenaean Age' or 'Mycenaean world' applied to Bronze Age Greece from the sixteenth to the twelfth centuries, the label is justified to the extent that the type of warrior society of great wealth, power and complexity which appears at Mycenae in the sixteenth century was widespread throughout Greece and in several of the islands during the following four hundred years. But cultural uniformity does not imply political unity, and the Mycenaean world was not ruled from Mycenae in the way that the Assyrian empire for example was ruled from Assur.

ACKNOWLEDGMENTS

I have been greatly helped in my work by the encouragement and advice of Professors M. I. Finley, R. M. Cook and A. D. Momigliano, and I am most grateful to them for wise guidance and valuable criticism.

I am also indebted to Mrs Irene Bosset for the painstaking care with which she typed a difficult manuscript; to Mr Evan Jones for his skilful work in preparing photographs for the book; to Miss Irmgard Kapner for helping me with the translation of several German language articles and books; and last but not least to my wife, to whom the book is dedicated, for her constant support and help.

To Professor R. M. Cook I am further indebted for the dating of vase-paintings, for helping me to obtain many photographs, and for his constant readiness to help me in many other ways with the archaeological sources. His help has been invaluable, and I am glad to have the opportunity of recording my thanks to him.

For providing me with photographs and granting permission to reproduce them I have to thank many museums, institutions and individuals, who are detailed separately in the Sources of Illustrations. In that list the sources of permission are the same as the sources of the prints unless otherwise stated, and I am most grateful to all of them.

Finally I should like to record my thanks to the staff of the Cambridge University Press, who have been extremely kind and helpful at every stage in the production of this book.

December 1972   P.A.L.G.

INTRODUCTION

This book is an attempt to trace the military history of the chariot and the mounted horse, both as they were represented in poetry and art and as they were used in reality, from the Dark Ages which followed the collapse of the Mycenaean world to the end of the sixth century B.C. The reason for my distinction between representation and reality is that our literary and artistic sources cannot always be taken at face value. In the case of the Homeric bards, and of the Late Geometric vase-painters who similarly depicted chariots in their battles, I argue that the warfare of their own experience can be revealed only by removing a simple and transparent but highly effective veneer with which they sought to heroize it. In the seventh and especially the sixth centuries it is true that vase-painting of at least two states provides us with a good many mounted warriors whose accurate portrayal from contemporary life need not be doubted. But even here the task of the military historian is not easy because he finds few who are actually shown in combat: it often requires a very careful analysis to deduce how the majority would have fought, and scant help is provided by what little remains to us of the contemporary poets.

Chapter I examines the war-chariot as it is treated in the Homeric epic, whose battle-scenes depict it in vast numbers (to the complete exclusion of the mounted horse) but reveal no conception of its proper tactical role. The real advantage of the war-chariot lay in massed attacks at speed. This is how it was used by the Mycenaeans and by the kingdoms of the Near and Middle East which maintained large forces of chariotry both in the Bronze Age and after the Mycenaean collapse. The Homeric picture could not be more different. There the warriors use their chariots merely as transport vehicles

INTRODUCTION

from which they dismount to fight on foot, and they are not equipped with either the lance or the bow, the two weapons which made chariotry so formidable an arm after the invention of a light and fast spoke-wheeled chariot in the first half of the second millenium. J. K. Anderson has recently argued that the epic could nevertheless represent realistic Greek practice in the Geometric period, but his evidence for the parallels which he sought in British and Cyrenaic chariotry does not stand up to close examination. Moreover the fact remains that if the use of the chariot for transport to and from the battlefield is not impractical (granted reasonable terrain), the same cannot be said for the individual taxi-service which operates in the middle of the battle itself. Finally the economic argument reinforces the tactical one. The Homeric poems know nothing of the complex, bureaucratic palace-administrations which enabled the great Bronze Age kingdoms to produce and maintain their large bodies of chariots. Beneath a transparent veneer of heroizing and archaizing the economic, social and political background of the poems is seen to belong to the Geometric Age no less certainly than the pair of throwing-spears carried by the chariot-borne warrior, and it has rightly been doubted that warriors in that period could have afforded the expensive luxury of a 'war-chariot' from which they would never actually fight.

The second chapter examines the chariot as represented in Attic Late Geometric art in the second half of the eighth century. A. M. Snodgrass has argued against the existence of any true chariot in mainland Greece after the Mycenaean collapse until the very end of the eighth century, when he cites a single sherd as evidence for the introduction of what he calls the canonical form of racing-chariot from the East. All other Geometric representations of chariots he dismissed as influenced by Mycenaean representations, by the epic, or by carts and wheeled vehicles of other uses. This chapter gives the first typological analysis of the representations, which demonstrates two facts: that even the earliest were modelled on contemporary racing-chariots which were basically the same as those raced by the Athenians and other mainland Greeks in the sixth and fifth centuries, and that racing-chariots had been known for a considerable time before their first appearance in Geometric art. It is important to distinguish between the uses of the chariot. Contemporary racing-chariots were familiar both to the Homeric bards and to the Late Geometric artists, but they were not used in war. Their appearance in the battle-scenes of the epic and of the vases is attributable to archaizing on the part of the bards and, under their influence, of the Late Geometric artists. One basic fact known to the bards about their poems' ostensible period was that chariots had featured in its battles.

If then the Homeric picture of chariotry is not based on a clear knowledge of Mycenaean warfare, or even upon an exaggerated picture of the chariot as used in Geometric Age battles or upon contemporary Oriental practice, is it all invention built on nothing more than the tradition that there had been war-chariots in Bronze Age battles, and attributable only to an attempt to heroize the epic picture by making all the nobles possess something which was a sign of the greatest wealth in the Geometric period? Chapter III advances a thesis which explains the primary use of the Homeric chariot as a means of transport for warriors who fight on foot with the javelin as their main weapon; which keeps the picture of the chariot as the *sine qua non* of a nobility who really are what Odysseus maintains, the only people who count in war or in government; and which reconciles these aspects, and the vast numbers of chariots envisaged, with the essentially Geometric Age background of the epic, which for all its exaggerations fails to approach the vast wealth and complex organization of the great Bronze Age chariot-using powers, and knows nothing of their palace bureaucracies or their feudal structure with its absolute kingship. I believe that the Dark Age bards have heroized and archaized warfare of their own experience simply by transferring to the more heroic chariot the military role of the contemporary mounted horse. Aristotle speaks of the military and political dominance of aristocracies of knights after the fall of kingship, and his statement is proved credible by archaeology. There is evidence in the Homeric poems themselves not only of the knowledge of riding but also of the suppression of the mounted horse in the narrative. And there is evidence from the seventh and sixth centuries that heavy-armed warriors paralleled Homeric practice by riding to battle accompanied by mounted squires who would hold their horses for them while they fought on foot.

The main subject of Chapter IV is the invention of the double-grip 'hoplite' shield and its effect on the role of the war-horse, but

INTRODUCTION

first I examine the properties of one of its predecessors, the incurved 'Dipylon' shield, which is much the commonest type in Geometric art. A weighty body of opinion dismisses it as I dismiss the war-chariot, as a piece of heroic property; and if it is right to do so, the value of Geometric art to the military historian is seriously undermined. Now the defenders of the Dipylon shield have discussed at length how it might have been made, but they have never asked why such a shape was chosen. If it was a real shield, there must have been good military reasons for reducing its protective area by cutting a large scallop from either side. I argue that there were two, both simple and readily comprehensible in the context of the contemporary weapons and of the fluid, unorganized type of battle depicted in Homer and on the vases. Then the double-grip shield was invented, and because it could not be slung round to protect the back it stimulated the development of the organized and disciplined phalanx of hoplites. And the phalanx in turn affected the role of the war-horse. As a transport animal, though still equally valuable before and after the battle, the horse was no longer able to operate in the battle itself until the phalanx had broken and it was needed for flight or pursuit. But if the new style of warfare limited the traditional role of the war-horse, it may also have suggested a new one: because the phalanx was so vulnerable in the rear and flanks, and because it was generally lost once it had been broken, its invention may have prompted the development of true cavalry, whose potential effectiveness against hoplites on suitable terrain is revealed by Thucydides' narrative of the Athenian expedition to Sicily in the later fifth century. In this chapter I also examine the sociology of the new style of warfare, and suggest how far and under what conditions the needs of the hoplite armies were likely to extend the class of heavy-armed infantry beyond the horse-owning gentry.

Chapters v and vi illustrate the evolution of the roles of the mounted warrior in the seventh and sixth centuries, mainly by means of a detailed, descriptive catalogue of the contemporary vase-paintings (which was last attempted by Helbig in his article of 1904). In the absence of all but a minute amount of literary evidence, the military historian must concentrate on the invaluable testimony of the artists. Even with their help of course he fails to get anything like a complete and continuous picture of Archaic Greek warfare either geographically or chronologically. Most of the vase-paintings belong to the Ripe Corinthian style, which provides evidence from about 625 to 550 B.C., or to the more prolific Attic Black Figure style of the sixth century; and even these must be treated with care to allow for possible heroizing and archaizing or for the dictates of fashion. Then again there is the problem already mentioned, that the majority of scenes depict the horsemen out of battle, and it is hard to deduce how they actually fought. All the same it has been possible to build up a picture of the mounted warriors at least of Corinth and Athens in the Archaic period, and on this basis the rival theses of Helbig and his recent detractor Alföldi are analyzed and shown to be equally wrong in treating mounted hoplites and true cavalry as mutually exclusive arms. Chapter v concentrates on seventh-century Corinth, Athens, and the knightly aristocracies of Euboea, for whose warfare I suggest an original reconstruction based on a fragment of Archilochus. Chapter vi continues the story of Corinth and Athens in the sixth century, and ends by examining the so-called 'Chalcidian' pottery and the East Greek sarcophagi, which go a little way towards filling the geographical gap at least for the second half of that century.

Chapter vii is part summary and part development of what has gone before, and in particular it examines what constitutional repercussions the military developments are likely to have had. First there is a brief outline of the history of horsemen in war as far as the evidence for the several states permits a reconstruction, and I suggest some external influences which may have contributed to the development of true cavalry in some of them. I then pursue the questions raised in Chapter iv, where I examined how far the hoplite reform was likely to change the sociology of warfare. How far is it likely to have produced a politically self-conscious hoplite class distinct from the horse-owning aristocracy, and what was its relation to the rise of tyranny and to trends to more democratic constitutions? Finally I have added an appendix which states in greater detail than was possible in the relevant chapters my position on the controversial question of the historical basis of the Homeric background picture, which is fundamental to my thesis about the Homeric warriors and their chariots. If it is true that Homeric warfare is not Mycenaean but a heroized picture of what the bards knew in the Geometric Age, the

INTRODUCTION

same should be true of other, non-military aspects of the basic picture. The Appendix outlines the evidence and suggests a pivotal date in the ninth century B.C.

I
THE CHARIOT IN HOMER

When we think of Homeric warfare we immediately think of the war-chariot. It is the *sine qua non* of the Homeric nobleman, and that is why Pandarus is made to give a good explanation for not having one with him at Troy: he had no less than eleven brand-new ones at home, and eleven magnificent pairs of horses to pull them, but he decided to come to Troy on foot against his father's advice because he feared that there might be a shortage of the good fodder which his horses were used to.[1]* But when we consider how the large numbers of war-chariots are used, we find that apart from a very few exceptions the Homeric poems reveal no conception of the proper tactical role of massed chariotry, as it was used by the Bronze Age kingdoms of the Near and Middle East and by the Mycenaeans.

There is, it is true, just the occasional hint of a realistic use of chariotry, and especially at *Iliad* 4.293-309, where Nestor is haranguing his forces before battle. The chariots are drawn up in the van, and Nestor urges them to keep in line: 'neither let any man, trusting in his horsemanship and manhood, be eager to fight the Trojans alone before the rest, nor let him fall behind, for thus you will be enfeebled. But whenever a warrior gets within reach of an enemy chariot, let him thrust out with his spear, since this is much the better way. In this way men of former time used to sack cities and walls' (303-8).

This passage however is very exceptional in three ways. The first is that in the whole narrative of the *Iliad* there are only three other allusions to massed chariot attacks, although it is in the massed attack at speed that the chariot is most effective as a weapon of war. In

* The notes for all the chapters start on p. 173.

Iliad 11.289 Hector, seeing the wounded Agamemnon withdrawing from the battlefield, calls to his own troops to 'drive straightway the whole-hooved horses against the Danaans'. Or in *Iliad* 15.352-4 Hector smites on his horses and calls aloud to the Trojans along the ranks: 'and they all cried out, and level with his they held the steeds which drew their chariots'. But in neither of these passages is there a direct clash of massed chariots: a direct clash appears uniquely in the *Iliad* in the last of the three 'massed chariotry' passages, *Iliad* 11.150-4, which is commonly held to be a late interpolation in which the *hippeis* are cavalry (see below, p. 55). Second, not only is this one of the very few references to massed chariots in action, but it is one of the very few references to any sort of fighting from the chariot, moving or stationary, in mass or alone: usually the warrior dismounts to fight on foot. And third, Nestor enjoins the use of the thrusting-spear, which may suggest a Mycenaean survival: the Homeric chariot-borne warrior's usual style is to throw his spears. Snodgrass can find only four occasions in the *Iliad* when even individual warriors fight from the chariot:[2] in one (11.531f) it is not explained how the spear is used; in another it appears as though the spear may have been thrust rather than thrown (16.377f: perhaps a thrust rather than a throw at 399, 404); but in the other two the warriors are clearly depicted throwing javelins and not thrusting with spears as Nestor advised. At 5.13 Phegeus from his chariot hurls a javelin at Diomedes, who is fighting on foot: Diomedes then topples Phegeus from the chariot with his return throw. And at 8.118ff we find Diomedes and Nestor in one chariot closing with Hector and Eniopeus in another. Diomedes hurls a javelin at Hector, misses him, but hits and kills his charioteer. To Snodgrass' four examples we may add the case of Euphorbus, described as an expert in fighting from the chariot; but he too is found throwing javelins (*Iliad* 16.809-11). Curiously Marcel Detienne offered this passage as an example of Nestor's advice being followed: 'he [Euphorbus] reaches out from his galloping chariot to strike an enemy warrior or driver with his lance'.[3] But on the contrary it is an example of how very exceptional Nestor's advice is. The lines which Detienne quotes only say (*a*) that Euphorbus excelled his contemporaries 'in the spear, in horsemanship and in fleetness of foot', and (*b*) that he had brought twenty men from their chariots (βῆσεν ἀφ' ἵππων). We are

THE CHARIOT IN HOMER

then told that Euphorbus was the first to 'let fly' a weapon at Patroclus (πρῶτος ἐφῆκε βέλος).

The very fact that the Nestor passage is so exceptional is a measure of the unfamiliarity with the effective role of the chariot in war. In the first place it is otherwise inconceivable that everywhere except in the few passages just cited such apparently vast numbers of chariots could be assigned to the role of mere transport vehicles for noble warriors who dismount to fight. Moreover, if their use for transport behind the lines is at least not impractical (granted reasonable terrain), the same cannot be said when they are found transporting individual warriors hither and thither through the thick of battle. And finally it is the javelin which is the main weapon of the Homeric chariot-borne warrior, and not the long thrusting-spear or the bow, the two weapons which made the chariot so formidable a weapon of war after the revolutionary invention of the light spoke-wheeled chariot in the first half of the second millenium. Before that invention the javelin had helped the bow to provide the fire-power of the heavy, slower-moving, solid-wheeled 'chariot' or war-waggon, which often appears equipped with a capacious javelin-container.[4] But it looks as though the increased speed of the new, lighter chariot meant that the javelin was considered to be too feeble and uncertain a weapon to remain effective. And so it was that the great Bronze Age chariot-powers either turned to the longer thrusting-spear and relied for success on the speed, accuracy and weight of their massed attack, or else they relied on the bow to provide more accurate and forceful fire-power than the javelin over a longer range. The Hittites were the great exponents of the first method, and the Egyptians, followed by the Assyrians, of the second.[5] And the chariot tactics of these two great powers, the Hittites and the Egyptians, are clearly and vigorously represented on the Abu Simbel reliefs commemorating the Battle of Kadesh in 1288 B.C.[6] T. G. E. Powell, presumably seeking to draw parallels between Celtic chariotry and Ancient Egyptian as well as 'Homeric' chariotry, makes the extraordinary statement that the Egyptian reliefs show no head-on clash of chariots, and that massed charges are in any case impossible.[7] He believes that the chariots were used in only two roles: first, before battle was joined in earnest, they drove up and down in front of their own lines exchanging arrows, 'but presumably

FIG. I
Hittite chariot in the Battle of Kadesh of 1288 B.C., from the Egyptian reliefs at Abu Simbel

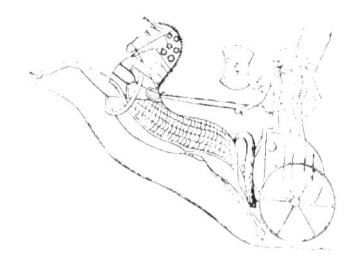

at a range which did not endanger the horses'; and later they were used again for pursuit by the winning side. Certainly pursuit of a fleeing enemy was an important use to which the Egyptians put their chariots, and scenes depicting this are very popular on the self-congratulatory Egyptian reliefs. But that the initial role of the Egyptian chariotry was as 'shock troops' for massed, head-on attack at full speed is clear from our Abu Simbel relief. A massed chariot attack could best be withstood by a similar force, and here we see the Egyptian and Hittite chariot-forces charging each other at full speed. The Egyptian chariots carry archers, and are equipped with quivers attached to the chariot-body, but the Hittites are armed with long thrusting-spears, apparently about seven feet long, and their chariots have no quivers or javelin containers (*fig. 1*).[8] And before the Hittite lancers can come within striking range of the Egyptian bowmen, both they and their horses are being decimated and thrown into disarray by their opponents' arrows. To return to the *Iliad*, I said that Nestor's advice was possibly a Mycenaean survival. There is no direct evidence that the Mycenaeans used massed chariots in the manner of the Hittites, but it is a sound conjecture. Monuments[9] and Linear B tablets attest the use of the chariot in war; and the very large numbers of chariots revealed by the tablets suggest that chariotry was a major arm, and make it very likely that massed chariot charges were as much a feature of Mycenaean tactics as they were among the other Bronze Age monarchies. According to M. Lejeune,[10] the series 'S-' tablets at Cnossos reveal that the palace magazines had in store more than a thousand pairs of wheels (*So*), more than three hundred chariot-bodies of type 242 (*Sf, Sg*), and at least forty chariot-bodies of type 241 (*Sf, Sg*). Series *Sc* is a long, mutilated list of men to whom are distributed chariots (type 240, i.e.

THE CHARIOT IN HOMER

FIG. 2
Sixteenth-century Greek war-chariot of type M1 on an engraved gem from Vapheio in Laconia

241 + wheels), horses and cuirasses. And at Pylos, what remains of series *Sa* attests that the palace had in store at least two hundred pairs of wheels, and no doubt the figure was very much larger: not only may there have been many more tablets, but many of the surviving tablets are mutilated, and in particular deprived of their numerals which appear on the right-hand edge. Such large bodies of chariots charging in a mass at full speed would be a formidable force; and it is incredible that such large numbers of so complex a piece of equipment can have existed merely for the use ascribed to chariots in all but the few exceptional passages in the *Iliad*. Moreover, the long thrusting-spear was the main weapon of the Mycenaean chariot-warriors as it was of the Hittites, with whom the Achaeans appear to have been in close touch if they are correctly identified with the Ahhijawa of the Boghaz-Keui records; indeed, the Tawagalawas letter is usually interpreted as meaning that the Achaean prince had visited Hattusas, the *haute école* of chariotry, to receive instruction in that art.[11] As Miss Lorimer notes,[12] all the monumental evidence points to the long thrusting-spear as the only spear used in Mycenaean warfare, except only for a fragmentary fresco from the Cnossos palace in which the rank and file appear to be aiming spears upwards. The only representations of spears in twos are on hunting scenes. Otherwise the thrusting-spear is the infantry spear with both the body-shield and the smaller shields of the Warrior Vase and Stele, and Karo rightly called it the indispensable weapon of the Shaft-Grave warrior, who is shown using it from the war-chariot.[13] It is not clear whether what the noble deceased of Stele 5 is holding in his hand as he drives down upon an enemy fleeing on foot is meant to represent the reins or a levelled lance,[14] although the former is more often suggested; but a long lance, apparently about nine feet in

length, is very clearly wielded by the chariot-borne warrior on an engraved sardonyx from Vapheio (*fig. 2*).[15] A chariot-borne archer appears once, on a gold ring from Shaft-Grave 4,[16] but this is clearly a hunting scene. The evidence of the representations shows the long thrusting-spear as the main weapon of the Mycenaean warrior both on foot and in his chariot (yet despite the representations Lejeune chooses to call the spears of the tablets 'javelots', although he admits that the ideograms give no indication of their size or use[17]). And therefore, since the Oriental chariot-using powers, the Syrians and Assyrians, with whom Greece was likely to come into contact in the Geometric period all seem to have used the bow,[18] it is possible that Nestor's advice is a true Mycenaean relic. If however the Nestor passage shows that the real, historical use of chariots in war in the Mycenaean Age had not quite disappeared from the poetic tradition, the fact that it is such an exception in Homer emphasizes how very faint a memory it was that survived the Mycenaean collapse: as G. S. Kirk notes, if even no more than a few Mycenaean battle descriptions had descended *verbatim* or had survived for any length of time in Dark Age poetry, the whole misconception about the use of chariots could never have been formed.[19]

The political and economic organization of the Homeric state similarly shows no real conception of the Mycenaean world as revealed by archaeology, and it is similarly incompatible with the existence of chariotry as a major military arm, and with the picture of the war-chariot as the essential possession of every nobleman. Just as there was no sufficient survival of information about Mycenaean Age chariot-battles for the reproduction of convincing battle-pieces showing chariots used effectively, there was no conception of the vast and complex bureaucratic palace-administrations which maintained the large chariot-forces of both the Greek and the Near and Middle Eastern chariot-using powers of the Bronze Age. Elena Cassin rightly stresses how the mass-production and maintenance of chariotry reveals a complex technology requiring the collaboration of various bodies of professionals and a centralized, bureaucratic administration to collect and control the raw materials, organize the work of the many specialist craftsmen, and distribute the new or repaired chariots: 'une économie de ce type ne pouvait subsister que grâce à un appareil administratif et bureaucratique très important

THE CHARIOT IN HOMER

FIG. 3
Chariot-borne warriors (including the 'Molione' siamese twins) on an Attic Late Geometric vase (**10**)

FIG. 4
Battle-scene on a Boeotian sub-Geometric vase (**45**) of the early seventh century

qui englobait dans un réseau serré toute la production du pays et se chargeait ensuite de remettre dans le circuit les produits manufacturés'.[20] Now it is argued in the Appendix that the political and economic organization of the Homeric state is an exaggerated and glamourized picture of conditions in the Greek communities in the Geometric period. Can we then say the same about the use of the chariot in battle?

In Geometric vase-painting of the late period, when figured scenes with chariots occur for the first time (from about the middle of the eighth century B.C.), it is certainly the case that where chariots appear in a military context they are treated in the same way as in the epic, as primarily a means of transport for armed warriors, with the exception that there are even fewer examples of fighting from the chariot. Snodgrass knows of two such examples,[21] and both are late (*figs. 3, 4*): vase **10** is Attic LG IIa (735–720 B.C.), and vase **45** is later still, Boeotian subgeometric and after 700 B.C. Not only is there no clash of massed chariots in Geometric art, but there is no example of even individual chariots clashing in battle: they all face the same way.[22] And even Snodgrass' two examples of fighting from chariots are dubious. On one at least (**10**) the chariot is undoubtedly stationary, and the Molione twin who is doing the fighting clearly has both feet on the ground (while his 'Siamese' brother has only one leg on the chariot). And the warrior who is poising his spear on board the

13

chariot of vase 45 may not be going to throw it until he has jumped down. Moreover it is never the lance or the bow but the javelin, or rather a pair of javelins, with which the chariot-borne warrior is armed; and on the odd occasion where a spear may be shown being used from the chariot, it is thrown (45). It is clear therefore that the Geometric artists were as vague, if not vaguer, than the Dark Age bards about the effective use of chariots in battle either in the contemporary Oriental powers or in the Mycenaean world. But can we believe J. K. Anderson's thesis, that the Homeric picture of chariots in battle is a true reflection of a reasonable Geometric Age usage as represented in the vase-paintings?[23] He accepts that the Homeric role was not the primary role of chariotry in any of the Bronze Age chariot-powers, but he seeks parallels in British and Cyrenaic chariotry to show that Kirk was wrong in denying that it was the primary role of any chariot-powers at all.[24] But there are fatal objections to Anderson's view, and a close examination of his references invalidates his parallels.

In the case of the British chariots which confronted Caesar, we can scarcely call the British a 'chariot-power': chariots are only a very small mobilized arm compared with the cavalry,[25] which outside Britain had completely replaced chariots in the forces of the Gallic Celts, as Anderson himself admits.[26] In Homer however the mounted horse is never once allowed to appear on the battlefield. This in itself does not of course prove that the Dark Age Greeks never used chariots in battle in the Homeric fashion, but it is very strange that such very large numbers of chariots, the only mobile arm, are used in Homer in a comparatively wasteful and ineffective transport role and to the complete exclusion of the mounted warhorse, which, as we shall discuss in Chapter III, was certainly known in the Geometric period. Moreover the parallel is not even exact in the matter of usage, except in so far as the javelin was the common spear-type, and both British and Homeric chariots conveyed their warriors to the battlefield. Once on the battlefield there are fundamental differences. Anderson himself notes the British trick of running out along the pole, which presupposes an open-fronted chariot; and he confesses that Diodorus' account is anachronistic, admitted to be on hearsay,[27] and on the look-out for Homeric parallels in Gallic society. Certainly Diodorus is guilty of anachronism in ascribing war-chariots to the Gauls, since it was only the British Celts who used them even as late as the first century B.C. (to judge from Caesar's silence). But there are more fundamental differences in the tactics themselves. First of all Diodorus himself makes no reference to Homer in his description of the 'British' tactics (5.29): the only point of comparison was simply that both the Gauls and the Homeric Greeks made use of the chariot in war (5.21). On the battlefield itself the usage is clearly not the same. Diodorus describes the role of the Gallic chariot (*a*) when engaging enemy *cavalry* and (*b*) before battle is joined. In the first case they hurl javelins and then dismount to fight with the sword. In contrast, the Homeric warriors and those of the LG vase-paintings normally dismount to throw their javelins; and when occasionally they do throw from their chariot, it is usually stationary. In the second case the chariot-borne warriors step forward on foot into no-man's land when the armies are arrayed ready for battle to begin, and they issue challenges to enemy champions for individual combat. Their chariots have only brought them to the front-line: they are not used for transport in the mêlée itself, as Homer would have it. And for a picture of what would happen to them if they were allowed to get embroiled in the infantry mêlée, we have the testimony of Tacitus' *Agricola*, 36.3. Caesar (on whom Diodorus may have based his account) gives another tactical use of the chariot in battle besides the initial wild drive designed to harry and confuse the order of the enemy ranks, a procedure which incidentally implies the hurling of many more '*tela*' than the maximum two of the Homeric warrior, and suggests that there was a large supply on board.[28] He describes the British chariots as working their way into the troops of cavalry (their own, presumably) and then depositing their warriors to fight on foot while they retire to a safe distance in case they are needed for a swift retreat. Here again, besides the cavalry problem, the British chariots may have transported the warriors into the thick of the mêlée, but not singly, and they did not wait beside the engaged warrior but immediately withdrew to a prudent distance. Finally, in contrast to Diodorus' comparison of the social status of warrior and driver in the Gallic and Homeric chariots, it is worth noting Agricola's very different observation, that the driver of the British chariot was the nobleman, and the *propugnator* merely his 'client'.[29]

Turning to Anderson's second parallel, we are initially on firmer ground. Cyrene could be called a chariot-power because her war-chariots were a major military arm. But was their primary role the Homeric one? Anderson's case rests on two passages. He first cites Aeneas Tacticus 16.14, and tells us that according to Aeneas 'the people of Cyrene and Barca and certain other cities used their two-horse chariots as troop-transports on long distance relief expeditions'. But this précis of Aeneas is misleading. Quite apart from whether or not this was the *primary* role of Cyrene's war-chariot force, Aeneas is talking about transport-waggons, two- and four-horsed ones, which are not brought into battle but remain as a bulwark for the fortified base-camp, and as a means of transport for the wounded (for whom a light war-chariot would scarcely be a very suitable or commodious vehicle!). What Aeneas says is this: 'It is said that the Cyrenaeans and Barcaeans ... made their rescue expeditions over long waggon-roads (τὰς ἁμαξηλάτους ὁδούς) in four- and two-horsed vehicles (ἐπὶ συνωρίδων καὶ ζευγῶν). And when they had reached the appointed place and the vehicles (τῶν ζευγῶν) had been parked in succession, the hoplites got out; and immediately forming up in battle-line they attacked the enemy with unimpaired strength. Hence, for those who have an abundance of vehicles (ζευγῶν), there is a great advantage in their soldiers' arriving both quickly and fresh to where they are needed; further, the waggons (αἱ ἅμαξαι) would be a ready bulwark (ἔρυμα) for the camp, and wounded or otherwise incapacitated soldiers could be conveyed in them back to the city.' Aeneas surely is not thinking of war-chariots at all, but transport-waggons.

Anderson's second authority is clearly writing about war-chariots. Xenophon explains that Cyrus 'abolished the Trojan chariotry and the method of managing a chariot still in vogue to-day among the Cyrenaeans, for in previous times the people in Media and Syria and Arabia and all the people in Asia used the chariot just as the Cyrenaeans now do'.[30] But I fail to see how this proves that the primary role of the Cyrenaic war-chariot was that of the Homeric one. In the first place, Xenophon also compares the Cyrenaean war-chariotry with that of the Asiatic powers, and we know that their chariot-borne warriors used the bow, a weapon never used in either the Homeric chariots or in those of the Geometric vase-scenes; and his assumption that three hundred chariots require twelve hundred horses is a further indication that Xenophon is not imagining a detailed comparison between Homeric and Cyrenaic usage. The point of contrast between the chariotry of all these other powers and the new *Cyrus*-chariot is the replacement of a lighter vehicle, used to carry fighting men beside the drivers, with a scythed chariot to be driven right at the enemy line, a much heavier, longer-axled construction carrying only a single occupant, the driver, encased all over in mail and further protected in a turret-like box. This is no sort of evidence that the Cyrenaic war-chariot had a primarily Homeric role in battle any more than that the Homeric chariot-borne warriors were 'the best men mounted upon chariots acting only the part of skirmishers (ἀκροβολισταί) and not contributing anything of importance to the victory'.[31] On the contrary, the word ἀκροβολισταί suggests that the Cyrenaic chariots relied on long-range mobile fire-power, probably supplied by the bow as in Cyprus whose cities were the only other Greek chariot-powers, and in Egypt, from where Cyrene most probably learnt the use of the war-quadriga.

It is clear that Anderson's attempt to find parallels in British and Cyrenaic chariotry fails to counter Kirk's basic objection to the Homeric picture of the chariot and pair as nothing more than a taxi-service for individual warriors in the battle itself: would so complex a piece of equipment ever be risked in the mêlée merely for this purpose, when the wounding of a horse by a stray weapon could easily put the whole apparatus out of action? And against the war-chariot in the Geometric period the economic argument reinforces the tactical one. As Snodgrass concludes, 'to suppose that warfare was actually carried on in that [the Homeric] manner at any time seems curious, but it is particularly hard to imagine that the warriors of the Geometric period, only just beginning to acquire an adequate protection for head and body, could afford the luxury of a "war-chariot" from which they would seldom if ever actually fight'.[32] The indications are that the war-chariot was 'heroic property' both in Homer and in Geometric art; that it had no place in Greek warfare after the Mycenaean collapse (apart from in Cyprus where Mycenaean culture and the palace-type organization escaped the collapse which occurred in the rest of Greece, and survived in close proximity to Oriental chariot-using powers); and that representations of the chariot in battle in Late Geometric art are influenced by the epic rather than that they and Homer are representing a genuine military use of the chariot in the Geometric period. Snodgrass goes further: he not only doubts the existence of war-chariots but of any chariots at all in Greece (outside Cyprus) from the time of the Mycenaean collapse until the latter half of the eighth century, a period in which there is a complete absence of representations of chariots; and he still further maintains that Late Geometric art was unfamiliar with the form of the true chariot until very near the end of the century, when he postulates the introduction of what he calls the canonical form of racing-chariot from the East,[33] a type represented on only one Attic LG fragment (*fig. 6*), and on a Boeotian fibula (which Snodgrass assigns to the seventh century B.C. but which is probably a forgery). He explains all the rest of the Geometric chariots as influenced partly by Mycenaean survivals, partly by the epic, and partly by wheeled vehicles of other uses, such as waggons and carts. That chariots are unlikely to have been used in battle I fully endorse; but I shall argue in the next chapter that both the epic and Geometric art show a clear knowledge of the form of the true chariot, which was used in the Geometric period for racing and for processions at the funerals of deceased nobles in whose honour chariot-races and other games were held. As for those chariots which appear on the battlefield in the epic or in Geometric art, I shall maintain that they are contemporary racing-chariots transferred to a military use by deliberately archaizing Dark Age bards, and by similarly archaizing Geometric artists influenced by the epic.

II
THE CHARIOT IN GEOMETRIC ART

It is true that there is neither direct nor representational evidence of chariots between the collapse of the Mycenaean world and the second third of the eighth century B.C. when they first appear on the Attic Late Geometric vase-paintings, and therefore it must remain unproved whether or not they were known continuously in Greece during the Dark Ages. Miss Lorimer pointed to three features common to the Bronze Age and Late Geometric chariots, the four-spoked wheel, central axle, and 'pole-end support';[1] but, as Snodgrass points out, all three could have been reintroduced to Greece from the Near East rather than directly inherited from the Mycenaean period,[2] although the continuity of the chariot through the Dark Ages is not unlikely, and Snodgrass' point about the absence of representations of chariots is worthless since there is an almost total absence of any representations until the LG period. But leaving aside the question of continuity, I believe that a careful examination of typology, context, and the size of the teams allows us to draw three reasonably safe conclusions: that certainly most, and very probably all, of the chariots of the Late Geometric vase-paintings (and not just Snodgrass' 'Egyptian' type, which I shall call G2) show familiarity with the form and use of contemporary racing-chariots which were basically the same as those raced by Athenians and other mainland Greeks in the sixth and fifth centuries; that this is true of the earliest Geometric chariots, which first appear in the sudden growth of figured representation marking the transition from Middle to Late Geometric, a little before the middle of the eighth century; and that racing-chariots had been known for a considerable period before their appearance in Geometric art.

In detail, I find that the chariots of the Late Geometric vase-

FIG. 5
The Rosellini chariot from fifteenth-century Egypt

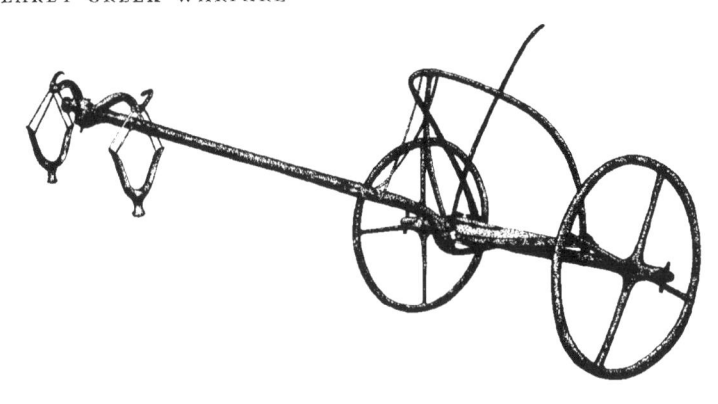

FIG. 6
Attic Late Geometric sherd (**8**) showing a Dipylon warrior driving a chariot of type G2

paintings readily divide into three main types, which I shall call G1, G2, and G3. The second type (G2) is represented by the couple of representations which are the only ones recognized by Snodgrass as true racing-chariots. This is the 'Egyptian' type, so called from the fifteenth-century, light, railed, 'Rosellini' chariot which it resembles (*fig.* 5).[3] In profile it has a single wheel, and a single rail at the front, shown curving backwards and filled with a lattice-work, presumably indicating wicker or plaited thongs. The two examples of this type appear on an Attic LG fragment (no. **8**, *fig.* 6), and on the Boeotian fibula which Snodgrass and Lorimer assigned to the seventh century but which is more probably a forgery (see above, p. 13, n. 22). Snodgrass may be right that this was a type introduced from the East near the end of the eighth century B.C. Besides G2 there are two larger type-groups, one very much larger. The G1 type is the long, squat, oblong 'box' with two wheels shown in profile and with a 'croquet-hoop' at either end (*fig.* 7). It usually contains two occupants, a war-

THE CHARIOT IN GEOMETRIC ART

FIG. 7
Chariots of type G1 being driven by Dipylon warriors on a vase of Attic LG Ib style (6)

FIG. 8
A rider whose two pairs of reins indicate a second horse appears in a procession of chariots of type G3a on vase 13 (Attic LG IIa)

rior and a driver (1, 2, 3, 4, 5), but sometimes only one (6, 7). Since sometimes the dead man's bier is shown on a similar-looking vehicle with two profile wheels (*fig. 26*), Snodgrass believes that it is not a chariot at all but a four-wheeled waggon. I shall postpone discussion of this type however, and concentrate first on my third type-group, G3, which is much the largest (*figs. 3, 8–15, 18*). There are variations within the group; but whatever Snodgrass may say about the G1 chariots, I believe that the G3 ones are genuine representations, more or less realistically drawn, of a contemporary racing-chariot which is the material ancestor of the central-axle mainland Greek racing-chariot of the sixth and fifth centuries, shown in fine perspective by the advanced artistry of agonal vases such as **46**, a Panathenaic Black Figure amphora (*figs. 16, 17*).

The G3 chariots are meant to represent the chariot with front and side rails. In strict perspective, the front rail would not appear as a wide loop but as a vertical line or slight loop, but the Geometric

21

FIG. 9
Rider in a procession of chariots of type G3*b* on vase **22** (Attic LG IIb)

FIG. 10
Procession of chariots of type G3*c* on vase **23** (Attic LG IIa)

artists never managed that degree of realism. The side rails are clearly shown as such on most of the G3 chariots (*c*, *d*, *e*, and *f*), and on a couple of vases (G3*e*: nos. **32**, **33**; *figs. 12, 13*) the artist tries to get some depth into his picture by showing a double side rail, presumably indicating the rail on either side in the same way that the far wheel is sometimes indicated by two concentric circles (e.g. **32**, **16**, **27**, **28**, **29**; *fig. 11*). But sometimes the side rail is shown as a loop at the rear (G3*a*), rather as on the G1 types; unlike G1 however, the G3*a* chariots have close affinities with the more realistic variations of G3*c*, *d*, *e* and *f* both in structure and context, and the homogeneity of the G3 group as a whole is clear. Unlike G1, the G3*a* chariot has only a single profile wheel, which is much larger in proportion to the chariot, and its loops are closer together. With one exception it has only a single occupant, usually unarmed and often wearing what came to be the standard robe of the racing driver, the robe worn by

THE CHARIOT IN GEOMETRIC ART

FIG. 11
Chariots of type G3*d* on vase **28** (Attic LG IIb)

FIG. 12
A single rider whose two pairs of reins indicate a second horse appears in a procession of G3*e* chariots on vase **32** (Attic sub-Geometric)

the famous Delphi charioteer (**18**, **9**, **13**, **14**; *figs. 8, 18*). Structurally the G3*a* chariots are most clearly shown to belong to the G3 group by a few representations which show the artists feeling their way to a greater realism: the loops of my G3*b* type (**20**, **21**, **22**; *fig. 9*) are not separate as in G3*a*, but they join at the bottom in an angle and mark a clear connexion between G3*a* chariots and those of G3*c*, *d*, *e* and *f*, whose rails are clearly shown one at the front and the other at the side. G3*c*, *d*, *e* and *f* are only slightly different conventions. G3*c* (**23**, **24**, **25**; *fig. 10*) differs from the others in showing the side rail at the side but making it a squashed, shrunken appendage to the base of the chariot instead of letting it come some way up the driver's body. The reason for this may be that the artist was not yet happy about showing much overlapping, and wanted the charioteer's body to stand almost clear of the side rail.[4] The G3*d* chariots show the front and side rails clearly in position as two loops (**27**, **28**, **29**, **30**, **31**; *fig. 11*).

23

FIG. 13
Procession of alternate riders and robed charioteers driving chariots of type G3*e* on vase 33 (EPA)

FIG. 14
Chariots of type G3*f* driven by robed charioteers on vase 37 (EPA)

G3*e* is very similar but shows a double side-rail as discussed above (**32**, **33**; *figs. 12, 13*); and G3*f* (**34**, **35**, **36**, **37**; *fig. 14*) shows a bit of breastwork at the front, with a smaller loop on top, otherwise the side rail is clearly and realistically shown as a single profile loop joining the breastwork quite high up, as in G3*d*. One vase (**26**) shows a transitional variant between *c* and *f* (*fig. 15*). It will be noticed that my sub-divisions of group G3 are arranged in ascending order of realism, to the extent that G3*a* is less realistic a portrayal of a chariot with front and side rails than G3*c*, *d*, *e* or *f*, and that G3*b* is more realistic than G3*a* but less so than the others. Now it may also be noticed that the more realistic groups are later in date than the less realistic ones. The G3*a* type appears as early as LG Ia–b (*c.* 750 B.C.), later only than the more primitive G1 pictures, and at a time when vehicles had been portrayed at all for not more than ten years or so, and ambitious

24

THE CHARIOT IN GEOMETRIC ART

FIG. 15
Chariots of a type combining G3c and ƒ on vase **26** (Attic LG IIa)

figured representation of any sort was in its infancy. The G3*a* convention continues down into LG IIb, but alongside it in IIa comes type G3*c* (**23, 24, 25**; *fig. 10*) portraying the side rail at the side for the first time; and in IIb the 'croquet-hoops' are found joining at the bottom (G3*b*) in a transitional convention from G3*a*, which no longer appears after IIb, to G3*d*, which is predominantly IIb (**28, 29, 30**; *fig. 11*) and extends into Early Protoattic (**31**). G3*e* is subgeometric (**32**; *fig. 12*) and EPA (**33**; *fig. 13*). And G3*f*, although an example of this more realistic convention occurs as early as LG Ib (**34**), and a transitional variant between *c* and *f* in IIa (**26**; *fig. 15*), is predominantly EPA (**35, 36, 37**; *fig. 14*), and goes well down into that period (**44**). The exceptions to a perfect graph of realism against time serve to emphasize the homogeneity of the whole G3 group: some painters achieved greater realism earlier than others, who remained happy with the more primitive and stylized convention. But the trend to greater realism as time passed is clear. In the more realistic of the G3 representations it is easy to see the artistic prototypes modelled on the material ancestors of the canonical Athenian racing-chariot which in the sixth century appears on such vases as **46** (*fig. 16*), and is similarly put into their epic battle-scenes by the Black Figure painters, as on the shoulder panel of that particular vase (*fig. 17*). And just as G3*a* and *b* are more primitive, less realistic conventions for the same chariot which is more realistically rendered in G3*c*, *d*, *e* and *f*, I shall

FIG. 16
Harnessing a four-horse racing-chariot on a sixth-century Attic Black Figure vase (46)

shortly endeavour to show that the still more primitive G1 types, the earliest chariots found only in LG I, are the artistic prototypes of G3, and based on the same basic sort of contemporary racing-chariot.

That the G3 chariots are racing-chariots is indicated by the fact that all except one have one occupant, and are often shown in a race or procession (nos. **13**, **26**, **18**, **30**, **22**, **31**, **33**, **20**, **35**, **36**, **37** all show a row of chariots with single, robed charioteers in a wholly unmilitary context; no. **9** is similar except that warriors appear on foot in the chariot-frieze). It is true that races and processions are difficult to distinguish on Geometric representations, so much so that Bronson refuses to accept any vase-painting as a certain representation of a chariot-race before his two Protocorinthian aryballoi.[5] But the galloping horses pulling the G3a chariots of Attic crater **9** (c. 750 B.C.) are surely racing (*fig. 18*),[6] and so too very probably are some others whose charioteers occasionally look animated even if the horses are staid and stylized (e.g. **18**). In any case, if they are not meant to be racing, the processions of chariots are surely processions in honour

26

THE CHARIOT IN GEOMETRIC ART

FIG. 17
A similar four-horse racing-chariot in a heroic battle-scene on the shoulder panel of vase **46** (*fig. 16*)

FIG. 18
Alternate Dipylon warriors on foot and racing-chariots of type G3a driven by the earliest robed charioteers on vase **9** (Attic LG Ia–b, *c.* 750 B.C.)

of the noble deceased before racing at his funeral games. Apart from the common appearance of robed charioteers, the frequency of three- and four-horse teams (e.g. *fig. 27*) as early as the third quarter of the eighth century is a strong indication of the knowledge of contemporary racing-chariots.[7] Groups of three and four plastic horses similarly appear on LG pyxis-lids (*fig. 19*).[8] A late eighth-century four-horsed chariot group with a single warrior occupant appears as a child's toy from a tomb in the Agora.[9] And a fragmentary group,[10] this time with an unarmed driver leaning forward as though plying the goad, and presumably representing a chariot in a race, was found in the same grave as vase **18**, whose animated robed charioteers drive three-horsed chariots. The four-horse chariot-race was apparently introduced to Olympia in the twenty-fifth Olympiad, *c.* 680 B.C., according to Pausanias;[11] and it had no doubt been practised as a sport much earlier. Old Greece also experimented with the three-horse team, and three-horsed pyxis-lids occur before the middle of the eighth century in Attica, although the triga never seems to have

FIG. 19
Attic Late Geometric pyxis with a three-horse handle

caught on as much in Old Greece as it did in Etruria after the Greeks had introduced it there.[12] The appearance of the three- and four-horse teams is especially significant for two reasons. The first is that they mark a technical advance on the simpler two-horsed variety, and this suggests that if we can put racing with the triga and quadriga back to the mid-eighth century, we can reasonably assume two-horsed chariot racing considerably earlier. The second is that the triga and quadriga are hardly likely to have been taken onto the battlefield in Geometric Age Greece. It is true that the Assyrians in the reign of Ashur-nasir-pal (885–860 B.C.) used the triga in battle,[13] but they, unlike the chariot-borne warriors in Homer and Geometric art, fought from massed chariots at speed. Here is an all-important difference. Bronson notes that the third and fourth horses are trace-horses, added to the yoked pair not for extra pulling power but for greater manoeuvrability, to enable much sharper turns to be made at speed (*fig. 20*). Now the ability to turn very sharply at speed is particularly valuable on the race-track where, as Nestor pointed out to Antilochus before the chariot-race at Patroclus' funeral games,[14] the ability to make the 180 degree turn as near as possible to the marker often gave the victory. The Assyrians however did not race their chariots, and Bronson confesses himself unable to understand why a three-horsed chariot should ever have been used in war,

FIG. 20
A fifth-century Boeotian clay model of a chariot with four horses (two yoked, and two trace-horses), containing a hoplite and a driver wearing a 'Boeotian' shield on his back

especially since the third horse was most likely to be shot first, as was Pedasus in *Iliad* 16.467–76. In the case of the Assyrian method of effective chariot-warfare, in which the chariots were fought from at full speed, the added manoeuvrability seems to me no less valuable than on a Greek race-course. But that warriors ever used a three-horsed, let alone a four-horsed, chariot merely for transport to and from the battlefield on which they dismounted to fight on foot, and where therefore the manoeuvrability afforded to a speeding chariot by a third horse really would be valueless, is surely extremely unlikely; and that they ever used such chariots for the transport of individual foot-soldiers in the midst of a raging battle is not only unreasonable but impossible and impractical. We may therefore safely conclude that the three- and four-horse chariots in Geometric art (like those in Homer) are an added indication that the racing-chariot was known in Geometric Greece before the LG period, but that its military use was a deliberate piece of heroizing whereby racing-chariots were transposed onto the battlefield, exactly as it was for the Black Figure vase-painters of nos. **46** (*figs. 16, 17*), **47** or **48** and for the maker of the fifth-century terracotta quadriga from Tanagra (*fig. 20*),[15] or the bronze artists of the famous Vix crater.[16]

On the basis of this detailed survey it is possible to counter Snodgrass' objections to the existence of any true chariot in Geometric

FIG. 21
Fifteenth-century Greek chariot of the quadrant-type (M2) on an engraved gem from Cnossos

FIG. 22
The ideogram for a chariot of type M3 on a Linear B tablet from Cnossos

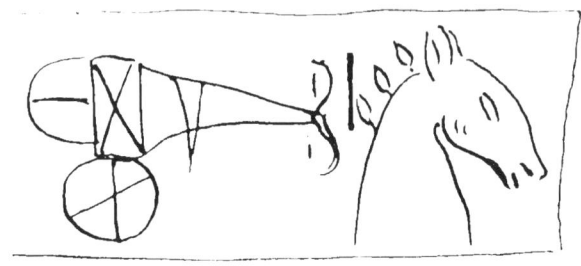

Greece until the introduction of the G2 type from the East towards the end of the eighth century. His first objection was that Mycenaean survivals were probably part responsible for the chariots other than the G2 type on the LG vase-paintings. But apart from the basic improbability of the survival of many representations of chariots through the Mycenaean collapse and through the Dark Ages for some four centuries (at least in sufficient circulation to influence almost all the Late Geometric chariot-painters!), there is no evidence of the imitation of Mycenaean technique, and no convincing representation of the commonest LH III type, Evans' so-called 'dual' chariot. In detail, four Greek Bronze Age chariot-types can be discerned from representations, as follows:

M1: A square-bodied type, found on the stelae, and depicted on the sixteenth-century Vapheio gem (see above, p. 11, *fig. 2*), and on the gold ring from Shaft Grave 4:[17] these last two show the chariot-bodies criss-crossed with lattice-work, indicating perhaps wicker or thongs? Four-spoked wheels.

M2: Quadrant-type (*fig. 21*):[18] the body is shown as the first

THE CHARIOT IN GEOMETRIC ART

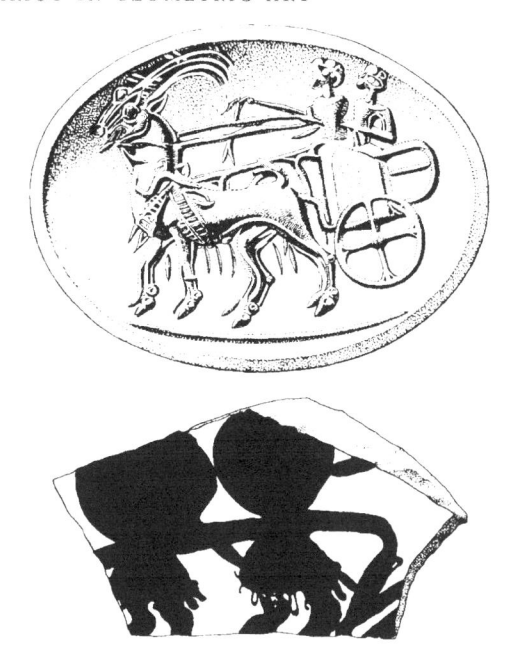

FIG. 23
Fifteenth-century
Greek chariot of
type M3 on an engraved
gem from
Lyktos in Crete

FIG. 24
The rail of a
Mycenaean
chariot of type M4
on a sherd of
c. 1200 B.C.

quadrant of a circle, as in the Hittite chariots of the Abu Simbel reliefs (see above, p. 10, *fig. 1*).

M3: By far the commonest type, Evans' 'dual-chariot'.[19] Type 240 of the Cnossos tablets (*fig. 22*), and standard in LH III. Rectangular in profile, with a large, semi-circular 'flap' projecting beyond the rear of the chariot. Sometimes the flap appears solid, sometimes open with a cross-bar (*fig. 23*). E. von Mercklin believed that the 'dual-chariot' was a non-perspective representation of the perspective quadrant-type (M2), but Lorimer has rightly objected that there are no quadrant-shaped flaps.[20] Nor is it at all likely that the flaps really do represent the side, and the rectangular part the front, of a type other than M2, since the existence of Bronze Age chariots with square sides and projecting flaps attached to the rear is certain. The Egyptians are shown using such chariots (semi-circular flaps, open except for cross-bar like *fig. 23*) on the same relief which shows the Hittite chariots as quadrants.[21]

M4: The 'Egyptian' type, so called from the fifteenth-century Rosellini chariot, built for lightness and speed at the expense of

31

FIG. 25
Model of an Archaic Greek chariot from Olympia similar to Geometric type G2

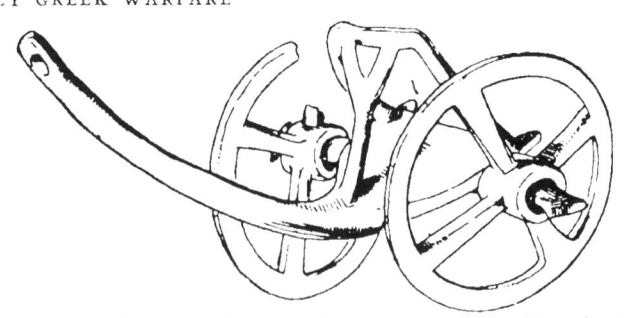

robustness. A chariot with a single curving rail looking basically like the Rosellini chariot (*fig. 5*) is rather optimistically reconstructed from the very fragmentary representations of the rail of a chariot on five late LH III sherds, two from Mycenae and three from Tiryns[22] (*fig. 24*).

Types M1 and M2 nowhere appear in Geometric art. The flap of M3 has been 'identified' with the rear croquet-hoop of some LG chariots, but Snodgrass himself remarks that if so the form is so highly distorted as to make 'Helladic' hardly a justifiable name for them. The G3c types are the only ones with anything like the projecting flap of M3; but they have nothing to do with M3: not only is the side loop of G3c clearly open, neither solid nor with the crossbar, but with the tall front-loop, single occupant and absence of box-body they are clearly a variation on the front- and side-railed chariots shown more realistically on G3*d*, *e* and *f*, where the side rail is allowed to come further up the driver's body. That leaves M4. If it has been correctly reconstructed as of basically the same design as Rosellini's chariot, it may well be that it represents the remote ancestor of the G2 chariot, known in the eighth century from only one late LG sherd (**8**, *fig. 6*), and appearing later on some models from Olympia (*fig. 25*)[23] and on the Boeotian fibula. Mercklin and Lorimer concluded that chariots of the G2 type were continuously known in Greece from LH III to the eighth century. Snodgrass, though similarly identifying M4 as the ancestor of G2 if only from the common Eastern source of the Rosellini type, claims that the G2 chariot, known only in the eighth century from the one late LG sherd (**8**), represents the first true chariot in Greece since the Mycenaean collapse, a racing-chariot type reintroduced from the East late in the century. Now this is curiously inconsistent with his argument that

THE CHARIOT IN GEOMETRIC ART

FIG. 26
Funeral scene with hearse and a procession of chariots of type G1 on an Attic LG Ib vase (6)

the rest of the LG chariots may have been influenced by surviving Mycenaean representations. He admits that none resemble M3; and certainly none resemble M1 or M2. And yet in the case of the one LG representation in which he accepts a resemblance to a Mycenaean type, he confidently states that it is based on a true, contemporary racing-chariot, because of its resemblance to some later Olympia models. He is surely right in the case of G2. And surely it is equally right to see the G3 chariots, which are even more clearly the ancestors of an even commoner sixth-century type, as representations of true, contemporary racing-chariots. Now it seems to me that one Mycenaean sherd from Tiryns, which appears to show part of a side rail at the back of an M4 chariot,[24] could just conceivably be representing a material ancestor of the G3 type, as shown most clearly on G3*d*, *e* and *f*. But if this is true, it does not alter the basic improbabilities that the Late Geometric painters were copying Mycenaean representations, and that they had the representations available to copy.

Snodgrass' second suggestion, that the LG chariot representations other than no. **8** were not based on contemporary models but were partly influenced by wheeled vehicles of other uses, such as waggons and carts, is similarly unconvincing. He argues that some two-wheel profiles (i.e. my type G1, plus nos. **10**, **39**, and **40**; *figs. 3, 7, 26, 27*) really portray four-wheeled vehicles, which cannot of course be chariots in the proper sense, and that similar-looking, single-wheel profiles may well be influenced by carts too. The argument is based upon three considerations: (i) that both types of representation, i.e. chariots showing single and double wheels in profile, appear together on the same vase (e.g. **10**; see above, p. 13, *fig. 3*), and it is hard to believe that the same artist used different conventions for a two-wheeled chariot on the same vase; (ii) that such heavy constructions as the bier on the Hirschfeld crater (**6**; *fig. 26*) suggest that the two wheels shown really do portray a four-wheeled vehicle since it would be impossibly precarious on two; and (iii) that other two-wheeled representations have every appearance of being a normal profile view as far as the body-work is concerned. Now it is true that in **10** a two-wheeled profile version of type G3*a* appears alongside a single-wheeled one; but it is not difficult to believe that these are alternative conventions for the same type of chariot for two reasons. First, the artist was evidently content to use two different conventions for a pair of horses: the extreme left-hand chariot of Snodgrass' illustration (*fig. 3*) has only a single horse (which is extremely unlikely in a yoked vehicle[25]), whereas the identical chariot in the middle shows two horses, as does the two-wheeled version on the right-hand edge. Moreover, the second wheel of the right-hand chariot is readily explained, since its warrior with his wide-winged 'Dipylon' shield needs more space than the naked figure in the left-hand one or the Molione with only one foot in their chariot in the middle, and perhaps it is because the elongated chariot of the right would look impossibly long for a single wheel that a second one was added. Exact parallels occur on nos. **39, 40, 45**, all more realistic-looking chariots, of body-types G3*f, d* and *e* but with two profile wheels: in **39** two warriors ride in the chariot in the old-fashioned manner, in **40** and **45** a panoplied warrior and unarmed driver, and in each case the chariots have been elongated to accommodate them, and a second wheel added for balance (see above, p. 13, *fig. 4; fig. 27*).[26] As to Snodgrass' second observation (ii), the bier of **6** would certainly be precarious on only two wheels (*fig. 26*). But even with the primitive draughtsmanship of this example of the earliest phase of the figured LG period (Ia), it is clear that the vehicle carrying the bier is very different from the chariots carrying the warriors: not only is

THE CHARIOT IN GEOMETRIC ART

FIG. 27
Four-horse chariot of basic type G3*d* but elongated and given a second profile wheel to accommodate two occupants *tandem* (**40**)

it much bigger and sturdier, but it is without the hoops which in the G3 examples are clearly seen to be a portrayal of the front and side rails, and which appear on the G1 chariots. Again (iii), that the two profile wheels really represent two-wheeled chariots and not four-wheeled carts is emphasized by the appearance of the axle on three of my seven examples of G1 (**1, 3, 4**) in which the whole of the chariot is visible (**2** being fragmentary), and two of those which do not show an axle are convincingly shown to be based on racing-chariots by their three- and four-horse teams (**7, 5**). The number of the horses is very significant. At least one G1 chariot (**7**), and most probably three (**42, 43**),[27] have teams of three horses, and one (**5**), which happens to be the most cart-like of the G1 examples, has a team of four; and it is highly unlikely that such teams will have been used other than for racing when they were not going to be used effectively in battle. It is not difficult to see the G1 chariots as primitive conventions for the sort of chariot with front and side rails which appears more realistically in G3*c*, *d*, *e* and *f*, but is shown with separate vertical hoops on the G3*a* examples. The oblong 'box' upon which the G1 warrior stands clearly represents the flat floor of the chariot, shown without regard for perspective as in the case of the chequered canopy over the dead man on the bier of **6** (*fig. 26*); and the lattice-work of the floor perhaps indicates criss-crossed leather thongs (as found in the Rosellini chariot). And finally it is hard not to see the tripods which stand beside the chariot of **5** as the prizes for a chariot-race, like those awarded for instance in the race at Patroclus' funeral games.[28]

This brings us to Snodgrass' last point, the influence of the epic on the chariots of Late Geometric art. There is no doubt that the artists were influenced to some extent by the epic, since recognizable characters like the Molione siamese twins occasionally occur,[29] as for example in the battle-scene of **10** (see above, p. 13, *fig. 3*). But it is inconceivable that the chariots of the LG vase-paintings, whose typology shows a variable but steadily increasing degree of realistic representation of what is basically the same side-rail chariot which finally appears in fine perspective on the sixth-century vase-paintings, are based not on contemporary chariots familiar to the artists but on what those artists have been able to reconstruct from hours of careful listening to epic recitals. It is true that the Homeric poems show a familiarity with parts and construction of a railed chariot, as I shall discuss below, but when all the scattered allusions are put together they do not allow even the painstaking modern scholars to produce a detailed reconstruction. And if the appearance of an occasional Molione or Ajax scene (Ajax on *fig. 4* perhaps) indicates an illustration of the epic, there is no reason to doubt that deceased noblemen of the eighth century were honoured by funeral games. After all, Hesiod tells us that he won a tripod in a poetry contest at funeral games organized by the sons of the rich Chalcidian nobleman Amphidamas.[30] And surely chariots were raced at the funeral of Amphidamas and of other wealthy nobles like the occupant of Agora Grave 12, who was buried with a terracotta racing-driver, and who had single, robed charioteers driving three-horsed chariots round his funeral amphora (**18**).[31] Other contests appear occasionally on the funeral vases,[32] but the chariot-race, or at least procession of racing-chariots, is the favourite scene, no doubt because it is the grandest and most expensive noble sport as well as a fine subject for the artist. And even if it could be argued that the two-horsed chariots of the vase-paintings represent epic and not contemporary practice, the frequency of three- and four-horse teams both on vase-paintings and pyxis-lids can hardly be attributed to the influence of the *Iliad* and *Odyssey*, which combined can muster only five mentions or allusions to teams of more than two.[33] Finally we must ask to what period the epic's knowledge of the racing-chariot and the picture of the funeral games belong. Bronson notes that there are no representations of chariot-racing from the Greek Bronze Age;[34] and chariots are practically never shown with a single occupant.[35] He notes too that the Oriental powers apparently never raced chariots, but suggests that the unforgettably dramatic races of the *Iliad*'s funeral games are

THE CHARIOT IN GEOMETRIC ART

evidence for the Mycenaean Age. Now it is perfectly true that despite the complete absence of representations the Mycenaean noblemen may have raced their chariots for sport, and that knowledge of the fact may be preserved in Homer. But since the Homeric poems show so very little familiarity with the social or economic or political conditions of the Mycenaean Age, or indeed its burial customs, it is far more likely that the *detailed* descriptions of chariot-racing are based, perhaps with some suitably heroic exaggeration, on contemporary life in the Geometric period. And in this connexion it is worth noting a point recently emphasized by M. I. Finley, that the tripods and 'glittering cauldrons', which were so popular as prizes both in Homer and in the Geometric vase-scenes, were extreme rarities until the Geometric period, when archaeology has revealed that they became notable treasures.[36]

I have said that the Homeric poems reveal a familiarity with the form as well as the use of a racing-chariot. Constructional details suggest the light, railed chariot, which could fit either the G2 or G3 type. There is no indication of a flap like that of Bronze Age M3, and although the Homeric chariot could be type M4, ignorance of the appropriate tactics and weapons is strongly against a derivation from Mycenaean or Oriental chariotry. The rails of the chariot are often referred to. Lycaon cuts the young branches of a wild fig-tree to make them.[37] And they are commonly spoken of in the plural (ἄντυγες),[38] but as only those of Hera's chariot are specified as 'double' they perhaps refer to the front and side rails of Geometric type G3. When the chariot is left, the reins are tied to the front rail to make the horses believe they are tied up,[39] or to the ἐπιδιφριάδος πυμάτης, which suggests the rail of the classical racing-chariot.[40] The mention of plaited thongs for the δίφρος of Hera's double-railed chariot,[41] and suggested by the epithets εὔπλεκτος and εὐπλεκέης,[42] may apply to the floor of the chariot (as of the G1 examples whose floor, shown vertically, is criss-crossed with lattice-work, nos. 2–7, *fig. 26*), or to the 'breastwork' (as shown on the G2 type and on no. **26**, *fig. 15*, type G3*c/f*), or perhaps even both. Miss Lorimer stresses the absence of the 'pole-end support' or *zygodesmon* from descriptions of chariots in Homer, and notes that when on two occasions teams break the pole,[43] there is no mention of any other attachment to stop them running away. There is however a mention of the fastening of the 'pole-end support' in the description of the assembling and harnessing of Priam's mule-car,[44] and it is clearly known in Homer; and perhaps we should not put too much weight on the two broken pole passages as evidence of ignorance of chariots so equipped. Miss Lorimer may of course be right in suggesting that the Homeric chariot reveals acquaintance with Ionian racing-chariots which she believes to have abandoned the traditional support,[45] although as far as her Olympic models are concerned it may be wrong to expect a rope *zygodesmon* to be shown on a model of the basic bodywork (*fig.* 25). It is true however that the eight-spoked wheel of Hera's chariot perhaps suggests the Eastern Greek type,[46] although there is unfortunately no clear indication of the position of the axle in Homer to help confirm it. Metal decoration is ascribed to some chariots, and this could conceivably indicate a Bronze Age or Oriental reflection;[47] but it is well worth noting that although the material of Hera's all-metal chariot is so supernaturally enhanced, the poet nevertheless kept to the ἄντυξ-type rather than giving her an Oriental box-bodied chariot. Moreover, despite the gold and silver adornment of Rhesus' chariot, it still has a front rail apparently, and is light enough for Diomedes to lift and carry single-handed.[48] There is no shortage of technical vocabulary for the horse-drawn chariot in Homer;[49] and I believe that there were light, railed racing-chariots in Greece in the Geometric period, and that the Homeric poems show an easy familiarity with both their form and use.

But even more strongly the evidence of Homeric technical vocabulary reinforces the economic and tactical arguments that the use of the chariot in war, as depicted in Homer and copied in Geometric art, is an invented one, based on mere knowledge that the Mycenaeans had used war-chariots, and achieved by putting all noble warriors into racing-chariots. As Delebecque concluded in his detailed analysis of the horse in the *Iliad*, the *combat* of chariots does not share the same abundance of technical vocabulary: 'pour d'écrire le combat proprement dit des chars il y a défaut total de vocabulaire technique ou simplement spécial'. And most significant of all is the fact that only one word in the whole of Homer is a technical word clearly distinguishing the functions of the two occupants of the war-chariot, and this word (παραιβάτης) occurs once only (when it is used in the plural in opposition to ἡνίοχοι).[50] It cannot be too strongly emphasized that this is the only occurrence of a word of technical appearance informative of the number of passengers. Here then is a very strong indication that whilst one-man racing-chariots[51] were familiar to the Dark Age bards who, like Hesiod, competed in poetry contests at the funeral games of great noblemen in whose honour they were both raced and no doubt driven in procession as on the LG vase-paintings (with their noble occupants sometimes armed, often not, often alone but sometimes driven by another man), the *war*-chariot with its two occupants has no place in the history of Geometric Age warfare outside Cyprus, but it is to be attributed to deliberate heroizing and archaizing on the part of the epic singers. In short, the light chariot was known and used for racing, but it was never brought into battle and never fought from, and therefore it is extremely unlikely that even where suitable terrain existed so precious an article was ever used merely for transport behind the lines, to save the nobleman from walking or riding on horseback.

III
THE HOMERIC *HIPPĒES*

The mention of the possibility of riding introduces my main thesis about the historical reality behind the Homeric picture of the chariot in war. If that picture is not based either upon a clear knowledge of the Mycenaean chariot-warfare or upon even an exaggerated picture of chariotry as used in Dark Age battles or upon contemporary Oriental practice, is it all invention based on nothing more than knowledge of the fact that war-chariots were much used by the Mycenaeans, and attributable only to a deliberate glamourizing of the epic picture by giving all the nobles the possession of something which in the Geometric period was a sign of extreme wealth? I believe that both these factors are present, but that there is a further factor which rationalizes the confusing role of the Homeric chariot tactically and socially and economically: it explains the primary use of the Homeric chariots as a means of transport, and the javelin as the main weapon; it keeps the picture of the chariot as the essential status-symbol of nobles who really are, as Odysseus states, the only people who count in war;[1] and it reconciles these aspects, and the vast number of chariots envisaged, with the essentially Geometric Age social, political and economic background of the poems, which know nothing of the palace-type bureaucratic administration or the feudal structure with its absolute kingship, the features common to all the great chariot-using powers of the Bronze Age. This further factor is acquaintance with the mounted war-horse. There is evidence that warriors who rode to war on horseback were militarily, socially and politically dominant in the Geometric communities, and especially in the suitable horse-rearing and horse-using terrain of the Ionian colonies in Asia Minor; and there is evidence in Homer not only of the knowledge of riding but also of the suppression of the mounted horse in the narrative. In short, I believe that the Dark Age bards have heroized and archaized warfare of their own experience by transferring to the heroic chariot the military and social functions of the mounted horse.

Before going on to consider the evidence in detail, it is worth stressing that, if this is so, it is not the only example of consistent heroizing and archaizing in Homeric warfare. There is an exact parallel in the case of the spear. The spear-type of the Homeric warrior is not the single, heavy thrusting-spear of the Mycenaean Age but the javelin, or rather pair of javelins, clearly attested by archaeology as the main spear-type of the Geometric period;[2] and yet the metal of the Homeric spears is invariably bronze. With the single exception of an allusion in one line of the *Odyssey* (19.13), all Homeric arms are of antiquated bronze, even the swords in which the superiority of iron would be most crucial. And yet archaeology has revealed that even the Protogeometric period (c. 1025–900 B.C.) was fully Iron Age, as Snodgrass conclusively demonstrated in his table of metal finds associated with Protogeometric pottery, which I here reproduce:[3]

	Bronze	*Iron*
Swords	1	20+
Spearheads	8	30+
Daggers	2	8
Knives	Nil	15+
Axe-heads	Nil	4

The completeness of the archaizing in Homer is very clearly emphasized if we set alongside the numbers of swords and spears of both metals in the epic (wherever the metal is indicated) the numbers of swords and spearheads of both metals revealed by archaeology in the period of the eleventh to the eighth centuries, the period to which the pair of throwing-spears undoubtedly belongs:[4]

	Homer		Archaeology (11th–8th centuries)	
	Bronze	*Iron*	*Bronze*	*Iron*
Swords	12	0	4	55+
Spearheads	121	0	13	53+

Now in the case of spears it is clear that the Dark Age poets knew the basic fact that the Mycenaean Age was the Bronze Age, but in the detailed battle-scenes it is the Geometric spear-type and usage which appear. The material has been changed into antiquated bronze, but the tactics remain Dark Age. And I believe that the same consistent archaizing has taken place in the case of the chariot in war. The material, in this case the mounted horse, has been archaized and heroized by conversion into the war-chariot. And the archaizing is so consistent that a mounted horse never once appears in a battle-scene any more than an iron weapon. But the usage of the Homeric chariot, and the social and political and military dominance of the chariot-borne warrior, reflect exactly the roles of the mounted war-horse and its rider in the Geometric period.

Aristotle speaks of mounted warriors as dominating the warfare of the early Greek cities at the time of the disappearance of kingship and the transition to an aristocratic republic, a transition for which the Homeric governments often seem poised: 'after kingship the earliest government among the Greeks gave political rights to the warrior class, and in the beginning was made up of the knights (ἐκ τῶν ἱππέων), for with the knights rested strength and superiority in war at that time'.[5] The keeping of horses is a sign of considerable wealth, as Aristotle also notes; 'and therefore in olden times the cities whose strength lay in their horsemen were oligarchies, and they used their horsemen in wars against their neighbours, as was the practice of the Eretrians and Chalcidians, and also of the Magnesians on the River Maeander, and of other places in Asia'.[6] Three points are brought out by Aristotle: (i) that the horse is a sign of wealth, a status-symbol; (ii) that supremacy in war and government rested with the knights in these early cities; and (iii) that this was the case, to judge from the choice of examples, especially where the terrain was suitable for the rearing and riding of horses. Eretria and Chalcis had broad plains, and so did the cities of Asia Minor. This last fact fits in well enough with the Homeric epic, which is Ionian. Indeed, it is perhaps worth noting that Colophon, without doubt one of Aristotle's 'other places in Asia', and compared with Magnesia for its horse-breeding and broad plains,[7] laid a very strong claim to Homer; and the Colophonian claim supports that of Old Smyrna, a typical East Greek coastal site to which archaeology has revealed the description of the site of Scheria as so remarkably close.[8] As to Aristotle's first and second points, they too fit the Homeric picture if we equate the Homeric chariot with the mounted horse of the Greek communities in the Geometric period. After all, it is the horse rather than the chariot which is the aristocratic symbol and evoked the eulogies even in the great chariot-using powers of the Bronze Age. As Elena Cassin noted with regard to the Oriental powers, the centralized palace-administration capable of supplying and maintaining large chariot-forces only partly accounts for the connexion between the war-chariot and the palace-type of society which ruled in Babylon as in all the Middle East in the second half of the second millenium: 'reasons of another sort make the chariot the typical product of this society: its intimate association with the horse above all, which became the personification of war and the chase, the activities of a class or caste'. And she went on to quote the words of the horse from the Babylonian Wisdom Literature, which amply testify to his importance and the esteem in which he was held: 'without me neither king nor governor nor prince races through the streets ... next to the king my box is placed'.[9] So highly did the kings rate their horses that they put them in the same category as the infant princes, harem-women and royal officers in describing themselves and their households; and horses became one of the most prized and precious riches of Babylon, a key-element in diplomatic gift-exchanges between Babylon and Egypt or the Hittites.[10] But whereas vast numbers of massed chariots meant a centralized palace-administration, whether in Babylon or Egypt or Hattusas or Mycenae, the horse as a widespread nobleman's possession was common both to the Bronze Age Kingdoms and to the very different Greek communities of the Geometric period, in which the chariot was at best an extremely exclusive and very precious object, but where the nobles, the owners of the larger estates, are all likely to have possessed horses, especially in the suitable areas. Moreover, the nobles who possessed horses in the Geometric period really did count in war and government, and far more so than the chariotry of the Bronze Age Kingdoms, which was never the only effective arm in battle. And the Geometric Age nobles were the effective warriors on the field of battle not only as a direct result of their horses and the tactical advantages afforded by them, but also because it was only they who could afford much in the way of good weapons and armour; and for this reason they will have counted most not only while fighting from horseback but also, if they used

43

FIG. 28
One of a file of riders on a thirteenth-century vase of Mycenaean style from Ugarit (Ras Shamra)

their mounts primarily as a means of transport, when they dismounted and fought on foot.

The credibility of Aristotle's statements is borne out by archaeology and by a knowledge of cavalry developments in contemporary Oriental powers, and especially those with whom the Asia Minor colonies would be likely to come into contact in the Geometric period. Mounted warriors had already appeared in Egypt in the thirteenth century, as we can see from a number of the great battle-reliefs of the nineteenth dynasty.[11] And a roughly contemporary mounted warrior belonging to a power more closely connected with Mycenaean Greece appears on a fragmentary crater from Ugarit (*fig. 28*).[12] This crater, in late Mycenaean style but apparently more likely to have been produced by an Ugaritian craftsman than imported, is unlike other painted Mycenaean vases of this type in showing not a frieze of chariots but a frieze of riders mounted on stallions. One of the riders is armed with a large poniard slung from his waist, and perhaps, as Schaeffer suggested, the frieze represents the defile of a detachment of Ugaritian cavalry. At any rate there is a gradual shift of emphasis from chariotry to cavalry during the first half of the first millenium. Mounted warriors appear on the Syro-Hittite reliefs in the Early Iron Age, the eleventh and tenth centuries, and on the contemporary reliefs from Tell Halaf; and by the ninth century cavalry is clearly a very important arm alongside chariotry in the Assyrian and other Near Eastern armies.[13] Similarly in Greece the mounted warrior is attested, however slightly, for the late Mycenaean Age centres, which were capable of producing and maintaining very large chariot-forces, their major mobile arm; and there is evidence of mounted warriors in the Geometric Age communities, which clearly were not.

THE HOMERIC HIPPĒES

FIG. 29
Terracotta figurine of a mounted warrior of c. 1300 B.C. from Mycenae

Whereas a mounted warrior never once appears in any of the Homeric battles, archaeology has revealed that they were known in Greece even in the *Iliad*'s ostensible period. A terracotta figurine of a mounted, conical-helmeted warrior holding in his right hand what appears to be either a scabbard or a quiver has been found with a quantity of LH IIIb pottery in a deposit at Mycenae (*fig. 29*), and it can therefore be dated to about 1300 B.C.[14] A second, exactly similar rider, except that he is divorced from his horse, has been found at Prosymna.[15] Snodgrass adds a third rider figurine, said to be from Mycenae and now in Oxford,[16] and Miss Lorimer mentions a fourth, a warrior from Kavousi in Crete and said to be sub-Mycenaean.[17] Perhaps even earlier than any of the terracottas is the evidence of an amphoroid crater with Cypro-Minoan script incised on top of the handles and assigned to the end of Mycenaean IIIa style (*fig. 30*).[18] One side of this vase depicts a conical-helmeted rider preceding a chariot with three unarmed occupants, behind which comes a 'groom' on foot holding a long sword (instead of the more usual parasol). The rider appears to be a horse-guard for the carriage full of dignitaries. A similar scene appears on the other side, except that this time the rider has no helmet. Now if there is this clear, direct evidence of clay models and a vase-painting not only for the practice of riding but also of mounted warriors in late Bronze Age Greece, perhaps we should look again at some of the tablets from the LM II palace at Cnossos (*c.* 1400 B.C.). There are many tablets registering the issue of corslet, chariot and horses, but one or two which have only the ideogram for corslet and horse.[19] And although Evans may have been right in suggesting that for brevity's sake the horse's head has been used to cover the chariot as well, it is at least conceivable that those tablets are recording the issue of equipment to riders, even

45

EARLY GREEK WARFARE

FIG. 30 Fourteenth-century Mycenaean crater depicting a carriage preceded by a helmeted horseguard and followed by a footguard with a sword

though the tablets are somewhat earlier than the earliest piece of representational evidence of mounted warriors. Finally there is an LH III sherd from Mycenae which may depict a cavalryman.[20] Unfortunately the top of his head is missing and we cannot tell if he was wearing a helmet, but he is clearly marked as a warrior by his greaves (and also perhaps by what may be the top of a shield appearing above the horse's back). He stands on the far side of his horse, but we cannot of course be certain that he was going to ride it rather than yoke it to chariot.

If Desborough is right in assigning it to the Geometric period, a crater used in a cremation burial in a miniature tholos tomb at Mouliana in Crete provides our earliest post-Mycenaean representation of a mounted warrior in vase-painting.[21] It was apparently the funeral vase of a nobleman who is depicted on one side engaging in the hunt, and on the other as a mounted warrior with ridge-crest helmet, a long spear, and a shield suspended by a telamon (*fig. 31*). A sherd from Vrokastro provides another but later Cretan Geometric rider, this time of the eighth century.[22] Since only the seat and legs of this rider are visible, it is impossible to know whether he was armed or unarmed, but another sherd of the same vase indicates a military context by depicting two warriors with swords, Dipylon shields and plumed helmets driving in a chariot. Any figured representation is of course very uncommon in vase-painting until the Late Geometric period (beginning about the middle of the eighth century), but then we find helmeted warriors holding single horses occurring quite frequently on Argive LG fragments,[23] and on one particularly fine crater from a late eighth-century grave at Argos near that which contained the helmet and bronze-plated bell-corslet.[24] In connexion with the motif of the warrior holding a single horse, it is worth noting that the motif of a man between antithetical horses which he holds by their bridles is not uncommon on LG vase-

THE HOMERIC HIPPĒES

FIG. 31
Mounted warrior on a vase from a cremation burial at Mouliana in Crete, possibly of the tenth century

paintings.[25] Sometimes the man is unarmed, but often armed, and sometimes he is a panoplied Dipylon warrior complete with Dipylon shield and two or even three spears. One such Dipylon warrior holding antithetical horses occurs on the Dipylon bowl from Thera, which also depicts (besides a bull) a man on foot armed with a sword, and two naked, unarmed riders; and although it is strictly impossible to be certain that the antithetical horses were not meant for chariots, the fact that the heavy-armed nobleman was often accompanied by a mounted squire on later representations makes it just possible that this may be the significance of the two horses here, especially perhaps since one of the naked riders holds a second horse, indicated by his two pairs of reins (as on vases **13**, **32**; *figs. 8, 12*). Sometimes too the motif of the antithetical horses is reversed, and we find two men flanking a single horse. One such representation on a beaker from the Ceramicus depicts two men armed with swords at their waists apparently training the horse, since one of them holds a whip.[26] Warriors actually riding reappear on some Attic LG and Early Protoattic vases (*c.* 735–675 B.C.). Unarmed riders, sometimes with a spare second horse, begin to break into the common processions of chariots as early as the LG IIa period, *c.* 735–720 B.C. (see above, p. 21, vase **13**, *fig. 8*; also vases **22**, **32**, **31**, **33**, *figs. 9, 12, 13*, for slightly later examples). A single rider occasionally occurs on the neck of Attic LG vases;[27] and a Chiot LG sherd features a rider who cannot be distinguished as armed or unarmed since only his legs are visible.[28] Two riders who have been supposed to be the Dioscuri appear on an Early Protocorinthian vase (*c.* 720–690 B.C.),[29] and an EPA pot gives us the first certain representation of horse-racing.[30] Two examples of armed riders breaking up the monotony of the usual chariot procession are known to me on Attic LG vases. On one (**38**: LG IIb) the warrior appears to be wearing a bell-corslet whose lower edge may be represented by the bulge below his navel.[31] He brandishes a

47

FIG. 32
Eighth-century mounted warrior on a rearing horse, from an Attic Late Geometric vase (41)

javelin and, like the unarmed rider of vase **13** (*fig. 8*), he is leading a second horse, with the difference that here the second horse is clearly represented and not, as on **13**, merely suggested by a second pair of reins. On a fragment of another vase (**41**), a warrior wearing a helmet like that found in the LG grave at Argos sits on a rearing horse (*fig. 32*): other fragments of this vase show four-horsed chariots. Another helmeted rider appears in a procession of chariots on an

THE HOMERIC HIPPĒES

FIG. 33
Pottery from the grave of an eighth-century Athenian who surely rode to war

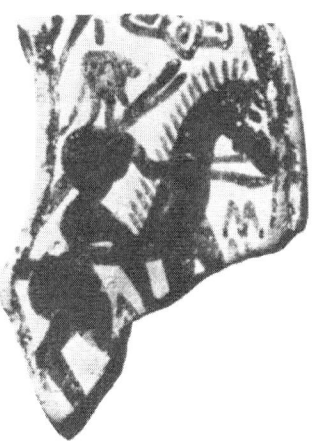

FIG. 34
Mounted warrior on an Attic Late Geometric sherd of c. 700 B.C. (A1)

MPA vase (A4). Then away from chariot-processions, a helmeted rider joins deer and sphinxes as a motif on an Argive LG crater from Tiryns of which two fragments survive.[32] Another occurs on the neck of an Attic LG vase, otherwise unfigured except for a frieze of birds round the belly, from the Ceramicus cemetery.[33] The neck-panel of a similar vase depicts a helmeted warrior leading his horse;[34] and a rider holding what may be a large sword appears on an LG scyphos

C   49

FIG. 35 Mounted foot-soldier in full armour on an Early Protoattic vase of the early seventh century (A2)

from a Dipylon grave, which also contained a terracotta horse and whose occupant surely rode to war (*fig. 33*).[35] A slightly later Attic sherd of *c.* 700 B.C. depicts a helmeted rider carrying twin spears (A1; *fig. 34*), and in the first quarter of the seventh century a panoplied mounted warrior occurs on the neck of an EPA vase (A2): he has a helmet, two spears and a heavily-bossed round shield (*fig. 35*). Panoplied riders also occur on the neck of what appears to be an Attic LG oenochoe in Toronto, but the figured scenes have been overpainted in modern times, and there is even some doubt that the vase itself with its linear decoration is genuine.[36] Boeotian mounted warriors appear on a couple of fibulae, both of which have been assigned to the LG period, but in my opinion this early dating is very doubtful: on one the rider is unarmed but qualifies as a belligerent by trampling down a prostrate man, and on the other the horseman is a heavy-armed warrior, complete with helmet, 'Boeotian' shield and single spear.[37] Several more knights have been found at Olympia. A rider with a long spear held horizontally above his head appears in relief on a bronze tripod-leg, assigned by Willemsen to the eighth century, and bronze figures of a helmeted warrior holding his horse by its bridle feature on the handles of tripod-cauldrons.[38] Then at the turn of the century (c. 700 B.C.) helmeted riders appear with 'centaurs' in a mythical scene on a gold relief in Berlin.[39]

Riders both armed and unarmed are also represented by Geometric and early Archaic terracotta figurines. Probably the earliest of these come from Asine in the Argolid where Frödin and Persson note that 'at the transition to the Geometric period [from the Mycenaean] appear some equestrian figures which differ clearly in type from the later Geometric ones'.[40] They are helmeted, and have large, plastically modelled eyes placed on either side of the beak-like face in the Mycenaean fashion. Later than these are two horsemen noted by Frödin and Persson among numerous miscellaneous finds from the Geometric period: one is headless, the other a helmeted warrior who holds a round shield in his left hand.[41] Hood doubted their Geometric dating and suggested that they were Archaic, but Snodgrass was content to call them late Geometric.[42] A considerable number of similar figurines have been found in the Argive Heraeum, and Waldstein describes three of them in detail.[43] One is a beak-faced, primitive figurine of a rider with a high helmet. The second is similar but with the addition of a large, apparently round shield. The third wears a peculiar helmet, rather like an American cocked-hat. And besides these he notes some forty-five fragments of similar figures, more or less broken. More heavy-armed horsemen come from Tanagra, Tiryns, Perachora and Tegea, along with some unarmed ones in the case of Tanagra, Tegea, and Perachora. They are variously dated, but most seem to belong to the seventh century, some perhaps a little later.[44] Excavation of the Agamemnoneion at Mycenae, where the cult began in the Late Geometric period, produced some twenty-five pieces of rider figurines of Argolid manufacture, several of them armed, and one wearing a helmet with a forward-curving peak like those on the Penthesilea shield from Tiryns (*fig. 41*).[45] And finally there is a bronze figurine of a rider in the Benaki Museum, Athens: it has been assigned to the eighth century.[46]

EARLY GREEK WARFARE

The Geometric representations of riders both armed and unarmed are admittedly not very numerous, but they are significant if seen in perspective. Figured representation, human or animal, is altogether rare in Geometric art; and, as I have already stressed, it is only in the Late Geometric period, from about the middle of the eighth century onwards, that the vase-painters begin to be at all ambitious in that direction. The rich Attic LG pottery provides most of the figured representations, and there we find chariots represented rather than mounted horses. And indeed the richness of the Dipylon graves makes it very likely that their noble occupants had possessed chariots which they used for racing, the noblest of all sports. But the old objections hold good against a military use. If they were used for war, it can only have been for behind the lines transport, and perhaps for pursuit and flight: the absence of bow or lance precludes an effective tactical military usage, no clash of chariots is ever depicted, and the mounted horse would be far more effective for transport on the battle-field itself as well as behind the lines and in pursuit and flight. It is not even the case that the vase-paintings show a smaller size or a different breed of horse for pulling a chariot and for riding, to help explain why the complex and expensive chariot and pair (or three- or four-horse teams in the case of some of the vase-paintings) should be risked in the Homeric role in battle, even if suitable terrain could be found. On vases where chariots and ridden horses appear together they are indistinguishable in size or in any other way (e.g. nos. **13, 22, 31, 32, 33, 38, 41**; *figs. 8, 9, 12, 13*); and indeed the same type of animal seems to have been used for both riding and driving until the fourth century or later.[47] Moreover there are other convincing indications that the chariots in the LG battle-scenes are 'heroic property'. For not only was the chariot a very prestigious possession to depict for a very rich man, especially perhaps at a time when even the lesser gentry may have possessed horses, but the favourite combat scene, identified as the Molione story and occurring no less than eight times in Geometric art, may indicate a very special piece of heroizing for the noblemen of eighth-century Athens, many of whom claimed descent from the Neleids of Pylos, and for whom the Molione motif may therefore have made what Coldstream calls a family crest.[48] And similarly the chariot pieces as a whole may indicate a more general expression of ancient heroic pedigrees, whilst the contemporary aspects of warfare may perhaps find expression in the sea-battle scenes.

If then we can believe Aristotle's statement about the superiority of the aristocratic knights in both war and government, we may turn to examine the internal evidence of the Homeric poems themselves, which not only reveals a knowledge of the mounted horse but also suggests that cavalry is being deliberately suppressed, and its role transferred to heroizing chariotry. Acquaintance with the practice of riding is clear from two unambiguous allusions in similes, one in the *Iliad* and one in the *Odyssey*. In *Iliad* 15.679–84 Ajax, striding mightily from deck to deck as he fights to repel the Trojans from the ships with his long ship-pike, is likened to a man who, 'well knowing how to ride, couples together four swift horses picked out of many, and rushes from the plain to the great city down a road full of people; many marvel at him, both men and women, and he, keeping his balance safely, jumps from one horse to another as they fly onwards'.[49] The simpler simile in *Odyssey* 5.371 alludes to ordinary riding as a common, well-known practice: we are simply told that the ship-wrecked Odysseus bestrode a ship's timber in the sea 'as though riding a swift horse' (κέληθ' ὡς ἵππον ἐλαύνων). Now it is significant that both these passages in which ἱππεύς is clearly and unambiguously a rider are similes, where the poet thinks of his own time. In the narrative however the picture is kept strictly archaized: just as all metal arms and armour are of bronze, so too if the warriors do not go on foot they invariably go by chariot, and never ride on horseback. And the distinction between narrative and simile was underlined by Aristarchus, who athetized the passage in the narrative in which Hector is given a quadriga (*Iliad* 8.185), but not the simile in which a quadriga appears (*Odyssey* 13.81–3): a contemporary note allowed in the latter is not allowed in the heroic, archaized narrative. Can we however go so far as to say that the only military use of the horse familiar to the epic poets was the use of the mounted horse, and that in order to archaize and heroize their picture Dark Age bards consistently suppressed the mounted horses and instead harnessed them to chariots? This possibility is certainly supported by E. Delebecque's detailed analysis of the horse in the *Iliad*. We have already noted how he contrasted the abundance of vocabulary for both horses and chariots with the almost total lack of technical, or simply special, vocabulary for the combat of chariots.[50] In particular he stressed the remarkable fact that only one word in Homer – παραιβάτης – is a technical word clearly distinguishing the functions of the two occupants of the war-chariot, and that it appears once only, at *Iliad* 23.132, where it is used in the plural in opposition to ἡνίοχοι. Otherwise both the usual words for 'homme de char' are the non-technical ἱππεύς and ἐλατήρ, equally applicable to charioteer or rider, and it is sometimes thought doubtful which is meant, as in the horse's cheek-piece simile of *Iliad* 4.141–5.

The suppression of the mounted horse in favour of heroizing chariotry in Homer is further suggested by three remarkable points which emerge from Delebecque's analysis. First there is the evidence in the narrative itself that the singer has been thinking in terms of the capabilities of the mounted horse. Second, there are often expressions which, taken in isolation, would naturally be taken as indicating the mounting of horses, and passages which have led careful modern scholars to understand that the poet was referring to cavalry. And third, there is the remarkable abruptness, confusion, lack of detail, and apparent embarrassment of the treatment of the mounted horse in the one episode in the narrative, as distinct from a simile, in which it appears. Of the first sort of evidence a good example centres on the ditch which the Achaeans dug to protect their ships. Hector scorns it, despite its great width and the pointed spikes, and says confidently that 'our horses will jump it easily at a bound' (*Iliad* 8.179). For horses to jump a wide ditch is possible if they are well-ridden and good jumpers, but materially impossible if they are dragging a chariot containing one or two men. In the event, Hector's own horses baulk at the fearsome ditch; and yet the narrative still speaks of the difficulty of 'leaping' it as well as 'crossing' it (12.50–9). Now the horses of Rhesus find no difficulty in jumping it; but they are being ridden by Odysseus and Diomedes, not pulling a chariot (10.564). Patroclus however actually jumps it in his chariot (16.380). In the case of Patroclus we might perhaps look to the immortality of the horses or the help of Apollo, but the fact remains that in the other examples the chariot is treated as able to jump as well as a mounted horse, an impossibility which cannot be explained away for the Trojan horses in general even if it can be explained in the case of an immortal pair, and which certainly indicates that the singer was thinking in terms of mounted horses of his own experience, but speaking in terms of chariots.

Of the second category of evidence, the expressions which, seen in isolation, would naturally suggest mounted horses, Delebecque cites as an example the passage where Diomedes is going after Aeneas' horses and tells his squire to 'leap upon the horses and drive them back to the Achaean lines' if he is successful in capturing them. In the event Diomedes is successful, and Sthenelus does as he was told – ἐπαΐξας καλλίτριχας ἵππους.[51] The expressions used here, and in Delebecque's other examples, are certainly unusual ones for the mounting of a chariot, and they suggest that the mounted horse is showing through the fabric of the narrative more than is usually allowed in Homer. To Delebecque's examples we may add those which have led Snodgrass to understand cavalry.[52] In the famous horse's cheek-piece simile (*Iliad* 4.141–5), Snodgrass noted that πολέες τέ μιν ἠρήσαντο | ἱππῆες φορέειν would be rather more easily understood of horsemen than of charioteers. He may be right that in this *simile* the bard meant his hearers to understand cavalry, but I think it unlikely, since although the art of riding was openly employed in the two similes already discussed, the reference was not to a military use of riding: warriors are carried on the battlefield only by chariots, and even when Diomedes and Odysseus ride Rhesus' horses back to camp when they have stolen them in a night-raid, the episode is treated with embarrassment, as we shall note below. The most significant fact about the cheek-piece simile is the typical ambiguity. Snodgrass cannot be sure. He points also to a distinction possibly intended between ἱππεύς of line 144 and ἐλατήρ of line 145, but as Delebecque has shown, both words can equally well designate 'cavalier' or charioteer.[53] Snodgrass also saw cavalry in *Iliad* 11.150–4, a similarly ambiguous passage. This passage has drawn special attention to itself for two reasons: it is the only allusion to a clash of chariots in Homer, and in some MSS it contains the unusual plural ἱππεῖς. On both these grounds Miss Lorimer called it a 'hoplite interpolation in which the ἱππεῖς are cavalry', while Snodgrass finds the singularity of the appearance of a clash of chariots sufficient by itself to indicate that ἱππεῖς means horsemen, 'whether or not Leaf and others were right in regarding the lines as a later interpolation'.[54] But I find it more difficult to believe that either 'Homer' (if we keep the lines) or an interpolator (if we athetize them) meant his hearers to understand cavalry in this single passage in the middle of a narrative battle-scene in the *Iliad*, when such pains are taken to emphasize that all the nobles have chariots. A clash of cavalry would be no less unique than a clash of chariots, but doubly so, both for the clash and for the introduction of the mounted warrior in battle. Careful modern readers, examining them in isolation, have discerned cavalry in such other ambiguous passages as *Iliad* 2.552–4 (Menestheus 'unequalled in arraying horses and shieldmen') or *Odyssey* 9.49 (Cicones 'skilled in fighting both ἀφ' ἵππων and on foot') or *Odyssey* 14.267 (the plain suddenly filled 'with footmen and horses'); but again it is extremely improbable that the audience suddenly envisaged horsemen, and surely inconceivable that the author of the lines intended his hearers to do so, and especially in the *Iliad*. As Delebecque points out, Homer transforms ἵπποι from its natural sense to multiply the words designating chariot. And in these passages in which cavalry has been 'detected', the heroizing veneer is more transparent than usual.

Finally we may examine the extraordinary episode of the nocturnal seizure of the horses of Rhesus by Diomedes and Odysseus (*Iliad* 10.465ff). It is the only episode in which the mounted horse appears in the narrative as distinct from a simile; but in contrast to the unambiguity of the similes, this narrative passage is remarkable for its obscurity, which is caused by the extraordinarily un-Homeric lack of details of the operation, and by the use of expresssions for 'mounting' which are elsewhere used for chariots. The central part of the episode runs as follows: while Diomedes was busy killing Rhesus, Odysseus loosed the horses, bound them together with thongs, and drove them out of the press, striking them with his bow because he had not thought to lift the whip from the chariot. Then he whistled as a sign to Diomedes, who had killed Rhesus and was pondering either dragging away the chariot containing the armour or else lifting it up and carrying it off in that way. Athene however dissuaded him from further risking his life. Then he jumped upon the horses, Odysseus struck them with the bow, and off they sped to the Achaean ships (498–514). Delebecque is right to notice the curiously un-Homeric suppression of circumstantial details, which is in sharp contrast to the minute repetition of details of the yoking of chariots in the rest of the narrative. There is no mention here of the bridling of the horses, which was surely a necessary preliminary to riding these strange and fiery thoroughbreds, especially in the dark. Nor are we told that Odysseus mounted: he may have driven the horses out of the press in the first instance without mounting, but he is certainly mounted when they gallop away to the ships; and when he gets back to safety he jumps down. Nor are we told that the horses were unbound again for the ride back to the ships; it is scarcely likely that they remained bound when both men had mounted. Then again there is the strangeness of the language used. 'Toutefois, le plus troublant peut-être est que ces obscurités semblent voulues par l'auteur. Celui-ci use d'expressions pour le cheval monté qui valent ailleurs et normalement pour le cheval attelé'. For example, Delebecque cites formulae used in lines 530, 513 and 529, and then concludes thus: 'L'auteur parle de cavaliers montés, mais pour le faire il emploie un style de chars...On ne peut pas supposer qu'il y ait là ignorance ou inadvertance, car nous savons au contraire que dans cet épisode l'auteur manifeste à des signes déjà remarqués non seulement des connaissances sûres, mais un véritable sens de cheval; on est donc bien obligé de croire qu'il a delibérément cultivé les obscurités semées comme à plaisir dans l'épisode, si exact en général et si coloré, des chevaux de Rhésos enlevés par ces deux cavaliers d'occasion, mais cavaliers consommés, que sont Ulysse et Diomède.'[55] It certainly looks as though some embarrassment was felt in dealing with the mounted horse in the narrative, and that the details were skipped over so that the hearer would soon forget them. The ambiguity of the expressions used in this passage is maintained in other passages, where the vocabulary applied to the yoked horses would seem more suited, by the corollary of the previous phenomenon, to the mounted horse.[56]

If Delebecque's points give rise to the strong suspicion that the mounted horse is being suppressed in Homer and yoked instead to a heroic war-chariot, that suspicion is strongly reinforced by an examination of the military role attributed to the Homeric chariot, for just as it argues in every respect (apart from one possibly genuine Mycenaean survival, the Nestor passage) against a familiarity with the chariot as a weapon of war, so too it argues with equal force for familiarity with the mounted horse. It is perhaps a measure of the

FIG. 36
A dismounted hoplite inscribed *hippobatas* preceded by his mounted squire, the *hippostrophos*, on an Early Corinthian vase of the late seventh century (C2)

FIG. 37
The same motif of the *hippobatas* preceded by his *hippostrophos* on an Early Protocorinthian vase (C1), nearly a century earlier than vase C2 (*fig. 36*)

deliberate heroizing of the Homeric picture that Telemachus is incredibly represented as driving down the Peloponnese and even over the mountains from Pylos to Sparta in a chariot.[57] As for the chariot's military role, apart from the fact that Homer shows no conception of the vast size or complex organization of the Mycenaean palace-administration capable of producing large numbers of war-chariots, we have already noted three tactical points against familiarity with the chariot in war: that it is highly improbable that large numbers of such expensive and complex pieces of equipment, if such there were, could have been restricted to transporting foot-soldiers as their primary role, as Homer suggests; that if it is at least not impractical that they were used primarily for transport behind the lines, and also for pursuit or flight, it is surely impossible that they could have been used individually for transport in the thick of battle; and finally that even on the few occasions when they are fought from, their warriors are not equipped with either of the weapons which made chariotry a formidable arm, the bow or the lance, but with the javelin, long obsolete as a chariot weapon in the great chariot-using powers. If however the bards were really thinking of mounted horsemen of their own experience, it accords remarkably well with our evidence not only that the horse, unlike the chariot, featured in considerable numbers in later Dark Age communities as an essential possession of nobles who really did count both in government and in war, but also that the mounted horse could and did fulfil a mainly transport role, and that, again unlike the chariot, it could be fought from effectively with the javelin, the main weapon in Homer and unimpeachably attested by archaeology as the main spear-type of the Geometric Age, at least from *c.* 900 B.C.

This last point is of course a minor one since the examples of fighting from chariots are so very few in Homer; but all the same it is worth noting that the effectiveness of the javelin from horseback is clearly demonstrated by its retention as a principal weapon of the cavalry squadrons of the classical city-states when the heavy thrusting-spear had long been revived for the organized hoplite infantry. Xenophon in particular is emphatic about its superiority, although later it alternated with the xyston as the favourite weapon of the Macedonian cavalry.[58] As to the primary role of transport, both to the battlefield and later for pursuit or flight, it is significant that after the Geometric period, when vase-paintings of horsemen begin to be more common, we find the horse very frequently used to mobilize a heavily armed warrior who dismounted to fight on foot, exactly as the Homeric warrior did, and who had with him a mounted squire to hold his horse (and sometimes a spare spear) for him while he fought, and to keep it handy so that he could remount quickly. The seventh and sixth century vase-paintings are fully discussed and illustrated in Chapters v and vi, and here it will suffice to mention a few examples. The squire's duty of manoeuvring the horses so that they were always at hand for the warrior to remount in an emergency is clearly expressed on an inscribed Corinthian aryballos, on which a dismounted hoplite is depicted with his squire, who remains mounted and holds the second horse (*fig. 36*): the warrior is termed *hippobatas*, and his unarmed squire *hippostrophos*.[59] This vase belongs to the last quarter of the seventh century, but a similar motif appears much earlier on an Early Protocorinthian aryballos which was painted not later than *c.* 700 B.C., and it almost certainly has the same significance (*fig. 37*). On both vases the positions of the heavy-armed warrior on foot and the unarmed rider preceding him are exactly parallel, the only difference being that no second horse is shown in outline on the earlier one. But in view of the many contemporary representations of chariots which show only a single horse we should not be surprised if the painter chose to leave the hoplite's horse to the imagination rather than blur the outline. Fragments of a Corinthian vase contemporary with the '*hippobatas–hippostrophos*' aryballos show hoplites mounted as well as their squires, along with hoplites fighting on foot (see below, p. 86, *fig. 46*). And the sixth century provides many more examples. W. Helbig listed a number of representations of squired warriors who dismount to fight, and he convincingly argued that the knights who according to Aristotle were militarily and politically dominant in the early Greek cities between the fall of kingship and the organization of the hoplite phalanx had been warriors of this type.[60] Some vase-scenes show the knight on foot taking leave of someone while his mounted squire holds his horse (see below, *figs. 63, 75*); some show both the knight and his squire mounted, and riding side by side (*figs. 55, 61, 73, 74*); some show the knight in the act of dismounting while his squire remains mounted (*fig. 62*); and in others he has clearly just dismounted (*fig. 56*). Other vases depict actual battle-scenes in which two dismounted knights are locked in combat whilst their mounted squires hold their horses on either side (*fig. 51*). And sometimes the action is still more interesting. On one Corinthian cup a similar duel has ended in the flight of one of the combatants (*fig. 50*). The mounted squire of the pursuer quickly rides up with his master's horse so that he can remount as quickly as possible, but it looks as though the defeated warrior's squire has panicked, because instead of waiting for his master he is riding away with both horses at top speed. In some of these scenes the characters are given mythological names either from the Homeric epic or elsewhere, whilst other vases are without inscriptions or other heroic identification. But all show the mounted warrior and his mounted squire in exactly the same roles as those of the Homeric chariot-borne warrior and his charioteer, and a recently published Corinthian cup of the first quarter of the sixth century actually shows the real war-horse and the heroizing war-chariot juxtaposed.[61] It depicts a heroic duel in contemporary hoplite equipment over a fallen warrior. The duellist on the left has a mounted squire holding his horse and a spare spear for him, but on the right we find a chariot performing more heroically the role which really belonged to the mounted horse. Now the exactness of this parallel has often been stressed; but we are always told of the abandoning of the chariot in favour of the mounted horse at the end of the eighth century.[62] I believe on the contrary that the evidence of the Homeric language, and in particular the fact that παραιβάτης is a hapax in Homer, underlines the other indications that the Dark Age bards were familiar with mounted knights accompanied by mounted squires but put them into war-chariots to heroize and archaize their picture; and I believe that the chariots in the LG battle-scenes have been influenced by the epic.

Finally there is the fact that the Homeric chariots are represented as transporting individual warriors in the thick of the fighting on the field of battle itself, and there is no doubt that its greater mobility, simplicity and manoeuvrability make that role a far more practical possibility for the mounted horse than for the chariot, which is even less likely to have been used for behind the lines transport when it would be impractical for use on the battlefield. If a later, non-Greek example of the practice of dismounting to fight on foot is worth quoting, a striking one is provided by Polybius' account of Hannibal's cavalry at Cannae, where, 'when the Spanish and Celtic horse on the left wing came into collision with the Roman cavalry, the struggle that ensued was truly barbaric, for there was none of the normal wheeling evolutions, but having once met they dismounted and fought man to man'.[63] It is also interesting to note that the squiring of a noble knight was apparently a practice of Celtic warfare too. Pausanias speaks of *trimarcisia*, a word presumably going back to the descent of the Celts into Greece in the third century, and indicating a group of three riders comprising a noble warrior and two squires who could supply him with fresh horses.[64] And for a famous example of inveterate enemies on horseback seeking each other out with heroic determination for individual combat in the thick of battle, we have Plutarch's story of Eumenes of Cardia and Neoptolemus.[65] At any rate it is clear from the Archaic Greek vase-paintings that there were squired knights who used their horses as the Homeric warriors used their chariots, primarily as a means of transport, and for pursuit and flight, in the days of hoplite warfare; and it is a reasonable assumption that in the pre-phalanx Geometric period battles were much more fluid, and allowed considerable movement of small groups or even individual mounted knights and their squires through the battle itself.

IV
DIPYLON WARRIOR, HOPLITE AND CAVALRYMAN

Our reconstruction of Geometric Age battles from the evidence of the Homeric poems revealed a fairly disorganized picture of clashes between heavily armed warriors who rode into battle and dismounted to fight, and who were attended by mounted squires whose task was to hold the warrior's horse for him while he fought, and to keep it at hand for him to remount quickly for pursuit or flight or to move about on the battlefield. This is not to say that no Geometric Age warrior ever hurled a javelin without first dismounting, or even that something in the nature of a cavalry charge never took place. But the Homeric horseman was essentially a foot-soldier, and instances of fighting from the 'chariot' either in mass or alone are extremely rare in the epic. Then for the second half of the eighth century there is the evidence of the Attic Late Geometric vase-paintings, and these reveal an exactly similar style of fighting. The heavily armed warriors almost invariably fight on foot in the Homeric fashion with javelins and sword. There are a few representations of mounted warriors, but none of them show fighting from horseback. Chariots occasionally appear in battle-scenes, but there is only one doubtful exception to the rule that the warrior dismounted to fight (*fig. 4*). Now we have argued that there were no war-chariots in use in Geometric Age Greece except in Cyprus, and that those which appear in the vase-paintings are heroic property. Snodgrass went further and similarly dismissed the 'Dipylon' shield, the commonest type, as another piece of heroizing, and if he was right, the value of the LG battle-scenes to the historian of contemporary warfare must be far less certain than he himself sought to claim elsewhere.[1] But the cases of the war-chariot and the shield are not parallel. It is not the form of the chariot but only its use in battle which is heroic. The vase-painters knew perfectly well what a chariot looked like. Their aristocratic patrons had racing-chariots in which they competed at funeral games and great festivals, and there is no good reason to doubt that they wore full armour while they drove them in procession in honour of the dead man before stripping to race them at his games. And similarly I believe that the vase-painters copied contemporary shields no less than contemporary helmets, swords, ships or chariots, and that the Dipylon type is a realistic and practical shield for the Geometric Age knight to have used.

What led first Webster and then Snodgrass to suspect the Dipylon shield as a heroic property was the common assumption that it is an earlier manifestation of the same type of shield which is usually called 'Boeotian' in Archaic vase-paintings, where it does undoubtedly become a 'romantic archaism'.[2] And for this reason they referred to both types as 'Dipylon'. But whatever their connexion, the two shapes are chronologically exclusive. The Dipylon with its incurved edges, much the commonest shield of the LG vase-paintings, disappears at the end of the eighth century or soon after, whereas the Boeotian form, an oval shield with scallops on either side, appears only in the seventh and commonly only in the sixth and after (e.g. see below, p. 126, *fig. 67*). And even if the two representations were identical, it would not follow that a shield which was an obsolete archaism in the seventh and sixth centuries had never been used in the eighth. It is useful therefore to judge the Geometric Age shield on its own merits without prejudice, and to forget for the present the later form. Now it is true that the Dipylon shield sometimes appears impossibly narrow-waisted (see above, p. 33, *fig. 26*), and Snodgrass objected that no contemporary shield was likely to have been so stylized. But that seems a strange argument in a style that is rightly called 'Geometric' and which stylized contemporary men, horses and chariots to the same degree. Snodgrass accepted the more realistic-looking round and rectangular shields as contemporary (*fig. 38*), but whereas circles and oblongs cannot be exaggerated in shape, no design could more readily lend itself to the excesses of Geometric convention than the incurved edges of the Dipylon, and it is noticeable that its greatest exaggeration appears in friezes of warriors where it makes a pleasing pattern. Moreover, if the incurved-

FIG. 38 Warriors with rectangular, 'Dipylon', and round shields on an Attic Late Geometric vase

edge shield was not contemporary, where did it come from? Webster maintained that the artists might have been copying surviving representations of the Minoan-Mycenaean figure-of-eight shield; but even if we could believe that sufficient representations survived from the sixteenth and fifteenth centuries, the incurved edges of the Dipylon are the very opposite of the convex curves of the figure-of-eight, and there is no evidence of any eight-shape in Geometric art, which would certainly have been quick to add so attractive a shape to its repertoire, and especially if it had been incorporated for the purpose of heroizing battle-scenes. And the Dipylon is no more a body-shield than it is eight-shaped. A likelier Mycenaean candidate for the *material* ancestry of the Dipylon shield is a shield with incurved edges of which only the top appears on a Mycenaean IIIb sherd from Iolcos;[3] but the commonest shield of the latest period of the Bronze Age was a small, rounded shield, and it is of course absurd to imagine that all the eighth-century painters of Dipylon shields were copying representations of a Bronze Age type known to modern archaeology by only the odd sherd.

At this point we should consider the possible purpose of the Dipylon shape of shield, since no-one seems to have done so despite all that has been written about the possibilities of its material evolution or artistic models. A possible method of construction for such a shape out of hide has been put forward by Miss Lorimer and followed by Ahlberg;[4] but as Lorimer pointed out, the rectangular shield that is also found in Geometric art could easily have been

FIG. 39
Clay model of a
Dipylon shield

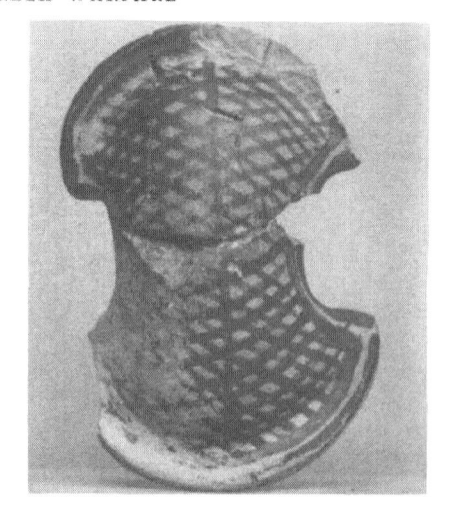

(outside)

(profile)   *(inside)*

produced by the addition of a pair of extra side-staves (*figs. 3, 4, 38*); and since a rectangular shield would give fuller protection than one with incurved edges, it is reasonable to ask why the latter type, which is so much commoner, was obviously preferred. Besides, it is just as likely that the Dipylon shield was made of wicker;[5] and whatever its material, if Lorimer and Ahlberg are right in believing that it was

DIPYLON WARRIOR, HOPLITE AND CAVALRYMAN

FIG. 40
A sea-borne attack on an Attic Late Geometric vase, showing Dipylon warriors fighting with both hands free and a warrior holding a small, convex, round shield (to the left of the ship)

a contemporary shield, there should be a better reason why it was chosen than an accident of construction. There is, and it is a very simple one. The clue is given by the fact that most Dipylon warriors, either fighting or marching or driving a chariot, are clearly shown with both hands free (*figs. 3, 4, 6, 7, 26, 38, 40*). The shield therefore must have been suspended from the shoulder by a telamon, and the advantage of the incurved edges was simply the greater freedom allowed to the arms. Very probably it had a single, central hand-grip, and no doubt it could be swung round from back to front to be manipulated as necessary, although no Geometric painting actually shows it being used in this way. Perhaps too it was sometimes allowed to hang on the front. But even more important in the unorganized warfare depicted both in Homer and on the vases was protection for the back,[6] and the elbow room which the Dipylon shield would afford for fighting and running – for it cannot have been easy to run or fight with the elbows banging against a shield which projected from either side of the trunk – goes far towards explaining its much greater popularity than either the round or rectangular varieties (*fig. 38*).

So far the Dipylon shield has been considered only in the two dimensions in which it appears in Geometric art, but another, secondary explanation for the incurved edges is revealed by the clay model of a shield in the British Museum,[7] which is clearly convex and which in every way suits the stylized shield of the vase-paintings and its possible construction (*fig. 39*). The painted lattice-work on the outside suggests a wicker shield, and cross-staves are clearly marked on the inside. And it can very readily be imagined fitting snugly on the warrior's back, its lower edge coming below the hips as the vase-paintings indicate, and its incurved sides allowing elbow room and yet providing greater width for the protection of the shoulders. No handle is indicated on the model, but there will almost certainly have been a central one at the strongest point, where the two diagonal staves of the basic framework crossed. Now a convex shield is clearly preferable to a flat one because it more readily

EARLY GREEK WARFARE

FIG. 41
A flat, clay, votive shield of Late Geometric date from Tiryns, supposedly depicting Achilles and Penthesilea, and showing warriors with small, convex round shields

deflects spears and arrows. And a convex shield which is round is best of all for this purpose. But not only is such a shield, if of any size, difficult to fight or run with when slung on the back, but when held in front by a single hand-grip it would effectively prevent the warrior from holding a second javelin in his left hand: to counter the convexity the hand-grip would have had to jut out so far from the inner surface of the shield that superhuman strength would have been needed to keep it upright. And that is why the only convex round shields shown held by a central hand-grip in Geometric art are very small ones (e.g. *figs. 40, 41*),[8] and one warrior is actually holding two javelins and such a shield in the same hand (*fig. 42*).[9] Large round shields are sometimes found, but they are necessarily flat, or nearly so, and therefore less effective as shields as well as less comfortable to wear on the back. The Dipylon design however surmounted the difficulty by enabling the left hand to grip a large convex shield close to its inner surface at the centre, and at the same

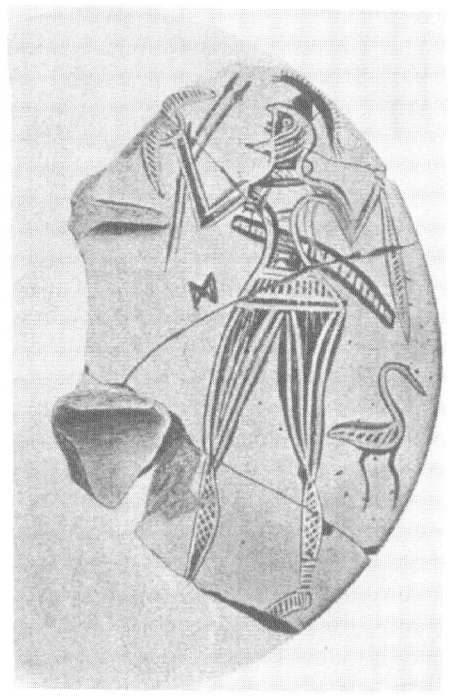

FIG. 42
Another Argive Late Geometric votive shield from Tiryns showing a warrior holding a small, convex, round shield and two javelins in the same hand

time a javelin which would protrude diagonally through the scallops on either side. And this is exactly what we find happening on an early seventh-century Protocorinthian aryballos from Lechaeum (*fig. 43*),[10] although the shields here are improbably large. At the same time however this vase-painting indicates why the scalloped shield became obsolete after the invention of the double-gripped 'hoplite' shield. The desire for a large and heavier shield which could be metal-faced and yet easily manipulated, which was both round and convex for the better deflection of blows and missiles, and which at the same time allowed the left hand to carry one or even two spears without giving up the protection of a shield held at the front, had led to the invention of a shield with an arm-band in the centre, which bore most of the weight, and a hand-grip at or near the edge. And exactly because the hand-grip had less weight to bear, it could be thinner, and this in turn made it even easier for the left hand to grip a spear at the same time. (It is less likely that the

FIG. 43
Battle-scene on an early seventh-century Proto-corinthian vase, showing how the scallops of the Dipylon shield enabled a warrior to grip a convex shield of large size by a central handle and hold a spare javelin in the same hand, and how the invention of the double-grip meant that the hoplite could hold a spare javelin with a large convex shield which was round

hand-grip was actually let go for this purpose, as Snodgrass suggested.) The invention of the double grip, first unmistakably revealed by vase-painters early in the seventh century,[11] soon made the hoplite shield universal. The need for the scalloped edges on a shield when it was being handled had disappeared; and the double grip meant that the new shield could not be swung round immediately onto the back, and thus their other purpose was removed. The inability to swing the new shield onto the back was of course a disadvantage, but it was far outweighed by its advantages, and neutralized by tactical developments as we shall see below (pp. 73 ff.). The active life of the Dipylon shield now came to an end. Artistically however it did not die but became what Webster and Snodgrass maintained it had always been, a heroic property, which recurred very frequently on Attic vase-paintings of the sixth century. At first sight the 'Boeotian' shield as it then appears on Attic Black Figure and on Boeotian coins might seem a different shield from the Dipylon of the Geometric vases. The scallops have become too small to serve any useful purpose, and the shield's rim often extends beyond them. And since the cutting of holes in a round shield purely for decoration is scarcely credible, it is reasonable to assume that their original purpose had been forgotten. But the connexion between them is illustrated by what I believe to have been the realistic form of the eighth-century shield, that of the clay model (*fig. 39*): stylistic convention was responsible for the impossibly large arcs of some of the Geometric vase-paintings, and ignorance of their purpose for the equally stylized scallops of Black Figure vases and of the coins.

So much has been claimed as the inevitable consequence of the invention of the double-grip shield, not only militarily but socially, politically, and psychologically too, that a discussion of its properties will be appropriate here. By way of a valuable counterpoise to the extravagant claims of Miss Lorimer and more recently of Detienne, Snodgrass revived Nierhaus' thesis that the adoption of the elements of the hoplite panoply, including the shield, was gradual and piecemeal;[12] and he further maintained that there was nothing which inherently tied the double-grip shield to phalanx tactics, and that the two innovations were not simultaneous. His first point is certainly convincing, but he seems to have overstated his further case: it would be truer to say that the double-grip shield was not impossibly ill-adapted to the unorganized warfare of the javelin era than that it did nothing to encourage the development of the phalanx, to which it was certainly better adapted. Snodgrass rightly criticized Miss Lorimer for restricting the use of the shield to the thrusting-spear of the developed phalanx. She maintained that a warrior could not hold a shield and a second javelin at the same time, but we have seen how the representations reveal the greater ease with which the left hand could do this when the weight of the shield was taken by the arm-band. And she was also mistaken in arguing that only the warrior's left side could be protected. As Snodgrass pointed out, the elbow's range of movement (coupled with a slight twist of the body) would be adequate to parry most blows aimed at the right-hand side. And against her objection that the size of a hoplite shield was restricted to a radius of the forearm's length, he could have added that this presupposes that the left hand invariably gripped the extreme outer-edge of the shield's rim, whereas in fact the vast size of some hoplite shields suggests that this cannot have been so;[13] and while some representations show the hand-grip fixed some inches away from the outer rim,[14] others reveal it as a large loop fixed to the strong rim but projecting some distance inwards (see below, p. 137, *fig. 72*).[15] Moreover there are early seventh-century representations which reveal the double-grip shield in use with the pair of javelins and with the sword (*fig. 44*),[16] of which the former had no place in the classical phalanx and the latter was resorted to only in an emergency when the thrusting-spear had been broken or lost. All the same, although it is clear that the hoplite did not materialize fully armed like Athene from the head of some military genius and immediately take his place in the developed phalanx of warriors advancing with single spears poised for the typical overarm thrust, a closely ordered battle-line can exist without the thrusting-spear, and Snodgrass went too far in trying to separate the invention of the double-grip shield and the development of the phalanx. The new shield had one aspect which I believe prompted the development of

FIG. 44
Protoattic vase of the early seventh century (A3) on which hoplites with the single thrusting-spear advance against another phalanx which is equipped with swords and pairs of throwing-spears (perhaps in the manner of seventh-century Euboean warfare)

the phalanx, and although the double grip is responsible for it, it is not what is usually alleged, that the shield covers not only the left side of its bearer but also the right side of the man next in line to his left.

It is of course true, as Thucydides explained, that the hoplite phalanx tended to move to the right because out of fear each man moved his exposed side as close as possible to the shield of the man on the right: they believed that the closest possible order would afford the best protection, and as the man on the extreme right wing instinctively moved further right, away from his opposite number on the enemy left, the rest of the battle-line followed him.[17] But this does not mean, as both A. Andrewes and W. G. Forrest have stated, that the shield jutted out to give frontal protection to the exposed side of the man to the left.[18] While a warrior could easily thrust his elbow out to the right to ward off a blow aimed at his own exposed side, he could not maintain the highly unnatural position of the elbow fully extended in front and the left hand held close to the stomach, the position which would be necessary to cover the right side of his neighbour. And in any case it is inconceivable that while fighting for his own life against an opponent who would be striking at his own exposed side, the warrior could be more concerned to protect his neighbour on the left. The same psychology which made the whole line move to the right would make each man move his shield to the right also. The significance of Thucydides' observation is that some lateral, not frontal, protection was obtained from the next man's shield, and that it was vital not to allow a gap to develop which might break the line, since a broken phalanx was as good as lost. The fact is that no shield held in the left hand except the long extinct body-shield of the Bronze Age could adequately cover a warrior's right-hand side, and indeed the more easily manipulated double-grip shield might do better than a similar-sized single-grip type. It was not then fear for the exposed side that prompted the development of the phalanx with the hoplite shield any more than with its predecessors. The real difference lies in the fact that the new shield could give no effective protection to the back. It is not that it had no telamon. Hoplite shields are sometimes depicted slung on a warrior's back when he is at rest or walking,[19] but never when he is fighting or running. The disadvantage of the double grip was that the arm could not be quickly disengaged for the shield to be swung round onto the back as the single-grip sorts had been; and since in any case it was hard to run with a large round shield catching the elbows, the hoplite shield was dropped in flight, and so produced Archilochus' poem and the harsh Spartan mothers' well-known injunction. If then the back became less easily protected, the answer was to keep such close formation that the enemy could not get behind the line. And thus the phalanx developed. Its initial development need not have been accompanied by the universal adoption of the single thrusting-spear as the main weapon. The warriors advancing from the left on a Protoattic vase are thus equipped in what is surely an early attempt to represent the phalanx, but those advancing from the right have swords and twin spears and they are no less closely ordered (*fig. 44*). The earliest phalanxes could well have been formed with the old Geometric Age weapons. The javelins would be thrown when the opposing lines came within range, and then they would close with the sword. This style may well have persisted in some areas, as among the aristocratic swordsmen of Euboea perhaps (see below, pp. 90–3), but generally the thrusting-spear soon asserted its superiority and simplicity, since sword-fighting probably required more skill and made it less easy to keep close order. And the javelin declined as a hoplite weapon, although it may have accompanied the thrusting-spear for some time.[20]

The first unmistakable representations of the double-grip shield belong to the first quarter of the seventh century, and from about 675 B.C. Corinthian artists began to depict phalanx battles in which opposing lines of identically equipped hoplites advanced with their spear poised for the classic downward thrust.[21] Besides the shield the hoplite panoply consisted of helmet, greaves, and often corslet. A sword was usually slung at the side, but the main weapon was a stout spear, some seven or eight feet long, with which each man struck, usually overarm, in an orderly way. Order was the essence of this new style of fighting, and the hoplites' aim was to break the enemy line while preserving their own. Clearly it was a very different style of warfare from what had existed in the eighth century, and its different military requirements and their possible social and political consequences must now be considered with regard to Aristotle's much quoted connexion of the hoplite reform with a trend to more democratic constitutions.[22] There seem to me to be three main differences: that it needed more men, that it needed less skill, and that it *could be* less expensive. With regard to the first, it is clear that the battle-line needed to be as strong and as wide as possible. If it was not wide enough it could be outflanked by the enemy, and if it was not strong enough it could be broken. And just as weight of numbers counted more than before, skill mattered less than it had done in the more individual, less organized 'Homeric' fighting. That is not to say that a highly trained hoplite force was not likely to be more successful than a poorly trained one, as Sparta's reputation amply testifies. But all the same, although training was necessary to be supremely effective, a smaller degree of skill would suffice for competence. As F. E. Adcock put it, it is hard to conceive a method of warfare that in peace made a more limited call on the time and effort of most citizens of most communities.[23] Now this in turn meant that a farmer who was not rich enough to enjoy the leisure necessary for the lengthy practice of arms could, with the minimum of training, become competent enough to take his place in the phalanx, and therefore the requirement of leisure and skill would not limit the availability of the greater numbers which the phalanx demanded. The expense of the hoplite's equipment was still great however, just as great if not greater than the arms and armour of the pre-hoplite warrior;[24] and although the odd state like Sparta may have provided the panoply,[25] in most the citizen was expected to provide his own. Expense therefore would limit the hoplite class to the richer sections of society, and Snodgrass' sound observations on this point, summarily dismissed in a footnote by Detienne, are a stumbling-block to the latter's extravagant claims that the hoplite reform signalled sweeping political changes by the 'promotion des ruraux'.[26] Even Aristotle writing in the fourth century stressed that 'the rich are hoplites, the poor not'; and on one occasion he distinguishes the hoplites from the 'demos'.[27] He does however make another point which gives the clue to the lesser social exclusiveness of hoplite warfare than of what had gone before when he proceeds to say that among the notables themselves there are differences of wealth, such as in the keeping of horses.[28] His style of warfare was not everywhere cheaper for the hoplite than the earlier style had been for the Dipylon warrior, but it could be, and sometimes it had to be; and the reason for this centres on the changing role of the war-horse.

The horse's role in transporting the warrior to and from the battlefield and for pursuit and flight continued to be valuable in hoplite warfare as in the earlier style, and Helbig was right to speak of the earlier aristocracies of knights as mounted footsoldiers. Alföldi claims that this was to disregard Aristotle's statement about military superiority as the basis for the pre-hoplite governments of aristocratic 'cavalry'. According to him, Aristotle explains that 'before the organization of heavy infantry, footsoldiers were powerless against cavalry: and this proves that the *hippeis* could not have fought on foot at this period.'[29] In fact however Aristotle says nothing about cavalry: he does not tell us how the *hippeis* had used their horses, but only that a hoplite force (as he knew it) is useless without organization, that the crafts and tactics connected with such matters did not exist in ancient times, and therefore the strength lay with the *hippeis*,[30] who are neutrally defined elsewhere as 'those who used horses in their wars against their neighbours'.[31] On the other hand, although he did not make it clear, Aristotle may have assumed that the pre-hoplite warrior class were true cavalry. If he did, it was a natural enough assumption for a fourth-century writer to make. But it is valid to ask how much he could have known about pre-hoplite warfare. Very probably he had little more to go on than the names of the aristocracies at Chalcis, Eretria and elsewhere. And certainly the weight of archaeological evidence coupled with that of the Homeric poems supports the thesis that the *hippeis* used their horses principally for transport. How then did the new style of fighting affect the horse's role? In the first place it removed its tactical role of transporting the footsoldier in the battle itself. When the fluid and mobile warfare reflected in Homer and the LG vases was replaced by organized phalanxes, the horse could only be used for transporting him behind the lines, and for pursuit and flight. It had lost part of its role, and the remainder was not perhaps as essential as the whole had been. But this does not mean that the remainder was no longer valuable.

While Alföldi's article is a useful counterweight to Helbig's view that true cavalry failed to develop in mainland Greece until the fifth century and until the fourth elsewhere, he was wrong to dismiss the whole idea of mounted hoplites on the grounds that as mere transport animals the horse's speed and manoeuvrability would remain unused, and that surely the Athenian 'naucraries' would not have gone to the expense of supplying pairs of horses and all the necessary equipment merely for that purpose.[32] It is true that the horse's manoeuvrability would be less used than before, but its speed would be valuable in enabling an attacking force to make lightning raids and arrive at their objective unawares before a defence force could be organized. Conversely a mounted defensive force would be better able to meet an invader rapidly before he could plunder villages or devastate crops; and it might delay him while reinforcements were being organized in the city. Both invaders and defenders would similarly benefit from arriving fresh at the battlefield; and the benefits of mounted flight or pursuit remain the same. As for the 'naucraries', if the lexicographer's dubious reference is reliable,[33] and if the naucraries had to maintain maritime defences, the advantages of keeping a mounted hoplite force (if such it was) are not hard to see. Ship-borne raids were common enough in Homer, and they featured in late eighth-century art (*fig. 40*).[34] And for a vivid illustration of the value of speed in launching an effective counter-attack we have the disguised Odysseus' description of an episode from his travels which he invented for Eumaeus: 'the cry came quickly to the city, and hearing the noise they came forth; and the whole plain was filled with footmen and horses and clashing bronze...they slew many of us with the sharp bronze, and others they led up to their city alive, to work for them perforce'.[35] Moreover, it is a mistake to think entirely in terms of a whole mounted phalanx and forget the individual point of view. Even where the majority of a hoplite force were without horses, for those of the landed gentry who were fortunate enough to have them the advantages of riding while others walked were not inconsiderable. Quite apart from the social distinction which horses and a squire would display for all to see before the gentleman had to dismount and join lesser mortals in the phalanx, the hoplite panoply was heavy, and it was clearly a personal advantage to arrive at battle unwearied by a long march. For flight in the case of defeat the personal advantage of having a squire at hand with a horse is an obvious one. In victory the horse will have made the journey home pleasanter and quicker for the weary man. It might also save his life if he was wounded; and if he died, he had a squire to throw his body over his horse's back and take it home to be wept over by his relatives. A final point may be suggested by a sixth-century Attic vase-painting which shows such a hoplite dismounting to join a phalanx which is advancing in battle-order, while his mounted squire holds his horse (see below, p. 112, *fig. 56*). Could it be that this mounted hoplite is an officer, who has just finished ordering his troops and is now joining his regiment for the battle? If so, he will have found his horse invaluable for getting round to marshal the troops, for seeing and being seen and heard more easily, and also for reconnoitring the ground beforehand. At any rate, there is ample evidence for mounted hoplites in the Archaic period, as the next two chapters will show. But the Attic vase-painting just mentioned does indicate what must have been the case in many states. In some areas, those with broad and fertile plains able to support many rich estates, there may have been sufficient horse-owners to produce a fully mounted hoplite army of the large numbers required by the new style of warfare, and in that case the new style will have been no less expensive than the old. But in most states the phalanx will have had to recruit the weight of numbers necessary for its effectiveness from a broader social stratum than the horse-owners, and in this case warfare will have become less aristocratic. And in turn, the changing sociology of warfare may, in some cities at least, have had political repercussions as Aristotle believed; but how great these are likely to have been, how they came about, with what time-lag, and in company with what other circumstances, are questions to be touched on in Chapter VII. For the present our concern is to discover how the mounted warriors fought, and they were the landed gentry. The war-horse was always an aristocratic beast, and even when the gentry had long since ceased to enjoy their once universal monopoly of effective warfare, wealth and government, Theophrastus' Man of Petty Ambition would give the rest of his accoutrements to his slave to take home after riding in a procession of the knights, but would continue to show himself off by putting on his cloak and clicking round the market-place in his spurs.[36]

So far the hoplite system of fighting has been discussed only with regard to the previous function of the war-horse, as transport for a warrior who usually dismounted to fight. But there are reasons to suppose that its introduction stimulated the development of true cavalry. Because success in a hoplite battle usually went to the side which first broke the enemy phalanx while preserving its own intact, any method of harassing a phalanx and causing it to disintegrate or weaken would be of undoubted value. And here was a role to which the manoeuvrability as well as the speed of the horse was well suited. Slingers, light javelineers and archers on foot were used for this purpose, but their mobility was limited, and once phalanxes were closely engaged their effectiveness against the enemy hoplites was limited by the danger of getting in the way of their own. To a mounted force of javelineers or lancers however a phalanx could be particularly vulnerable. It is true of course that a well-ordered phalanx would not easily be broken by a head-on cavalry charge, although sixth-century vase-paintings occasionally show such attempts being made (see below, p. 123, *fig. 65*). A frontal attack would find the hoplites well protected by their shields and armour, and the line would present a formidable array of spears. And although the demoralizing effect of a cavalry charge is not to be lightly discounted, the Archaic Greek cavalryman was not a Mediaeval knight. It was not the case, as is commonly supposed, that a phalanx could only be broken by a charge of lancers and that the lancer needed stirrups.[37] Stirrups did of course give lancers a firmer seat, but the Parthian cataphract cavalry which operated with such devastating effect against the organized Roman infantry in the first century B.C. bore lances so long that the Greeks called them barge-poles, and yet they had no stirrups. Both the cavalryman and his horse were encased in heavy iron mail, but whereas the Mediaeval knight was armoured all over, the cataphract was denied thigh armour under his mailcoat because grip was all-important.[38] Clearly bareback riding and lancers are not incompatible, and although Xenophon in his own time preferred the javelin, Alexander had both lancers and javelineers. And there were cavalrymen who thrust rather than threw their lances in Archaic Greece too, as the sixth-century Attic vases will testify (e.g. below, pp. 121ff, *figs. 64, 67, 70, 71*). But the Archaic Greeks did not have the mighty chargers of Iran or of Mediaeval England which could bear the vast weight of armour necessary for protection in an attack against a wall of spears, and without that protection a head-on charge against an organized hoplite phalanx would be wasteful. But the head-on attack does not exhaust the possibilities of effective cavalry action against a phalanx, which, though strong in front, was vulnerable on the wings and especially in the rear.

A flanking attack on an advancing phalanx could well break it up by forcing the hoplites on the wings to wheel outwards to defend themselves and so lose contact with the centre and, unless well trained, with each other.[39] And if the cavalry could ride round behind the line before it had time to reform and make a square, the nature of the hoplite equipment reveals how vulnerable it would be. While hoplites were engaged with an enemy, and could not turn to defend themselves, they could not swing the double-grip shield onto their backs: and unlike the 'Homeric' warriors they were often less skilled in arms and trained only to operate in line. No hoplite commander could afford to let the rear of an advancing phalanx go unprotected if the enemy had cavalry. If he himself was weak in that arm, he had either to make his stand in a place which was unsuitable for cavalry or in which natural or artificial features protected the flanks, or else he must form a square, which in turn meant weakening the ranks facing the enemy phalanx and thereby lessening their chances of success in the frontal assault. On the other hand, if he too was strong in cavalry, he could still concentrate all his hoplites against the enemy phalanx by relying on his own horsemen to protect his wings and rear from the cavalry of his opponents. And so pure cavalry battles would develop on the wings. So far however we have discussed the effectiveness of cavalry only against hoplites organized in the phalanx, and it was even more effective if it could catch them disorganized. That is most probably how the Thessalian cavalry managed to defeat Anchimolius' Spartan hoplites at Phalerum in 511 B.C., since Herodotus tells us that they attacked the Spartan camp:[40] the Spartans were probably not able to form up quickly enough to deal with this unexpected cavalry attack of such strength. Once bitten however the Spartans were twice careful. And when they next invaded Attica, this time by land, they no doubt remained in readiness to deal with cavalry since they rapidly put the Thessalians to flight when they attacked.[41] Cavalry were also of great use in pursuit once a phalanx had been broken, and especially since the hoplite could not easily run with his shield on his back. Equally they could hinder a victorious phalanx from following up its victory since hoplites in pursuit would rapidly lose close order and become vulnerable to horsemen. And for the same reason an army weak in cavalry could be prevented from foraging.

As Frederiksen has recently shown, to underestimate the possible effectiveness of cavalry in hoplite warfare is to disregard Thucydides' careful account of the Syracusan cavalry in the great Athenian expedition to Sicily in the later fifth century.[42] His narrative illustrates all the roles which I have outlined, and fully explains the Athenian generals' constant requests for cavalry reinforcements;[43] and it also reveals how the very nature of hoplite tactics might have prompted the development of true, organized cavalry. It was because they were weak in cavalry that for the battle before Syracuse in Spring 415 B.C. the Athenians carefully chose a position where they were protected by walls, houses, trees and a marsh on one side, and by cliffs on the other, so that they could not be taken in the flank or rear by the enemy horsemen, and could concentrate their whole force for a frontal attack.[44] And the strategy was rewarded. With its cavalry neutralized the Syracusan phalanx was broken. All the same, the cavalry was able to hold back the pursuit. Running after the fleeing Syracusan hoplites the Athenians lost their close order, and the Syracusan horsemen were able to isolate the disorganized groups and attack them from all sides. As Thucydides explains, '[The Athenians] did not pursue [the Syracusan hoplites] far, for the Syracusan horsemen, who were numerous, interposed, and whenever they saw *hoplites advancing from the ranks*, attacked them and drove them back. The Athenians pursued *in a body as far*

DIPYLON WARRIOR, HOPLITE AND CAVALRYMAN

as they safely could, and then returned and raised a trophy'.[45] As to the effectiveness of cavalry against retreating hoplites who had no cavalry of their own to cover them, many examples could be cited from Thucydides' narrative, and it was a point specifically stressed by Nicias in his speech to the Athenian troops before this particular battle.[46] Then again, when they were not actually engaged, the Athenians were confined to camp by the enemy cavalry which was constantly in readiness to attack foraging parties or groups of stragglers.[47] And the difficulties of marching in open country dominated by cavalry are amply illustrated by the narrative of the Athenians' last march towards Camarina. For although the Syracusan cavalry were still no match for a phalanx in a frontal engagement, the account reveals how they could slow down and harry a column on the move, could force an engagement in a position unfavourable for the enemy, and once engaged, by requiring the enemy to mount all-round defence, could weaken the strength of the phalanx which had to face their own infantry.[48] Now to return to the Archaic period, it cannot of course be assumed that cavalry as it was known in Sicily in the late fifth century developed all at once. And if Thucydides' narrative reveals its potential effectiveness in hoplite battles under favourable conditions, it must be remembered that not every state had terrain as suitable for horses as the Sicilian plains. When for example the Pisistratids so successfully sent the Thessalian cavalry to attack the Spartan force under Anchimolius on the plain of Phalerum, Herodotus tells us that they had previously 'cleared the plains and made the country practicable for cavalry'.[49] And although anyone who has ridden a sturdy Welsh cob will know not to overrate the difficulties of riding in difficult country, Greek horses did not enjoy the benefit of horseshoes and were more easily lamed.[50]

For contemporary evidence for the military roles of the horse in Archaic warfare we must turn to archaeology, and in particular the vase-painters. Contemporary literary evidence is slight, and although the poets do speak of warfare their testimony is inadequate and obscure. And the vase-paintings themselves, though they do provide a considerable number of military scenes, fail to give us anything like a complete and continuous picture either geographically or chronologically; and even when they are abundant they must be treated with caution. In the first place the vast majority of them are

Attic and Corinthian, and neither of these cities was as renowned for its horsemen as the two great Euboean cities, or those of Asia Minor with its broad plains, or of Thessaly or many of the Western colonies. 'Chalcidian' vase-painting goes a little way towards filling this geographical gap for the second half of the sixth century at least, although its origins are controversial and it may be the work of Greek artists who had settled in Etruria, or of a Greek colony in the West, rather than the product of the Euboean city itself. On the other hand Chalcidian colonies will have taken with them the warfare and institutions of their metropolis; and Greek tactics and armour were imported by Etruria along with vase-painting techniques and models.[51] (And for this reason even Etruscan Black Figure itself may not be entirely irrelevant to the military historian of early Greece, although a study of Etruscan warfare lies beyond the scope of this work.) With the exception of the odd Clazomenian sarcophagus and one or two other items of the late sixth and early fifth centuries, East Greek painting is not very helpful; and Boeotian prefers non-military scenes for its Black Figure phase. The fact is that apart from Corinth and Athens most Greek cities either produced little of their own pottery, or little or none has been found, or else if they did produce some their tastes apparently dictated non-military subjects. All the same, Athens and Corinth were not without warhorses in the Archaic period, and it was surely not for nothing that the Athenian upper class rejoiced in the same name as the aristocratic Eretrian *Hippeis*, a name which unlike the new-sounding *Pentacosiomedimnoi* had no doubt been in currency as a status-term with military and social significance long before it became a timocratic class-term under Solon.[52] Even here however the picture falls far short of what we should wish. The evidence of both cities is thin for the seventh century, very thin in the case of Athens, although Attic Black Figure provides a much better picture for the sixth, and the Ripe Corinthian painters make a very valuable contribution for the three quarters of a century from *c.* 625 B.C. until the style fades about 550 and leaves us completely in the dark. Then again there are the problems of fashion and of heroizing. If for instance a period is without representations of cavalry, does it mean that there was no cavalry or simply that other subjects were preferred? Arguments from silence are dangerous, but the silence of cavalry may be significant if other types of warfare are not neglected at the same time. As to heroizing, it cannot always be assumed that vase-painters were representing contemporary military practice. Some scenes are marked as heroic by inscriptions, and others not so inscribed may also be heroic. Sometimes a scene from mythology is readily recognizable, and sometimes a readily recognizable archaism is present, such as a 'Boeotian' shield. In all cases the military historian must try to estimate how far the heroizing is likely to have affected the representation. It may extend to items of dress or equipment, or to their use and tactics, or to both or to neither. Individual cases must be decided on their individual merit, but it is perhaps fair to say that artists will generally have found it easier to portray what they saw. Often an inscription may be the full extent of heroizing. Or with regard to equipment, it may be confined to the simple expedient of a Boeotian shield. On the other hand we have already seen that the war-chariot was an archaism whose *form* is the contemporary racing-chariot but whose *use* is clearly 'Homeric'. With all these reservations in mind, I now turn to a detailed analysis of the evidence.

V
MOUNTED WARRIORS IN THE SEVENTH CENTURY

Corinth

Until the Ripe Corinthian period, which begins in the last quarter of the century, the evidence of Corinthian vase-painting for the use of the horse in war is scanty. There is considerable interest in riding, and among all the Orientalizing repertoire which makes human figures a comparative rarity riders do have a firm place as favourite Protocorinthian motifs. Sometimes they appear singly among other motifs;[1] and sometimes, particularly in the more detailed artistry from the middle of the century onwards, they are racing.[2] But although there is the occasional Bellerophon who aims a spear as he rides his winged steed at the Chimaera,[3] there is no evidence of cavalry on Protocorinthian vases. There is however evidence for mounted infantry, and it spans the whole of the seventh century. The earliest is the Early Protocorinthian aryballos (C1) of *c.* 700 B.C., already mentioned and illustrated in Chapter III (see above, p. 58, *fig. 37*). It depicts a heavy-armed warrior on foot, fully equipped with round shield, sword, single spear and crested helmet. The inside of his shield is not shown to prove it, but he is very probably a hoplite, and he certainly carries the single spear rather than the pair of javelins. And preceding him is an unarmed rider. Now the arrangement of these figures makes them the almost exactly similar prototypes of the hoplite and his unarmed, mounted squire who are inscribed as *hippobatas* and *hippostrophos* on the Early Corinthian aryballos (C2) of the last quarter of the century (*fig. 36*). The only differences are that the later vase is inscribed, that the inside of the warrior's shield is shown, and that the squire is shown leading his master's horse which appears in outline on the far side of his own. Otherwise the illustrations are identical, and they are surely to be

MOUNTED WARRIORS IN THE 7TH CENTURY

FIG. 45
Hoplite duel
flanked by
mounted squires
on an Early
Corinthian
aryballos of
the late seventh
century (C3)

interpreted in the same way. The single horse of the earlier presents no problem. The earlier artist may simply not have wished to blur the clarity of his drawing by adding a second outline. And the same may be true of a fragmentary EC aryballos from Perachora (C3), which shows a hoplite duel flanked by antithetical unarmed riders who are surely mounted squires but are not shown with second horses (*fig. 45*). There are several later representations of youthful riders similarly flanking hoplite battles without second horses indicated, and Helbig suggested that the hoplite and his squire shared the one horse.[4] But it seems highly unlikely that a hoplite would impair the usefulness of his horse by encumbering it with the weight of another body besides all his own armour. In an emergency of course, if one horse had been killed or wounded, both master and squire may have shared the same horse, but to do so normally would be to lessen the chances of successful flight or pursuit and to cut down the range of the horse while increasing its chances of going lame. At any rate, no vase-painter to my knowledge ever bore witness to the practice, whereas many showed the squire separately mounted. And Helbig appealed in vain to his bronze from Grumentum which, with the boy perching precariously on the very back of the horse's rump and the helmeted but shieldless rider with his bent spear, cannot be taken seriously: at most it may have been an amusing cartoon of a return from a disastrous battle.[5]

Pairs of horses appear on other vases. On C4, the famous Chigi olpe of *c.* 650–640 B.C., the main frieze depicts hoplite phalanxes marching against each other, and below it a subsidiary frieze presents

FIG. 46
Mounted hoplites and squires on an Early Corinthian vase of c. 625 B.C. (C6)

a procession in which a racing-chariot is followed by several unarmed riders, each leading a second horse shown in outline.[6] And while it is impossible to prove that these pairs of horses are not meant for chariots, it is conceivable that their youthful riders are the squires of dismounted hoplites like those who are fighting in the frieze above. A row of three similar riders, youths wearing the chiton and holding a spare horse, appears on C5, a fragmentary Transitional Corinthian dinos of c. 630 B.C. recently published by D. Callipolitis-Feytmans. This time however the riders carry a single long spear over their shoulders; and since no artist wishing to show pairs of cavalrymen side by side would have failed to indicate the presence of the second rider at least by showing a second spear, these horsemen are no less clearly the squires of mounted hoplites than their counterparts on several later, Middle Corinthian vases, for example C9 and C10, where their masters are shown engaging in battle (see below, pp. 97f, *figs. 50, 51*). And in fact Callipolitis-Feytmans plausibly suggests that a hoplite duel may have featured on a lost section of C5 too. Then early in the last quarter of the century, sherds of an Early Corinthian vase from Perachora (C6) show hoplites actually mounted as well as their squires (*fig. 46*). On one fragment a panoplied warrior, complete with helmet, round, emblazoned shield and single spear, is riding to the left, and the outline of a second horse indicates the presence of his squire riding at his side. And another fragment shows a mounted, unarmed squire holding his master's horse exactly as on C2 (*fig. 36*). Another panoplied horseman, mounted and with a second horse shown in outline, appears on C7, an aryballos fragment of similar date, or perhaps even earlier (*fig. 47*). He wears helmet and

MOUNTED WARRIORS IN THE 7TH CENTURY

FIG. 47
Another Early Corinthian mounted hoplite, whose outlined second horse indicates the presence of a squire riding at his side (C7)

FIG. 48
A clumsy Early Corinthian painting which provides a rare illustration of a hoplite fighting from horseback (C8)

greaves, carries two lances and a whirligig-blazoned shield, and he too is perhaps a mounted hoplite accompanied by his squire. Lastly the extraordinarily clumsy drawing of one large EC aryballos (C8) shows a combat between a panoplied hoplite on foot and an identically equipped rider who is aiming his single lance overarm (*fig. 48*). Now the rider appears to be sitting side-saddle, and it may be that he is in the process of sliding down from his horse to fight his enemy on foot. On the other hand he may have been imagined astride by an artist who was inexperienced in showing figures overlapping and in profile, and simply wished to show both legs. Both explanations are possible. In favour of the former is the fact that Corinthian art had managed to depict riders properly in profile for at least three quarters of a century, and the showing of both legs of a rider meant to be astride would be unique at this period. In favour of the latter, the curious drawing of the shield may be significant: the inside is turned outwards, and the arm is shown outside it. And there is no sign of a squire to hold his horse, although this would certainly have been too much to expect from so poor an artist. At any rate, if the rider is not dismounting, he provides the only example of a warrior fighting from horseback known to me in seventh-century Corinthian art, and one of the extremely rare examples in the whole of Archaic Greek vase-painting of any rider fighting with the hoplite shield, let alone the rest of the hoplite panoply as well. The reasons for this will be fully discussed in the next chapter (see below, pp. 102-3, 130-2). Here it will suffice to note the basic improbability that a horseman thus equipped regularly fought as a cavalryman rather than as a hoplite, although in an emergency he would have done so.[7] Of regular cavalry forces there is as yet no decisive seventh-century ceramic evidence, and although it is true that military scenes are altogether comparatively few, all battles (with the possible exception of C8) are fought on foot.

Athens
By themselves the Attic Late Geometric horsemen with their various items of arms and armour indicated both a knowledge of riding and a military use for the mounted horse in the later eighth century, but little more. No rider appeared in a battle-scene, and although a rider (perhaps wearing a corslet) brandishes a spear as he rides in a procession of chariots on one vase (**38**), the context will not justify the conclusion that he fought from horseback in battle, while his second horse may suggest the squired warrior who dismounted to fight in the Homeric fashion. Certainly all warriors in the LG battle-scenes fight on foot (with the possible exception of one who appears to be poising a spear ready for action while still mounted on a chariot, *fig. 4*); and the fact that the LG horsemen are without the items of armour enjoyed by the heavy-armed warriors of these scenes, particularly the shield, is not evidence of cavalry since they are frequently shown without arms at all. One sherd of *c.* 700 B.C. (A1) does show a rider, who, if anyone, is likely to have been a cavalryman

(see above, p. 49, *fig. 34*). He wears a helmet and carries two spears. But once again, he is not shown in battle, and since the rest of the vase is missing there is not even the possibility of contrasting his equipment with that of other warriors to see if the absence of the shield may be significant (unless the rounded shape of the upper part of his body is meant to indicate a round shield): the two spears which he carries are neutral evidence since they are still standard equipment for infantrymen.

The seventh century proper also fails to provide clear evidence of true cavalry; and although there is much interest in riding,[8] battles continue to be fought exclusively on foot. In the first quarter however military scenes of any sort are very few,[9] and while chariot-processions are still common, their occupants are no longer warriors but exclusively non-military, usually robed charioteers. Among the favourite motifs of this period are the choirs of men and women (now carrying branches), which continue from the LG period; but new Orientalizing motifs predominate, and there is little advance in narrative scenes except for the exploits of lions and human-horse hybrids. All the same, Early Protoattic does give us at least one military horseman (A2), and he is our first panoplied rider (see above, p. 50, *fig. 35*). He has a helmet, twin spears, and a heavy-looking, round shield with a large central boss and with smaller bosses studded all round the rim. And although we cannot be certain how he fought since he is simply depicted sitting on his horse and is given no context by the otherwise unfigured vase, it seems most probable that he dismounted and fought on foot like the similarly equipped warriors advancing from the right on vase A3, which reveals the hoplite shield in use with the twin spears as well as the single thrusting-spear of the warriors advancing from the left (see above, p. 72, *fig. 44*). A rider with a similarly large round shield is provided by a clay model from the Ceramicus. The way the shield lies on the arm clearly indicates the hoplite double-grip, and its size suggests that its owner was another mounted infantryman of the first half of the century.[10]

The battle-scene of A3 is only one example of a revival in the popularity of battle-scenes which takes place in the more vigorous Middle Protoattic phase (*c.* 680–630 B.C.), and once again the only fighting that is done is done on foot. The odd helmeted rider occurs in MPA, as on vase A4, and although the helmet is his only military feature and he is depicted simply riding behind a totally unmilitary chariot driven by a robed charioteer, his presence may suggest the use of the horse as transport for warriors like those fighting on foot on the frieze beneath. Other vases too feature both riders and hoplites, but the riders are unarmed and it would be specious to try to connect the motifs. The most that can be said is that riding was popular and that all fighting is done on foot. There is no clear evidence of cavalry until the much more prolific Black Figure style is getting under way in the sixth century. On the other hand Protoattic is not at all common, and its preference was increasingly for non-military scenes and particularly mythological narrative, exemplified by the LPA Nessos amphora in Athens (c. 615 B.C.).[11] And the same is true of the earliest Attic Black Figure. Even where the Gorgon painter includes a duel scene in full, contemporary hoplite panoply among the extensive mythological repertoire of his famous dinos, it is flanked by 'Homeric' chariots.[12] This vase was painted c. 590 B.C., and it is only from the end of the first quarter of the sixth century that the almost total military silence is finally broken and Archaic Attic vase-painting begins to make a valuable contribution to military history.

Euboea

For the style of warfare which could be expected in contemporary Euboea a fragment of Archilochus is extremely valuable. The displaced aristocrat himself, who probably thrived in the middle of the seventh century,[13] may well have fought as a hoplite in the classical manner: the single thrusting-spear is more likely to have inspired fragment 2 than a javelin, and the shield which he so gaily abandoned may have been a hoplite shield (although of course no-one believes that pre-hoplite shields were never forsaken for greater speed in flight).[14] Elsewhere however he speaks of javelin warfare between Parians and Naxians.[15] And he never mentions the war-horse. But what he has to say about Euboean warfare may be highly significant: there will be but few bows and slings, 'and it will be the weary work of swords, for this is the sort of battle the spear-famed Lords of Euboea are masters in'.[16] Now the spear-famed Lords of Euboea were surely the knightly aristocracy, the Eretrian *Hippeis* and the

MOUNTED WARRIORS IN THE 7TH CENTURY

Chalcidian *Hippobotae*; and these two cities were among Aristotle's examples of the connexion between the military supremacy of horsemen and early aristocratic constitutions.[17] But Archilochus says nothing about horses, and the sword was the least likely weapon to use from horseback. No true cavalry in Greece from the sixth century to Alexander ever used the sword as their weapon.[18] Most preferred spears, either javelins or lances or the xyston; and the bow, which was also effective from horseback though less used by Greek cavalry, was expressly avoided in Euboea according to Archilochus. W. G. Forrest believes that the style of warfare to which Archilochus referred must be developed hoplite warfare,[19] but this too is very far from certain. The Abantes of the *Iliad*'s Catalogue could have been hoplites since they are described as spearmen who longed to rend the corslets of their enemies with their ashen spears;[20] but this highly formalized description may not have been chosen for any particular relevance to Euboean warfare, even if it could be referred to Archilochus' day. And while it is true that hoplites often carried a sword as well as their thrusting-spear, it was resorted to only in an emergency, and Archilochus' poem is hardly referring to so secondary a weapon. Then there is a piece of ceramic evidence which may be relevant. A Late Geometric amphora, painted in the Attic manner but found in Eretria and most probably a local product of *c.* 700 B.C., depicts a frieze of helmeted warriors equipped with large, round, emblazoned shields and with twin spears.[21] And finally there is Strabo's report of an agreement between Chalcis and Eretria not to use long-range weapons (τηλεβόλα) in a war over the Lelantine Plain,[22] which may have been the dispute referred to by Herodotus and Thucydides as having split Greece into rival camps, and which almost certainly belonged to the seventh century.[23]

Strabo found this agreement recorded on a stele (perhaps a copy of the original) which he saw in the sanctuary of Artemis Amarynthia near Eretria, and there is no good reason to suspect it. Forrest did so on the grounds that Archilochus' poem proved that the Lelantine War was a hoplite war, and therefore an agreement to ban obsolete weapons was equivalent to banning pikes in favour of gunpowder. But the argument is not valid. Archilochus' poem is evidence against rather than for the hoplite's thrusting-spear, and in any case archers and slingers are not incompatible with the developed phalanx tactics: on the contrary, the Scythian foot-archers who commonly accompany hoplites on Attic vases of the later sixth century were presumably not without value,[24] and there is no lack of evidence for seventh-century archers and slingers in hoplite warfare.[25] At any rate, although there is no proof that Archilochus was referring to the Lelantine War in particular, the agreement on the stele does tally with what Archilochus tells us, and such agreements, either tacit or formal, may have been a regular feature of Euboean warfare. And if so, there could be one very good reason for them which is chivalrous in a very basic sense. If the *Hippeis* and *Hippobotae* rode their horses to war, as they surely did, the horses would be the chief sufferers from missiles,[26] and it could have been to save these precious beasts from unnecessary harm that τηλεβόλα were banned. Now the well attested use of war-horses is not irreconcilable with Archilochus' failure to mention them or his stress on the sword as the primary weapon if the Euboean lords were knights in the 'Homeric' sense and dismounted to fight on foot. If 'Chalcidian' is not after all a misnomer, Chalcis still had squired mounted hoplites in the second half of the sixth century on the evidence of her vase-painters (see below, pp. 136f, *figs. 73, 74, 75*); and the knights of the seventh century may also have dismounted to fight on foot, though not with the thrusting-spear. Archilochus called them 'spear-famed', but the hoplite spear is incompatible with the sword as primary weapon, and perhaps the Late Geometric vase provides the explanation for the epithet (if indeed it is not merely a poet's stock-epithet): the spears of the Euboean lords may have been the two javelins, which were thrown before the warriors came to grips with their swords;[27] and if the warriors of the vase are the knights, they are shown on foot with a vast shield that was hardly intended for use from horseback. All this is not to deny that the Euboean cities may have had true cavalry forces as well. If Plutarch's story is worth anything, and if it applies to this period, Chalcis won a victory with the help of the Thessalian Cleomachus against the Eretrian cavalry, which is what Chalcis apparently feared most;[28] and perhaps this cavalry and the Thessalian cavalry which overcame it were true cavalry like that which defeated Anchimolius' expedition against the Pisistratids on the plain of Phalerum in the late sixth century. There is nothing incompatible in mounted infantry and true cavalry. Athens for example had both arms in the sixth century, and the Euboean cities may have done the same in the seventh. Perhaps the younger nobles formed a corps of light cavalry. But cavalry must remain little more than hypothetical. Archilochus' fragment is reliable contemporary testimony for the warfare of the Euboean lords in the seventh century, and it suggests that the *Hippeis* and *Hippobotae* rode to battle but fought on foot with their famous swords.[29]

Other States
For the role of the war-horse in the *East Greek* states which had large territories the evidence is disappointingly meagre and ambiguous. Callinus of *Ephesus* would probably have helped if more of his work had survived, but as it is his only references to fighting methods are exhortations for every man to throw one more javelin before he dies and to step forward manfully 'grasping the spear and protecting his stout heart under the shield'.[30] Snodgrass suggests that the last phrase indicates a hoplite shield, but it is far from certain.[31] *Colophon* was almost certainly among the 'other places in Asia' mentioned by Aristotle along with Magnesia, Chalcis and Eretria as having had aristocratic governments of knights in early times. But Mimnermus provides scarcely more information for his city than Callinus did for Ephesus. Presumably in the spirit of *laudator temporis acti* he praises the valour of a warrior whom his elders described as 'routing the serried ranks of the Lydian horsemen in the plain of Hermus with his spear, and rushing forward in the forefront, defying the missiles of the enemy in the thick of bloody war ... going like the ray of the sun'.[32] It is impossible to be certain, but the hero does not sound to have been mounted himself, and the only reference to horses is the description of the Lydians as ἱππομάχοι. He may have been a cavalryman, but he may also have been a knight in what I believe to have been the Euboean style, and dismounted to fight like some of the squired knights of the Clazomenian sarcophagus at the end of the next century (see below, pp. 143–5).

For *Lesbian* warfare of the end of the century there is the evidence of the aristocratic Alcaeus, who describes a house full of the items of the heavy panoply in which he and his friends were presumably going to fight.[33] He lists bronze helmets with horse-hair plumes, shining bronze greaves, linen corslets, hollow shields, Chalcidian blades, and belts and tunics. And with all this equipment he was more likely to have fought on foot than from horseback. Whether or not he fought as a hoplite in the phalanx is impossible to know. Spears are not mentioned, and D. L. Page concludes that he must therefore have fought with sword alone since the spear, whether for thrusting or throwing, would have been one of the most important items in the armoury and the least likely to be excluded from the list.[34] On the other hand, all the items mentioned were *worn*, the sword in a scabbard presumably (slung from the shoulder by a belt), and they were all personal and permanent pieces of equipment. Perhaps the hoplite's single thrusting-spear may have been thought of as a more personal weapon than javelins, which were expendables and might even less merit special mention, but neither sort was an item of dress. The epithet of the shield fits the convex, hoplite shield well enough, just as the *rhipsaspia* story suits the double-grip,[35] but neither indication is decisive. On the other hand it would be surprising if so useful an invention as the double-grip had not been adopted in Lesbos by the end of the seventh century, and Page has exaggerated the 'old-fashioned' nature of the equipment which Alcaeus describes.[36]

Finally we must return to mainland Greece, and *Sparta*. Tyrtaeus gives valuable evidence for his city's adoption of hoplite equipment and tactics in the seventh century,[37] and also for the value of light-armed slingers and javelineers in phalanx warfare.[38] But he does not mention horses in war, only a chariot in one fragment which is clearly a heroic poem.[39] In the fifth century however the three hundred hoplites who made up the royal guard and formed the élite corps of the army were called the *Hippeis*,[40] and the ancestry of this title is suggested by an ivory fibula-plaque of the third quarter of the seventh century from the sanctuary of Artemis Orthia (*fig. 49*). It depicts a rider armed with a large, round shield and a single, stout spear, and Miss Marangou is probably right in suggesting that the representation was based on a mounted hoplite.[41] There is as yet no decisive evidence of seventh-century Spartan cavalry, although Helbig was wrong to take Thucydides, 4.55, as 'expressly stating that Sparta organized a cavalry corps for the first time in 424 B.C.'.[42] Thucydides says only that to form a corps of cavalry and archers was παρὰ τὸ εἰωθός, and this can hardly be taken as the final word on the

MOUNTED WARRIORS IN THE 7TH CENTURY

FIG. 49
A Spartan mounted warrior on an ivory fibula-plaque of the later seventh century

Archaic period, when Artemis Orthia reveals that archers at least were not uncommon.[43] And it is not impossible that a rider on a fragmented ivory plaque of *c.* 600 B.C. may have been a cavalryman. The representation as reconstructed in *Artemis Orthia* is absurd.[44] All that is certain is that the plaque shows a tunic-clad rider with a single spear, and (if that dubious fragment really does belong) that the top half of a warrior with a round shield appears in the top left. The latter may have been a second horseman riding behind the first (although not of course on the same horse since no leg is visible on its flank), and if so (and that means excusing another set of horse's legs on artistic grounds), the plaque is perhaps more likely to have depicted, as Dawkins maintained, a knight and squire.

VI
MOUNTED WARRIORS IN THE SIXTH CENTURY

Corinth
In vase-painting of the Ripe Corinthian style illustrations of horses in a military context become much commoner, and particularly during the first half of the sixth century before this brilliant style fades, and ceramic evidence for Corinthian warfare fades with it. But unfortunately for the military historian the scenes of actual fighting are few, and sometimes it is difficult to assess how the armed riders would have used their horses. All the same there is enough decisive evidence to show that both Helbig and Alföldi were wrong to treat the mounted hoplite (a term which I shall use for men in hoplite armour who dismounted to fight on foot in the phalanx) and the true cavalryman (who fought from horseback) as mutually exclusive. For Helbig there were only mounted hoplites and their mounted squires, whereas for Alföldi all armed horsemen were true cavalry, and the very idea of mounted hoplites was to be dismissed out of hand. In fact we shall find that Corinth had both equestrian types as did Athens, where Black Figure pottery, superior both in the number of its representations of horsemen and in its far greater number of battle-scenes, will make a much clearer picture.

A clear illustration of Corinthian mounted hoplites is the battle-scene on C9 (*fig. 50*), a vase already mentioned in Chapter III. As Helbig noted, it gives a very vivid illustration of the roles of the *hippostrophos* and the *hippobatas* of the EC aryballos, C2 (see above, p. 58, *fig. 36*).[1] In the centre two hoplites have been fighting, and the left-hand one is running away. The squire of the victorious warrior now rides up leading his master's horse ready for him to mount for the pursuit. But the retreating hoplite's squire has panicked, or at least his horses have; and instead of waiting for his master to mount

MOUNTED WARRIORS IN THE 6TH CENTURY

FIG. 50
Middle Corinthian cup of the early sixth century showing hoplites in battle while their mounted squires hold their horses (C9)

he is galloping off with both horses, while three bearded and naked men, one with a javelin (ψιλοί ?), run to intercept him, and the front one is shown catching at the runaway's bridle. Now Alföldi, who does not mention this vase, would have to argue that the youthful riders are not the squires of hoplites but the companions of warriors who were the 'successors of the chariot-borne warriors, who acted both as cavalrymen and infantrymen, although not in the phalanx but in a loose tactical formation with the *hippostrophos*'.[2] This at any rate was his interpretation of C2. Now it is true that the same warrior may sometimes have fought from horseback as well as dismounting to fight on foot (as perhaps the warrior of C8, *fig. 48*), although this would not of course have been, as Alföldi maintained, according to any either real or 'Homeric' charioteering method. But it is inconceivable that hoplites would have been operating ineffectively outside the phalanx so long a time after Corinthian vases had revealed the introduction of that organized style of warfare, and yet Alföldi maintained that the *hippobatas–hippostrophos* 'Rottengemeinschaft' was contemporary with the vase-painting which depicted it. The only possibility of keeping Alföldi's explanation would be to argue that the painters of both the EC aryballos (C2) and the MC cup (C9) had been deliberately archaizing by depicting pre-phalanx usage in post-phalanx equipment. But there is nothing to suggest that C2 is not contemporary; and although the later vase does have mythological scenes on the other side, the battle-scene of C9 gives every appearance of a cross-section of a phalanx battle: both hoplites are using the single thrusting-spear of the developed phalanx tactics and not the weapons of the individual pre-phalanx warfare. And we have already discussed Alföldi's general objections to the theory of mounted hoplites, and found them to be groundless. Among other

97

FIG. 51
Mounted squires waiting with their masters' horses behind the lines during a hoplite battle on a Middle Corinthian cup (C10)

examples may be cited C10, an MC cup on which hoplite duels are flanked by a mounted squire who similarly holds a spear (a spare for his master perhaps, or perhaps for his own defence), and leads a second horse (*fig. 51*). Here the artist was apparently trying to indicate a phalanx by a plurality of overlapping duels, and again the scene has no archaizing or heroizing features. A contemporary vase illustrated by Alföldi does admittedly have inscriptions (C11). On both sides it presents a pair of duelling hoplites, Ajax and Aeneas on one side, Hector and Achilles on the other, and each duel is flanked by mounted squires who are similarly holding second horses but this time are without spears. And a similar scene on an LC vase also has inscriptions which may have been intended to heroize it although they make nonsense (C12). But even here the heroic features are confined to the inscriptions. On neither vase is there so much as a Boeotian shield to detract from the contemporary appearance of the warriors; and the fact that the mounted squires even of C11 are dressed only in the tunic is an indication that they belonged to contemporary warfare, since a painter who included mounted 'squires' only for the purpose of illustrating heroic practice would surely have given armour and arms to no lesser personages than the other Ajax and Hippocles, Sarpedon and Phoenix (as indeed at least one Attic artist did on vase A14, where rival goddesses are also present holding a spare spear for their favourites). Moreover, although the duellists may be heroic individuals, a battle between two phalanxes was scarcely more than a duel on a grand scale, and certainly there is no reason to doubt that the non-heroic examples represented crosssections of phalanx battles in which the mounted squires and spare horses were drawn up in reserve behind the lines, ready to help the hoplites either in pursuit or flight when one of the phalanxes broke, or when they had to retire wounded.

For true cavalry there is one unequivocal vase-painting, and I have

MOUNTED WARRIORS IN THE 6TH CENTURY

FIG. 52
Helmeted Corinthian cavalry riding into a hoplite battle on a wine-jug of the early seventh century (C13)

a

b

not found it mentioned by any previous writer. In the centre of a continuous battle-scene which goes right round a large MC oenochoe (C13), a hoplite battle is represented by three hoplite duels and an archer who is kneeling and shooting (*fig. 52a*). And from either side a line of three horsemen is riding into battle. Like the hoplites they all wear helmets, but unlike them they have no other armour – no shields, corslets, greaves or swords. Of the three riding in from the right (*fig. 52b*), the first into battle is aiming his single spear apparently at the back of the hoplite at the right-hand edge of the central battle. The second and third have not yet poised their spears, of which the second has one, the third two; and the latter is glancing behind him as he rides. Now it is possible that the artist was intending to show the horsemen attacking each other on the wing of the phalanx battle; but it may also be that the phalanxes are being attacked where they are most vulnerable, in the rear, and if so this scene would illustrate how the introduction of phalanx warfare may have prompted the development of the horse's military role in the creation of organized cavalry. At any rate, these horsemen are clearly a squadron of true cavalry and not mounted hoplites. Helbig conceded that sometimes mounted hoplites might fight from horseback in pursuit; but these warriors are neither pursuing nor fleeing since the hoplite battle is still raging in the middle, and in any case, if they had been hoplites, they would scarcely have dispensed with their corslets, swords and greaves for this purpose even if they had left their shields!

Of other armed riders there are several examples, but none of them are actually shown fighting, and it is often hard to be sure of their role. And it is less straightforward than is sometimes claimed to use as criteria the presence and absence of shield or greaves, the number of spears, or a second horse. Of armoured riders four categories may be distinguished: (i) those without shields, unattended by squires, and without a second horse shown in outline on the inside of their mounts (C14a, C15); (ii) those similarly unsquired and single-horsed but carrying shields (C14b, C16); (iii) those with shields and a second horse (C17–C23); and (iv) those who are like the last but have a tunic-clad squire clearly shown riding the inside horse (C24). Then finally there is a large category of unarmoured horsemen, usually ephebes, usually wearing only a tunic, and invariably carrying a single spear. Now the horsemen of the first category, if they are going to fight at all, must surely fight from horseback. The relevant side of C14 (*fig. 53a*) depicts a helmeted rider like those on C13 (*fig. 52*). He rides towards a furious battle of three hoplites fighting over the body of a wounded fourth; and in contrast to their full panoplies he wears only a high-crested helmet and carries two spears. And he similarly contrasts with the four mounted warriors who form the motif of the other side of the vase and have blazoned shields and greaves (*fig. 53b*). Without shield and greaves he is not going to dismount to fight, even if there were someone to hold his horse for him. And his two spears, though not in themselves a criterion of the cavalryman, are more necessary to him than to a hoplite: it cannot have been very often that a hoplite would be unable to extract his spear from a corpse, but a horseman, if a lancer, might sometimes have had to let go or be pulled from his horse, or if a javelineer, he would not always be able to retrieve his spears. For similar reasons the horseman who leads the mixed force of hoplites and unarmoured cavalry on C15 must also be a cavalryman: he wears a red corslet over his white chiton, but unlike the hoplites who are following him on foot he has no shield. Similarly too the helmeted rider holding a spear and looking over his shoulder on the subsidiary frieze of a very worn MC cotyle (C25).[3]

MOUNTED WARRIORS IN THE 6TH CENTURY

FIG. 53
A helmeted cavalryman, hoplites in battle, and three mounted hoplites on a Middle Corinthian vase of the early seventh century (C14)

The other three categories of armoured riders who are not actually fighting, those with shields, are less straightforward. One basic fact is that they are almost all fully equipped to fight on foot in the phalanx: besides helmets, all have round shields and one or two lances, and with two possible exceptions all have greaves. Is it likely then that they fought from horseback equipped in this way? It will be useful to consider first the properties of the separate items of the equipment, and then of the panoply as a whole. To take first the greaves, it is sometimes stated that their presence indicates mounted infantry because the much hard riding and very firm seat required by the cavalryman would cause them to cut into the horse's flanks. But this is not necessarily so even of metal greaves. Surviving examples from the sixth century reveal that they were closely moulded to the rounded shape of the calf-muscle, and since the two edges came very close to meeting at the back they would not therefore dig into the horse.[4] Moreover it is the thighs which provide the horseman's main grip, and they were the only part of the otherwise completely mailed Parthian cataphract to be left unprotected.[5] Then to put the matter beyond doubt there are several Attic representations of greaved horsemen who are unmistakably cavalrymen in action (e.g.

A74, A76, A79, A80, A95; *figs. 69, 70*). All the same, if some cavalrymen wore greaves, others just as clearly chose to leave them off. Now the argument from absence is only valid if it can be reasonably certain that the painter's omission was deliberate and not unconscious or careless, and this is reasonably certain on those of our vases which not only reveal in general a careful attention to detail but specifically point a contrast between greaved hoplites on foot and cavalrymen without them.[6] And in fact just such a contrast appears on both C13 and C14a, which have already been mentioned as depicting shieldless horsemen who are unmistakably true cavalrymen (*figs. 52, 53*). If then some cavalrymen chose to forgo the protection of greaves for what was the part of a rider's body most accessible to the infantryman's thrust, there were good reasons for it, and two are not hard to find. Although it was the thighs which provided the main grip, the lower legs also helped, and bare legs would undoubtedly be more secure against lathered flanks than legs encased in shiny, rounded metal. But more importantly, the bare leg would give greater sensitivity in applying the 'aids' which control the horse's movements, and for the cavalryman in battle manoeuvrability, and in particular the ability to turn rapidly, were of the greatest importance. There were then good reasons why the cavalryman of C14a went without greaves, and therefore when we find on the same vase four mounted warriors who have both shields and greaves identical to those of the hoplites fighting on foot, the indications are that they were mounted hoplites (*fig. 53b*). It is true of course that no second horse or squire is depicted to show who could have looked after their horses while they joined the phalanx, but they are not actually shown on the battlefield, and the artist could simply have wished to depict well-to-do hoplites as they were wont to travel.

The presence of a shield is also an uncertain criterion. Without a shield a horseman is not going to fight in the phalanx, but the converse is not necessarily true. The difficulties of holding a hoplite shield while fighting from horseback can be exaggerated. The armband would make it possible for the left hand to hold the bridle or a spare spear, and besides the EC aryballos C8 (*fig. 48*) there are one or two Attic Black Figure vase-paintings which show cavalrymen fighting and holding what is almost certainly a hoplite shield (A52, A94, A95; *figs. 64, 71*). And perhaps the Corinthian riders of the single other vase of category (ii) are cavalrymen too (C16). In contrast to the hoplites fighting on the other side, these riders are unmistakably without greaves, and the unusual direction of the cavalcade's progress suggests that the artist was a careful draughtsman who paid attention to detail: of all the Ripe Corinthian cavalcades of horsemen with shields I know only of this one which progresses from left to right and therefore requires the inside of the shield to be shown. And although no tunic or corslet is shown and an artistic preference for nudity must always be suspected, greaves are often shown on otherwise nude hoplites; and the absence of a corslet, while serving to point a further contrast with the hoplites on the other side, may explain why this rider, if a cavalryman, wanted the protection of a shield. The fact remains however that the overwhelming majority of cavalrymen depicted in action in Archaic Greek art (both armoured and unarmoured) are without shields. And the reason for this is surely that the hoplite shield was more trouble than it was worth for the limited protection which it afforded. It was a clumsy and weighty burden for a cavalryman to whom speed and manoeuvrability were so important. Unlike the infantryman, the rider could not easily swing his shield over to protect his front or right simply because the horse's neck and shoulders were in the way, and protection for only the left side was poor compensation for the virtual immobility of the left arm. And all in all a cavalryman who wanted protection for his body would do much better to wear a corslet and forget the shield, like the Attic rider of A32 (*fig. 59*).[7]

The next problem is the role of the second horse, since much the largest category of armoured horsemen (iii) comprises those with shields and with second horses shown in outline. Three basic possibilities need to be considered: that the second horse was riderless, that it had a similar rider, and that it had a dissimilar rider. If it was riderless, why should a horseman take along a second horse? Alföldi's recent article has suggested two answers to this question, one possible but highly improbable, the other frankly incredible. He maintained that horses' backs would rapidly become too sweaty to provide the cavalryman with a firm enough seat, and therefore these Corinthian warriors rode into battle with two horses and every so often jumped across from one to the other. Now not only is this a gross exaggeration of the problem of a slippery seat (and the rider's tunic which

FIG. 54
A Middle Corinthian crater showing a hoplite battle on one side and on the other three mounted hoplites, whose outlined second horses indicate the presence of their mounted squires (C20)

usually covers the thighs would be fairly absorbent),[8] but it would be physically impossible to try to fight while at the same time managing a shield and a second horse as well in the heat of battle. And it is not surprising that no Greek writer or artist ever bears witness to such a practice. Alföldi's only 'parallel' for cavalry who may have gone into battle with two horses was the 'Tarentine' cavalry of the first century B.C.; but Livy's account of Philopoemen's confrontation with Nabis does not say that the Tarentines actually engaged in battle with their two horses, only that Philopoemen sent to the van of his marching column 'the Cretan auxiliaries and those whom they called the Tarentine cavalry, each leading two horses with him' in case of an attack by Nabis;[9] and in any case Tarentines were by definition light-armed javelineers who did not come into close contact with the enemy and therefore would not have risked presenting too good a target with two horses.[10] Alföldi's other and less impractical suggestion emerges from his quotation of Pollux's definition of ἄμφιπποι, that they had two horses fastened together and jumped from one to the other from time to time in order to cover longer distances without tiring them out.[11] But it seems highly improbable that we should transfer this explanation to our panoplied horsemen of sixth-century Corinth. Now at this stage it is necessary to distinguish the *Desultortechnik* of Alföldi's μεταβάται (which requires two horses) from simple dismounting. Among all his quoted representations of men vaulting from horses (from many Greek cities and periods), only a few of them have two horses; and of these all are youths, not one is armed (let alone heavily armed with a shield!), and none are actually shown leaping from one horse to another. There is only one possible exception, and that is the Attic 'Siana' cup (A37) of the second quarter of the sixth century (see below, p. 117, *fig. 60*): it presents a frieze of heavy-armed warriors who may be vaulting from or onto their horses, of which a second is shown in outline, or they may simply be walking or running beside the horses, since a single hoplite on the bottom of the cup is similarly prancing by himself without a horse. But the warriors are certainly not jumping from one horse to another, and the second horses in outline may either suggest pairs (or even ranks) of warriors running with their horses, or else – and this would be more in tune with other representations of the Siana cup generation and with other paintings by the same artist – we may be intended to imagine the warriors' squires on the inside horses, youths perhaps like the one who appears at the far right of the frieze and whom the decorated band was not wide enough to show mounted: the top of it touches the horses' heads and the warriors' helmets as it is. Now it was clearly useful for a mounted warrior to learn to mount and dismount rapidly whether he was going to fight from horseback or not. And no doubt they practised and displayed this skill, which made an artistic motif. Sometimes, as on the fifth-century clay shield from Corinth illustrated by Alföldi, a heavily armed warrior was shown jumping down from his (single) horse.[12] But more often a mounted squire was shown holding his master's horse while he dismounted, as on an Attic lekanis-lid (A7), which was painted by the same artist as the cup mentioned above (A37), and depicts the mounted hoplite dismounting to join the phalanx (*fig. 56*).[13] And here too we have a clue to the purpose of the unencumbered boys who are shown riding or jumping to the ground while leading a second horse on some of

Alföldi's illustrations: they might have been simply displaying equestrian acrobatics, but if they were the squires of heavy-armed warriors they would need to practise controlling two horses at once. At any rate, as far as our panoplied Corinthian horsemen are concerned, it is highly improbable that they were planning to jump so encumbered from one horse to another, and certainly impossible that they were going to take them into battle single-handed. There is however the further possibility that the second horse, if riderless, may signify cavalry exactly because hard riding and the likelihood of wounds would make it useful for the cavalryman to be able to ride out of battle and change horses. But even so he would need someone to look after the spare horse no less than the Huntsmen and Masters of Hounds who provide the only modern equivalent; and if our Corinthian warriors were rich enough to have two horses to take to battle with them, it is unlikely that they would not have taken their own squires. And in fact the single vase of category (iv), C24, shows an unarmed, youthful squire on the inside horse (*fig. 55*).

If then it is unlikely that their second horses were riderless if our Corinthian warriors were riding to battle, we come to the other two basic possibilities. The modern student might expect that if an artist chose not to show the inside rider's outline in order not to blur his main human figure, both riders are more likely to be similar than dissimilar. On the other hand, the Corinthian artists (and their customers) may have been so accustomed to the sight of mounted panoplied warriors attended by mounted squires that they usually felt able to take the latters' presence for granted, and only rarely bothered to show them as on C24 (*fig. 55*). And if the outlined second horses do indicate squires, there are other indications that those armoured warriors with shields, if they were going to fight as they are shown equipped, were mounted hoplites rather than squired cavalrymen. The first is that the only armoured warriors on Corinthian or Attic vases who have two horses also have shields, whereas those without shields, who are clearly therefore not equipped to dismount and fight in the phalanx, invariably have only the one horse. And the sole exception to this statement is provided by an Attic vase of the second quarter of the sixth century which depicts two mounted hoplites flanking a duel between two identical hoplites on foot and holding the duellists' horses for them.[14] Now these mutually

MOUNTED WARRIORS IN THE 6TH CENTURY

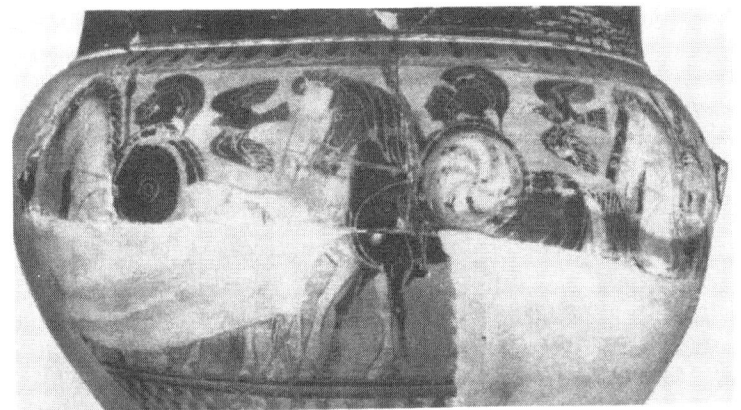

FIG. 55
A Late Corinthian vase (575–550 B.C.) which clearly shows the squires riding alongside the mounted hoplites instead of merely indicating their presence by the outline of a second horse (C24)

exclusive coincidences are surely not without significance, and although a second horse could technically be a spare for a cavalryman, it appears that only those who are equipped to fight on foot have the second horses and the squires who would be needed to take care of them. Then mounted hoplites are further indicated by the extreme rarity of any fighting with large, round shields from horseback in the whole of Archaic vase-painting, whereas there is a considerable number of fully panoplied riders with second horses on Ripe Corinthian vases, and an equally considerable number of battles on foot between identically panoplied hoplites. On vases C20 (*fig. 54*) and C23 for instance, it is very likely that the panoplied riders shown on the one side were riding to a battle in which they would dismount and fight on foot like the exactly similar hoplites on the other.[15] And we may recall the contemporary vases which unequivocally testify to the practice of hoplites fighting while mounted squires hold their horses: their number is in closer proportion to the number of panoplied riders of categories (iii) and (iv), and further points a contrast with C8, the solitary possible example of such a warrior fighting from horseback (*fig. 48*). Finally we have already observed why there were so few examples of any horsemen fighting from horseback with the hoplite shield in Archaic art, and it is even less likely that our Corinthian warriors regularly did so when equipped with the rest of the panoply. At any rate I know of only one other example besides C8 of a panoplied rider fighting with a hoplite shield in the whole of Archaic vase-painting, a lancer who is lunging at a mounted Amazon on a late sixth-century Attic vase, A95 (see below, p. 132, *fig. 71*), and his singularity is in marked contrast to the numerous contemporary examples of shieldless armoured cavalrymen in action (e.g. A74–A80, *figs. 69, 70*). Now Anderson supposed that mounted hoplites might 'sling the great shield out of the way onto the back' in order to engage the enemy on horseback.[16] But I can find no example of this practice in Archaic art; and although a warrior might ease his left arm by slinging his shield on his back while riding at the walk,[17] it would be impossible to ride fast or fight with a great hoplite shield in that position exactly because its diameter would be much greater than the length of the back from the neck to the base of the spine. Certainly the shields of our armoured Corinthian riders of categories (ii) – (iv) are much too big; and in any case there is not even a single example of any Corinthian warrior with a shield, either mounted or on foot, who is not holding it.

In conclusion then there is a combination of three indications to suggest that most of the mounted warriors of my categories (iii) and (iv), if they are going to fight as they are shown equipped, will dismount to fight on foot like the hoplites on the other sides of C20 (*fig. 54*) and C23. The horsemen of these vases along with those of C17, C18, C19 and C21 (all MC vases) have the full hoplite panoply of greaves, helmets and shields (and they may also have corslets hidden under their shields), and an LC vase, C24, also shows the mounted squire (*fig. 55*). On three vases they have only a single spear, C19, C20 (*fig. 54*), C22, and although those of the other four have two (C17, C18, C21, C23), a second spear to be carried by the squire as a spare for his master (and also perhaps for his own defence) is no proof of cavalry. The horsemen of one LC vase, C26, have the full panoply except for the greaves, but since there are no hoplites on foot on this vase, there is no way of telling if the omission may have been deliberate as there was in the case of C16, where the single-horsed warriors' lack of both greaves and corslet made a clear contrast with the hoplites fighting on foot on the other side. The horsemen of C26 therefore I tentatively class as mounted hoplites, and those of C16 (although they have only single spears) as cavalrymen. So far however the method of fighting has been assessed only on the assumption that the horsemen always fought as they are shown

MOUNTED WARRIORS IN THE 6TH CENTURY

equipped. And although the warriors of categories (iii) and (iv) would scarcely have taken all that equipment to war unless they were preparing to fight as hoplites, the presence of a squire would enable them to leave in his charge not only their horses but also their shield and even their greaves if they wanted to fight as cavalry. Some at least may have set out prepared to do either or both according to circumstances. On unsuitable cavalry terrain they might have joined the phalanx, or where cavalry could be effective they might have assumed that role. Certainly most of the landed gentry who kept horses will have been competent horsemen, and they might have practised fighting both as hoplites and as cavalry. And in this case the two spears which some of the mounted hoplites carry will have been more valuable. But all this is pure hypothesis. Two facts only are certain: that there were mounted hoplites and there were squadrons of armoured cavalry; and on balance it seems easier to believe that the cavalrymen of C13 and C14 (*figs. 52b, 53a*) were exclusively cavalrymen rather than that they had stripped down to tunic and helmet from the full panoply of the hoplites on foot and of the mounted hoplites who also appear on C14 (*fig. 53b*).

Of the final category of armed horsemen, those unarmoured but carrying a single long lance, there is a large number of examples, but the majority may not be relevant to the military historian. They were a favourite motif of the Ripe Corinthian vase-painters throughout the full period from 625 to 550 B.C. Sometimes they appear singly, merely in a context of animal motifs (C27, C28b, C29). Sometimes there are two riding one after the other (C30a, C31, C32), sometimes three (C30b, C33b, C34, C35, C36, C37), and sometimes more, so that they fill the whole circumference of the vase (C38, C39). Occasionally two appear antithetically, flanking a non-human motif (C40) or in one case a group of three similarly nude men on foot who are apparently conversing and each holding a spear (C28a, on the other side of which is a single rider with a lance between two cocks). One or two of these riders, as on the last-mentioned scene, appear to be nude, but most of them wear the chiton, and all are beardless youths. None however are shown in an unmistakably military context; but although none are unmistakably hunting either, some at least are almost certainly racing, as on C30b, on which the riders are galloping flat out, and two have goads instead of the spears carried by the other three. Three vases however have military scenes as well as the light-armed riders, and this may perhaps suggest a military significance although of course no connexion can be taken for granted. C34 has three of the riders walking to the right on one side, and on the other a heroized departure scene featuring a chariot, a hoplite on foot and a heavily armed horseman. C39 has three friezes one above the other, and the middle one shows a file of light-armed riders beneath a hoplite battle-scene. And the third, C33, is more explicit in having a line of galloping riders on one side, and on the other two identical riders antithetically flanking a hoplite duel over a corpse, probably marked as heroic by its inscription. Now Helbig's interpretation of any scene in which mounted ephebes flanked a duel was that they were hoplites' mounted squires. But unlike those of C10 (*fig. 51*) and C12, these mounted youths are not shown with a second horse; and there are several similar examples, of which some have no heroic identifications (C41, C42), some have inscriptions which are presumably heroic (C33, C43), and occasionally there is a Boeotian shield (C44). If then these are mounted squires, it is necessary to suppose that the artist left the second horse to the imagination, since we have already dismissed Helbig's suggestion that hoplite and squire regularly had only a single horse between them. And certainly this explanation is likely enough. But it is also perhaps just possible that they are light-armed cavalrymen waiting behind the lines, or even that the motif of the duel flanked by antithetical horsemen combines the two ideas. It is true of course that no Corinthian vase known to me shows unarmoured riders actually fighting as on the Attic lekanis-lid A7 (*fig. 56*), but a similar mixed force of hoplites and light cavalry may be indicated by C15, of which one side depicts a helmeted horseman leading a file of five running hoplites followed by an unarmoured, tunic-clad rider with a lance, while the other has an unarmoured rider, similar to the last, at the front and rear of five more hoplites. These riders are surely not squires, and they give every appearance of cavalrymen accompanying an infantry phalanx, perhaps on the wings. And if that is so, perhaps some of the similar riders, who must have been a common sight to have inspired so many scenes on Ripe Corinthian vases, were neither riding to the hunt nor practising to be mounted squires (as those leading a second horse on C45 and C46 surely were), but were light cavalrymen. At any rate, in the absence of fighting scenes there can be no absolute proof of Corinthian unarmoured cavalry, but C15 makes it a strong probability; and that probability is reinforced by contemporary Attic vases which show exactly similar cavalry in action.

Athens
Early Attic Black Figure vase-painting maintains an almost total silence on contemporary warfare. Its preference was for mythical and Orientalizing creatures, sometimes as purely decorative motifs, sometimes in narrative scenes; and its favourite contemporary activity was revelling rather than fighting.[18] But when the military silence is broken from the end of the second decade of the sixth century, the war-horse is immediately represented. The story begins with a couple of sherds from the Acropolis, belonging to the third decade or perhaps a shade earlier. One of them (A5) depicts a panoplied rider, probably one of a cavalcade since the legs of a horse and rider preceding him are also visible. He has a large, round, blazoned shield, twin spears, a stilt-crested helmet and possibly greaves too; and although there is no sign of a second horse or squire, a cavalcade is not a battle, and his equipment suggests that this warrior dismounted to fight on foot like the hoplites shown duelling on other fragments of the vase. The unarmoured rider of the other sherd however appears to be a true cavalryman (A6). Only his outline is distinguishable, but he is certainly aiming a single lance overarm for a downward thrust or throw; and since he appears to be holding a small shield of uncertain shape in front of him, he is a cavalryman rather than a hunter, and to my knowledge the earliest Attic cavalryman who is actually shown fighting from horseback. Then the evidence for military horsemen becomes much greater and clearer once we are firmly into the second quarter of the century: both mounted hoplites and true cavalry are found, and of the latter there are both armoured and unarmoured cavalrymen.

The Naples lekanis-lid already mentioned (A7) provides valuable evidence for mounted hoplites and unarmoured cavalry (*fig. 56*). The subject is the Greek army marching to sack Troy, but there is no obvious archaizing or heroizing either in items of arms and armour or in tactics: there is not so much as a single Boeotian shield, and the

FIG. 56
An Attic Black Figure lekanis-lid of 575–550 B.C. depicting light cavalry riding at the head of the army and mounted hoplites dismounting to join the phalanxes while their squires hold their horses (A7)

advancing hoplites, fully panoplied and with single spears, are clearly shown in phalanxes. Behind each of the two phalanxes comes a mounted hoplite, perhaps an officer who has finished making his dispositions, and he is shown dismounting to fight with the identically equipped hoplites of his phalanx while his squire, a mounted unarmed youth wearing a chiton, takes care of his horse for him. Similarly dressed youths (without armour or shields) ride at the head of the advancing army, but they have no second horses and are not acting as squires. They ride abreast, and each is poising a javelin for an overarm throw. Clearly they are a squadron of light cavalry, whose task in battle would be to harass the enemy phalanx, to deal with its cavalry, to lead the pursuit in the event of victory or to try to hinder it in the event of retreat.

Other vases of this period depict both these types of horsemen, the mounted hoplite and the light cavalryman, but not generally both at the same time as A7 does. Among the other evidence for the former, there are some scenes which depict hoplite duels flanked by the mounted, unarmoured squires holding the second horse, as on A8, where one of the squires may hold a spare lance but the other appears to be unarmed. The duel is inscribed and perhaps therefore heroic, but the equipment is completely contemporary. Then there are at least two Siana cups, A9 and A10, which depict hoplite duels on the

MOUNTED WARRIORS IN THE 6TH CENTURY

outside while the circular field of the bottom inside features a mounted tunic-clad youth who carries a lance, leads a second horse, and is almost certainly to be interpreted in the context of A7 (*fig. 56*) as a hoplite's mounted squire. A vase from the Athenian Agora (A11) shows a hoplite on foot preceded by his mounted squire leading a second horse exactly as on the Corinthian *hippostrophos–hippobatas* aryballos, C2 (see above, p. 58, *fig. 36*). Then there are other vases which show a mounted hoplite and his squire riding side by side. There is just enough of a dinos fragment of *c.* 570 B.C. from the Acropolis (A12a) to indicate a cavalcade of panoplied warriors with the head and shoulders of a youth wearing only the chiton riding on their inside. And later in the second quarter of the century a funeral amphora (A13) features a single, similar pair (except that here the inner rider is an older man, bearded and wearing a felt hat). And if the warrior of the sherd might be thought a possible cavalryman since he has two spears (although a squire often carries a spear, and the rim of a shield is just visible), the clearly panoplied warrior of the later vase will surely dismount to fight with so large a shield; and since only a single spear is visible between the two of them, the inner rider will certainly be an unarmed squire rather than a light cavalryman. A different combination of horsemen side by side is provided by another fragment of the Acropolis dinos (A12b), on which both riders of each pair in a cavalcade appear to be similarly armoured, and they may perhaps be heavy cavalry. Whether they had the hoplite panoply or not is impossible to say since only their helmeted heads and the tips of their spears are visible. If they had no shields they were surely cavalrymen. And if they were panoplied, the absence of an obvious squire in a cavalcade does not alter the probability that in battle they dismounted to fight. What is certain is that a mounted hoplite would not have been wasted as another's squire in contemporary warfare, and the scene on A14, where mounted hoplites are shown flanking a hoplite duel and holding the duellists' horses for them, is clearly marked as heroic by the presence of a goddess standing behind each duellist and holding a spare spear for her favourite. There is less doubt about the rider of A15: he is equipped in the standard hoplite manner with helmet, greaves, large round shield and single spear, and the second horse shown in outline indicates the presence of a mounted squire. Last may be mentioned

FIG. 57 Light cavalry about to engage alongside a hoplite battle on an Attic Bf cup of near the middle of the sixth century (A17)

the Vatican's merrythought cup of about the middle of the century (A16), which shows on each side a hoplite dismounting while a mounted youth accompanies him as on A7 (*fig. 56*). The squires wear chitons (and one has a little cap), and they hold the lances while their masters dismount unencumbered by weapons.

What was suspected in the case of some of the Corinthian horsemen armed with a single spear – that they were not all mounted squires for hoplites – is proved beyond question in the case of Athens in the second quarter of the sixth century since light cavalry is depicted in action. Besides the horsemen leading the army on A7 (*fig. 56*), a cup in Taranto (A17) shows two hoplites locked in combat while two mounted youths wearing only the chiton ride up from either side and attack each other with javelins poised for an overarm throw (*fig. 57*). The left-hand youth has only one javelin, but the other is holding a spare one in his left hand, which also manages the reins. And they are clearly attacking each other and not the hoplites since their horses' forelegs disappear behind the infantrymen. Now this scene may provide an alternative explanation for those armed but unarmoured riders who are shown flanking hoplite duels, not fighting themselves but not holding a second horse either. Unless painted spears have worn away, this cannot of course be the explanation of the unarmed riders flanking duels on A18 and A19: they are very probably mounted squires, and if so we must imagine second horses, as we may also be right to do on A20, where two hoplites stand facing each other while the mounted youths standing at either side

MOUNTED WARRIORS IN THE 6TH CENTURY

FIG. 58
Greek mounted javelineers riding against barbarian horse-archers on an Attic Bf vase of c. 565 B.C. (A30)

give every appearance of being in attendance. But those riders who have spears, like the bearded horsemen of A21, could perhaps represent light cavalry ready to operate on the wings of a phalanx battle indicated in cross-section by the two duellists. And what is a possibility for the riders of A21 becomes a virtual certainty for those of A22 and A23. Both these vases depict three hoplites almost frontally in close order while a frontal chiton-clad rider armed with a lance appears on either wing (all four unarmoured except for the rider of the right on A22, who wears a helmet as well as the chiton and has no visible weapon). The bearded, tunic-clad rider who carries a spear on the inside of a Siana cup (A24) but has only the one horse unlike those of A9 and A10, if the warriors on the outside give him a military context, may also be a cavalryman; and the same may be true of the files of four identical riders cantering on one side of A25, A26 and A27 while hoplites battle on the other. On another Siana cup (A28) the mounted, chiton-clad youths are found galloping among hoplites running on foot, and these too are surely cavalry. And finally there are others besides those of A7 and A17 (*figs. 56, 57*) who are actually fighting. Among a frieze of apparently unconnected subjects including a boar-hunt and a hoplite duel flanked by chariots, a cothon in Munich (A29) features two mounted youths galloping to the right with javelins poised for an overarm throw, and they are as likely to be cavalrymen as hunters. But there is no such doubt about the riders on a roughly contemporary dinos of *c*. 565 B.C. from the Acropolis (A30), which presents our earliest certain illustration of cavalry fighting cavalry (*fig. 58*). Twelve Greek javelineers, all bearded, wearing tunics and felt caps and carrying a spare javelin in their left hand while they hurl one with the right, are charging ten barbarian horse-archers. As Anderson noted, the vase may have been dedicated in honour of some Athenian nobleman who lost his life in an Athenian enterprise in the Hellespont; and this frieze may show

FIG. 59
An armoured Attic cavalryman of the second quarter of the sixth century wearing a bell-corslet (A32)

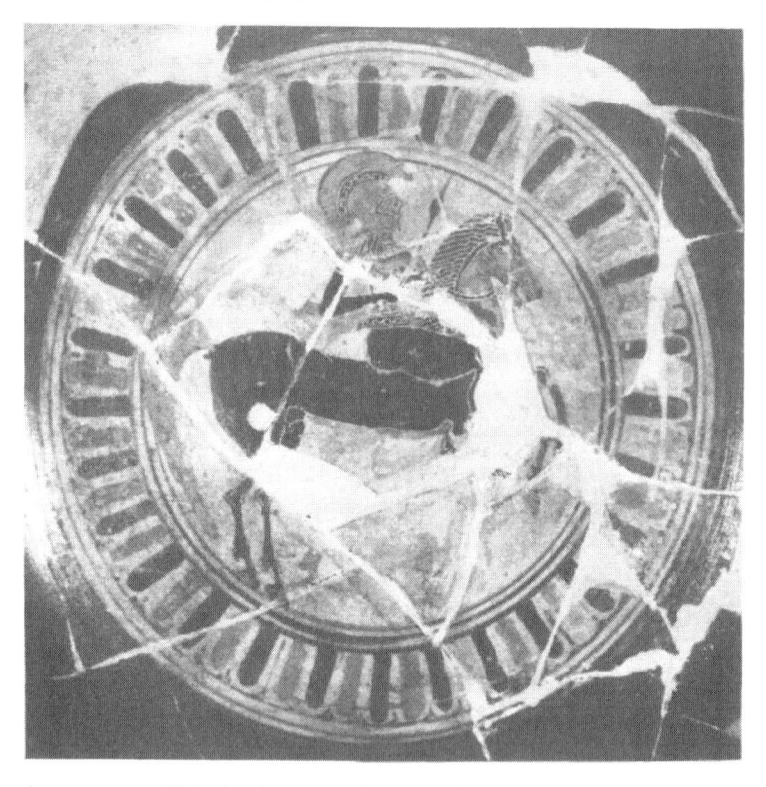

the context of his death, while the main decoration may have been intended to compare it with the fate of a hero of the Trojan War.[19]

Armoured cavalry too is clearly attested for the second quarter of the sixth century by at least three vases, A31, A32 and A33. The first of them shows a helmeted horseman in battle, about to ride down a hoplite who advances on foot to meet him. On neither of the other two vases are the cavalrymen actually shown in action, but they are without shields and therefore not equipped to fight on foot. A32, an otherwise undecorated cup, depicts a single rider on the circular field inside (*fig. 59*). He carries a single, long lance, wears a helmet and a fine bell-corslet, and is probably without greaves. A33 has a cavalcade of four similar cavalrymen riding to the right, except that they are without corslets: they wear helmets and tunics (and probably no greaves), and carry single lances. A fourth vase already mentioned

MOUNTED WARRIORS IN THE 6TH CENTURY

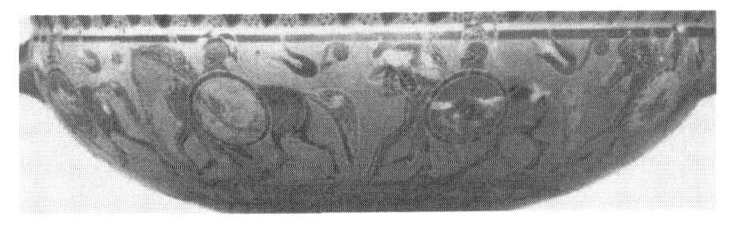

FIG. 60 Hoplites exercising with their horses on an Attic Bf vase of 575-550 B.C. (A37) by the same painter as A7 (fig. 56): the second horses shown in outline suggest mounted squires

(A22) shows a frontal, helmeted rider stationed on one wing of a hoplite phalanx while an unarmoured rider is positioned on the other, and he too will be a cavalryman although he has no visible weapon. Other vases depict unsquired horsemen either riding or leading single horses, but all are holding shields, and most are probably mounted hoplites. This is true at least in the case of the fully panoplied warriors riding on A34, running with their horses on A35, or standing with them in the heroic scene of A36. None of these warriors are shown with squires who could hold their horses for them while they fought, but they are not battle-scenes. The hoplites of A35, who are running with their horses, are shown in pairs, and they are probably engaging in military exercises. And the same may be the case with the warriors of A37 (*fig. 60*), a vase already discussed as being Alföldi's main evidence for his extraordinary 'Metabatai-Desultortechnik' thesis. It shows single hoplites walking or running with their horses, and second horses are shown in outline: perhaps these second horses indicate pairs or ranks of hoplites running with single horses as clearly shown on A35, but more likely in view of their painter they suggest mounted squires whom the field is not wide enough to show. The motif of warriors on foot with their horses was much better adapted to the narrow bands of cups like A35 and A37 than riders would have been, and the width of the band no doubt dictated the preference. And in the case of A37, the likelihood that the second horse indicates a mounted squire is reinforced by the same artist's similar motif on his lekanis-lid (A7), on which he had space to show the mounted squire (*fig. 56*).[20] The riders with large, round shields on A38 however are likely to have been a detachment of cavalry, if indeed they fought at all as they are shown equipped. If they did not, it might be argued on Helbig's thesis that they were the squires of mounted hoplites who had left their shields to fight as cavalry, but this would be a very far-fetched explanation,

EARLY GREEK WARFARE

and especially so since the other side depicts panoplied hoplites fighting on foot with their shields. In contrast to the hoplites, the riders have no armour at all, neither helmets nor greaves, and are therefore both ill-equipped to fight on foot and sufficiently unburdened to be able to manage so large a shield in the manner of the similarly unarmoured Scythian cavalryman shown in action on vase A94 of the last quarter of the century. But examples of any riders using the large hoplite shield from horseback are so extremely rare that the protection which it afforded cannot generally have been thought worth the trouble of carrying it even by otherwise completely unarmoured cavalrymen, of which there are a great number. And this fact reinforces the probability that the panoplied horsemen with shields were mounted hoplites.

Moving to the evidence of the second half of the sixth century we shall find that the following pattern emerges. From near the end of the second quarter the unmistakable representations of cavalry steadily increase throughout the rest of the century, and in particular the representations of cavalry in battle; but whereas the cavalrymen of the third quarter are almost exclusively unarmoured, the last quarter provides a striking proliferation of heavy cavalry, armoured but shieldless. Panoplied horsemen who are equipped with the large hoplite shield continue to be depicted with mounted squires in the third quarter, but they are almost invariably shown unsquired in the fourth. Most of these appear to be mounted hoplites, but there are a few examples of horsemen with hoplite shields who may also be cavalrymen besides the extremely rare riders shown actually using a hoplite shield from horseback in battle.

Hoplite duels flanked by mounted squires have all but disappeared by the middle of the century,[21] but mounted squires in non-heroic contexts are not uncommonly found riding side by side with their masters, holding their horses for them while they dismount, or bringing their horses to them as they prepare to depart to battle. In mythological contexts we find vases like A40 continuing in the third quarter a motif which appeared in the second on A41 and A42, the pursuit of Troilus by Achilles. Troilus is invariably depicted as an unarmoured youth, sometimes carrying a spear, sometimes unarmed, and riding away leading a second horse while Achilles, dressed as a hoplite, runs after him on foot. Even these scenes however may not

FIG. 61
Hoplite and squire riding side by side on an Attic Bf amphora of c. 560 B.C. (A45)

be entirely without significance since the painters had to have some reason for depicting their subjects in the guise of a hoplite and a mounted squire, whose contemporary military reality is attested by other vases of at least the second and third quarters of the century. Moreover it is worth noting that not all hoplites preceded by mounted youths with second horses are necessarily Achilles and Troilus, and we may contrast two vases of the second quarter of the century in this respect: on A42 the artist left no doubt about their identity by showing all the features of the story, but on A43 the motif is surely just a hoplite and his squire, and there are no heroic identifications. And even where there is clear heroizing such as the presence of the chariots in the chaotic battle-scene of A44, the hoplite who enters the battle from the far right is surely not Achilles pursuing Troilus but simply a *hippobatas* preceded by his *hippostrophos*, who not only reveals the true identity of the Homeric 'charioteers', but enjoyed a similar (if somewhat reduced) role in the days of the warfare to which his master's hoplite equipment belonged. Of non-heroic scenes, a Lydos amphora of roughly the middle of the century (A45) depicts what is surely a hoplite and his squire riding side by side, and here the squire is unusually the outer rider (*fig. 61*). The inner rider has the full hoplite panoply and carries a single spear (whose shaft is shown protruding beneath the horse's belly), while his youthful squire wears only the chiton and also carries a spear. A similar vase of the Lydos school (A46) has the same

FIG. 62
Hoplite dismounting while his squire holds his horse on an Attic Bf vase of the third quarter of the sixth century (A48)

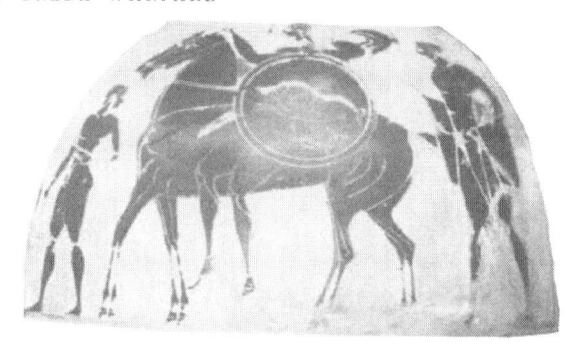

FIG. 63
A hoplite and his mounted squire (who has both horses) bid farewell to their families before departing for battle on an Attic Bf vase of 550–525 B.C. (A50)

motif reversed: the unarmoured squire (who in this case is bearded) is the inner rider of the pair. And a third shows a departure scene in which a youthful mounted squire leading a second horse bids farewell to two other youths and an old man (A47). Vases A48 and A49 both belong to the third quarter of the century and both illustrate the mounted hoplite and his squire side by side, the former gliding down from his horse (*fig. 62*). The warrior of both vases is equipped with helmet, greaves and a round, blazoned shield of very large size. On A49 he holds two spears in the same hand as his shield, and grasps his horse's mane with his right to steady himself. His squire wears a chiton and a 'Scythian-looking' bonnet, but is surely not a Scythian archer as suggested by Miss Richter:[22] he is clearly unarmed and his bonnet scarcely makes him an archer; and in any case Scythian archers on Archaic Attic vases are almost invariably footsoldiers, whereas mounted Scythians (e.g. A79, A94) are spearsmen.[23] On A48 the warrior is unarmed except for a sheathed sword whose

MOUNTED WARRIORS IN THE 6TH CENTURY

FIG. 64
A battle with cavalry and hoplites on an Attic Bf cup of early in the third quarter of the sixth century (A52)

scabbard just protrudes from beneath the lower rim of his shield, and his squire holds his spear for him (*fig. 62*). A hydria of the same period (A50) depicts a departure scene on either side, and the scenes are almost certainly connected (*fig. 63*). On the one, a panoplied hoplite takes his leave of two robed men, while on the other a mounted youth wearing a tunic and carrying a lance does the same; and since the latter is leading a second horse like his counterpart on A47, he will be the squire of the hoplite, who will ride to the battlefield. The similar mounted youth leading a second horse and depicted between two robed and bearded men and two women on A51, an earlier vase of about the middle of the century, is also likely to be a hoplite's squire, although this vase (like A47) does not show an equivalent scene for the hoplite.

For true cavalry engaging in battle with hoplites on foot, a vigorous scene is provided by A52 (*fig. 64*). This band-cup was painted probably early in the third quarter of the sixth century, but it has

E*

EARLY GREEK WARFARE

been considerably restored and some of its details cannot be accepted with certainty. On one side the chiton-clad rider who is charging from the left against either a hoplite or a mounted archer is also wearing a helmet, and if the details of his equipment are genuine, he is one of the extremely rare cavalrymen who use a hoplite shield in battle. With his right arm he is poising a long, single lance for an overarm throw, and he has a small, apparently 'hoplite' shield on his left (of which only the upper part above the elbow is visible, thus indicating the double-grip). An equal rarity in Archaic art is the Greek mounted archer, bearded and tunic-clad, who rides up and bends his bow at him (or less probably at the back of the hoplite on foot). Then the rest of the cavalrymen on this side and all those on the other are unarmoured spearmen, apparently all youths (unlike the archer), and all wearing only the chiton. All have a single, long lance, which some thrust underarm while others hurl overarm; and one of the latter has engaged his fingers in a throwing-loop. The tactics are not altogether clear, and sometimes the cavalry may be attacking hoplites, sometimes each other; and it may be that the artist envisaged a cavalry battle taking place alongside a clash of infantry. A clear example of a detachment of light cavalry charging an organized hoplite force is provided by another band-cup, A53 (*fig. 65*). Four tunic-clad riders, of whom the first three have their single lances poised for an overarm throw, are about to clash with a phalanx of five hoplites advancing to meet them from the right. More light cavalry in action against hoplites appear on A54, an amphora which depicts two riders trampling fallen hoplites in what looks like the mounted pursuit of a routed phalanx. One wears a chlamys, the other a chiton, and the latter is thrusting underarm with a lance at a fleeing hoplite who is turning to protect himself with his shield. On A55, a Lysippides vase of *c.* 530 B.C., a crouching hoplite is caught between two, probably bearded, chiton-clad horsemen. They may conceivably be meant to be attacking each other since the artist superimposed the hoofs of the forelegs of both horses over the hoplite, but the angle of the single spears which they are poising in their right hands for an overarm thrust or throw suggests that they are aiming at the hoplite rather than at each other. Another Lysippides vase of similar date (A56) shows a cloaked and bearded rider helping in the rout after a hoplite battle and preparing to hurl

MOUNTED WARRIORS IN THE 6TH CENTURY

FIG. 65
Light cavalry charging a hoplite phalanx on another Attic Bf band-cup of the third quarter of the sixth century (A53)

his lance at a fleeing hoplite who turns to defend himself as on A54 and A72 (*fig. 68*). And a work of the Amasis painter (A57) also shows light cavalry operating against hoplites. A hoplite duel is raging in the centre. To the left a hoplite rushes against a rider wearing a tunic and a conical cap and carrying a single lance, who pulls up his horse with a jerk in the face of the violent attack. To the right the exact opposite is happening. A similar cavalryman is galloping flat out in pursuit of a fleeing hoplite, who is about to be overrun and is turning to lunge at his pursuer with his lance. Neither of these riders however has yet poised his spear for action, unlike the similarly chiton-clad cavalryman of a band-cup fragment, A58. The sherd does not allow us to see his target, but he is clearly leaning back and aiming his long lance for a throw, while behind him a panoplied hoplite on foot turns and defends himself against an unknown assailant (probably not a cavalryman but another footsoldier, to judge from the angle of his spear). The battle-scene of another band-cup (A59), this time complete, is marked as a heroic scene by the inscriptions which name two of the hoplites as Hector and Ajax, and by the Boeotian shield carried by the latter. But even so we should perhaps be wrong to dismiss the scene as irrelevant to contemporary warfare. Even 'Ajax' and 'Hector' are not single duellists but members of opposing phalanxes of three, and the single Boeotian shield is the only archaism among the equipment of all six hoplites. To left and right of the phalanxes come the light-armed, auxiliary troops, an archer and a javelineer both on foot (and Athens was not unacquainted with Scythian archers at this time). Then from far left and far right mounted youths ride up carrying single spears, two from the left and three from the right. Now it seems unlikely that these riders should be interpreted as mounted squires since they have no spare horses and there are not enough of them to go round; and although their nudity is hardly realistic, what the artist had in mind as he planned his composition could well have been contemporary Athenian light cavalry squadrons, which he had seen arrayed behind the phalanx to protect its rear, or preparing to operate on the wings, or waiting to be of use in pursuit (like the riders of A54), or to cover a retreat. Another battle-scene clearly marked as mythological but even more clearly based on contemporary warfare is the Amazonomachy of A60. The battle is being fought by Greek light cavalry

MOUNTED WARRIORS IN THE 6TH CENTURY

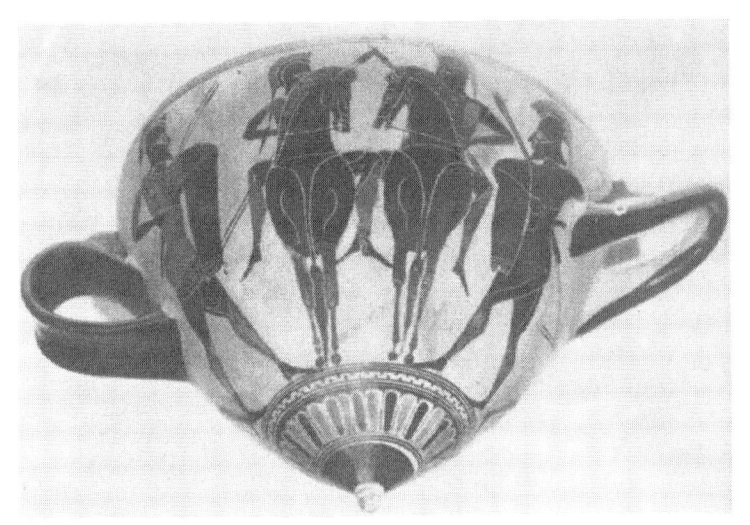

FIG. 66
Two armoured
Attic cavalrymen
of the third quarter
of the sixth
century on vase
A64

against Amazons on foot who have hoplite shields and lances, and apart from the identity of the latter there are no eccentricities of equipment or tactics. The Greek horsemen, bearded and wearing only the usual tunic, are fighting with lances either hurled overarm or lunged underarm at the hoplites.

As in the second quarter of the century, there are horsemen in the third who are unmistakably light cavalrymen although not actually engaged in battle. Recalling A22 and A23, one side of A61 indicates cavalry stationed on the wings of a phalanx by showing a frontal mounted youth with chiton and single lance on either side of four hoplites closely ordered in line abreast. The other side shows light cavalry and infantry mixed: of five frontal figures there are two panoplied hoplites on foot, a bearded, chiton-clad rider with a single lance between them in the centre, and a mounted youth similarly equipped on either flank. Another bearded light cavalryman appears in a departure scene on a roughly contemporary vase, A62. Wearing the chiton and carrying two spears, he sits on his horse between two elderly men to whom he is bidding farewell, while two hoplites walk away on the far left of the scene. More light cavalrymen, this time riding among hoplites on foot in what may be a scene of pursuit, appear on the shoulder panel of A63. Then finally a mastos in the British Museum (A64) gives a rare example of armoured riders

125

FIG. 67
Unarmoured cavalrymen thrusting at retreating hoplites on an Attic Bf wine-cup of the last quarter of the sixth century (A65)

without shields in the third quarter of the century. The two cavalrymen, who are shown frontally, have tunic, greaves, helmet and two lances (*fig. 66*).

Attic Black Figure of the last quarter of the century continues to depict light, unarmoured cavalry, often in action, and usually fighting infantry rather than each other. The battle-scene on a cyathos (A65, *fig. 67*) begins with a youthful, chiton-clad cavalryman making an underarm lunge with his single lance at a hoplite who crouches to defend himself and thrusts at his assailant's horse with his spear. Then further round the vase a second and similar horseman rides up behind a hoplite who is dispatching a fleeing enemy. He holds his lance ready for an underarm thrust, and appears to be helping in the pursuit of retreating infantry. Two similar cavalrymen are taking part in a hoplite battle on A66, but they are not fighting on the same side as in the last scene. The battle centres round a hoplite duel over a corpse. The duel is marked as heroic by the Boeotian shields of the duellists, but otherwise they have the full panoply of contemporary hoplites. From either side a light cavalryman rides up, wearing chiton and chlamys and poising a single lance for an overarm throw: the angle of their javelins indicates that they are riding to attack each other, although the rider from the left is trampling a hoplite who tried to stand in his path. A later vase, A67, recalls the similar cyathos A65 by depicting a chiton-clad cavalryman similarly lunging with his lance at a hoplite who crouches to defend himself, except that this time the hoplite has a spotted chiton which presumably makes him a barbarian. Then on the other side the scene is the same except that the nationalities are reversed, since the hoplite

MOUNTED WARRIORS IN THE 6TH CENTURY

FIG. 68
Attic Bf plate of
c. 500 B.C. showing
a light cavalryman
helping in the
rout of a hoplite
phalanx (A72)

has a plain chiton and the rider a pointed cap. A departure scene is the subject of A68, which depicts a youth wearing chlamys and petasos, carrying two lances, and looking back over his shoulder as he leads his single horse away from an old man sitting on a stool. And he is clearly departing for battle and not to the hunt since a panoplied hoplite stands on the extreme right of the scene. A69, a slightly later vase belonging to the end of the century, depicts the back view of a mounted youth armed with two spears who stands between two hoplites on foot, one of whom is walking away and glancing back over his shoulder. A70, roughly contemporary, presents an identical scene except that the horseman is shown frontally. A71 has a hoplite on foot apparently caught between two cavalrymen who are like the horsemen of A69 and A70 in having two lances, but unlike them have 'Scythian' bonnets. A72 (*fig. 68*) shows a bearded, light cavalryman who appears to be helping in the

FIG. 69
A clash of armoured cavalrymen on an Attic Bf fragment of the late sixth century (A74)

rout of a phalanx after a hoplite engagement, and he recalls the similar scenes of A54 and A56. And finally A73 of the early fifth century shows a cavalryman standing with his horse between two hoplites: he is bearded, wears the chlamys, and carries three lances.

Armoured cavalrymen without shields like the single rider of A32 (*fig. 59*) become common only in the last quarter of the century, and now they are often shown actually fighting. And unlike the contemporary unarmoured cavalry they are often shown fighting each other as well as infantrymen. Not infrequently vase-paintings depict some or all of their cavalry as Amazons, but many other scenes are entirely 'Greek'; and even in the case of Amazons, their mythological identity does not automatically mean that their equipment and manner of fighting owe nothing to contemporary Attic cavalry. Of combat scenes which are entirely Greek and have no archaizing or heroizing features we may cite first a fragmentary cup, A74 (*fig. 69*), which depicts two cavalrymen clashing on rearing horses over the body of a fallen hoplite. Each wears a heavy helmet, a chiton, a short cape and greaves and is poising a single lance in his right hand for an overarm thrust or throw. Similar 'all-Greek' scenes of cavalrymen meeting over a fallen hoplite occur on A75 and A76 (*fig. 70*). On A75 they wear the chiton, chlamys, helmet and greaves, but unlike those of A74 (*fig. 69*) they both have two spare lances in their left hand (which also holds the bridle) while they prepare to use a third in their right: one is lunging underarm, the other aiming an overarm throw, and since both are clearly aiming not at each other but at the hoplite in the centre, they are both on the same side in the battle. On A76 in contrast, the horsemen are clearly enemies charging

FIG. 70
Armoured lancers engaging over a fallen hoplite on a late sixth-century Attic Bf vase (A76)

each other with lances levelled, and like the cavalryman of A32 (*fig. 59*) they wear metal bell-corslets over their chitons (*fig. 70*). Besides their helmets (one with a flat crest, the other stilted), they wear greaves and have swords slung at their sides from the shoulder, and one has a second lance in his left hand. A corslet is also worn by the Greek cavalrymen in similar scenes on A77, A78 and A79, but their mounted opponents are respectively an armoured Amazon inscribed as 'Penthesilea' (being attacked by 'Achilles'),[24] an unarmoured Amazon, and a Scythian cavalryman (also unarmoured, and wearing a high-pointed cap). On A80 another mounted Amazon (unusually shown wearing greaves) attacks an armoured Greek lancer without corslet as he tramples an Amazonian hoplite. More armoured Greek cavalrymen, mounted but not fighting, appear on A81 and A82. The former depicts a frontal horseman with helmet, chiton, greaves and two lances, while panoplied hoplites stand with their shields on either side of his horse. And the single riders who form the motif on either side of A82 are similarly equipped except for the addition of a corslet and the absence of greaves. Then there are vases which depict cavalrymen leading their horses. A83 for example is a departure

129

EARLY GREEK WARFARE

scene in which a panoplied hoplite is taking his leave of an old man sitting on a stool while on either side a cavalryman stands holding his horse: both horsemen wear a helmet, chlamys and greaves (no sword, shield or corslet), and are armed with a lance. Another departure scene on A84 shows a helmeted and bare-legged cavalryman with two lances standing on the far side of his horse, and a man and woman standing to left and right. And other vases like A85 and A86, the former an early Red Figure work, simply show the helmeted warrior holding his lance and standing with his horse in no particular context. Now all these cavalrymen were Greek, but there are also many vases which depict armoured Amazonian cavaliers out of battle, and A87, A88, A89 and A90 (if indeed this last really is an Amazon) will provide a representative selection. All wear helmets and carry one (A87) or more usually two lances (A88, A89, A90), and wear a chiton (A87, A88, A90) or a chlamys (A89); most have swords at their sides (A87, A88, A89), and none have greaves.

At this point it is necessary to reconsider for some Attic vases the problem already tackled for Corinthian. In the case of all the armoured horsemen discussed above it is usually clear that they are cavalrymen, whether they are actually shown fighting or not, since without shields they are ill-equipped to dismount and fight on foot. But it is not always as easy to determine the roles of those who are found riding or holding a horse with a round shield either held or slung behind their backs. A few of these are found in the third quarter of the century besides those panoplied horsemen with mounted squires who were noted as being almost certainly mounted hoplites; and more are found in the last quarter when squired mounted hoplites have virtually disappeared, and when they are greatly outnumbered by the shieldless armoured cavalrymen who appear so commonly both on and off the battlefield. Now although the absence of a shield is a good guide to a cavalryman, its presence is not of course an absolute criterion of a mounted hoplite; but two points can be restated: (i) that it would be impossible to fight from horseback with a large shield of the usual hoplite type hanging on the back, although of course it cannot be assumed that a warrior thus equipped when leading his horse or riding slowly would not hold it in battle;[25] (ii) that while it is not impossible to fight from horseback while holding a hoplite shield on the left arm, the extreme

MOUNTED WARRIORS IN THE 6TH CENTURY

rarity of examples is in sharp contrast to the large number of shieldless cavalrymen shown in action (both armoured and unarmoured). Besides the helmeted spearman of A52 (*fig. 64*) who rode into the attack holding a fairly small but apparently hoplite shield, two cavalrymen of the last quarter of the century are shown fighting with hoplite shields on A94 and A95. On A94, a hoplite on foot is caught between Scythian horsemen who are about to hurl their lances down at him. Both riders are unarmoured, wearing only chitons, peaked headdresses, and swords or daggers at the waist; and the cavalryman riding from the left is unmistakably carrying a large, convex, emblazoned hoplite shield on his left arm: the realistic position of the shield, which completely hides the arm, clearly indicates that the artist envisaged the double grip. It does seem odd that if an artist had seen hoplite shields used by riders, he was able to portray the bridle passing impossibly over the face of the shield before disappearing behind the Scythian's right thigh. But perhaps this one carelessness should not be allowed to detract from the realism of the rest, and there is no reason to doubt that even so large a hoplite shield was occasionally used from horseback, as for example by one of the mounted barbarians of A96 (probably Thracians): one has the Thracian pelta, but the other has a convex, round shield hanging on his back, and since both are unarmoured they are unlikely to dismount to fight. The cavalryman shown in action with a hoplite shield on A95 however is definitely Greek, although he is clashing with a mounted Amazon over a fallen Amazonian hoplite (*fig. 71*). And he is fully panoplied. Wearing helmet, greaves, and a bell-corslet over his chiton, he carries a large, round shield on his left arm, and although his body obscures the centre of the shield, the position of his elbow indicates that his arm passes through a *porpax*, and he manages both the bridle and a spare lance in his left hand (as we should expect the Scythian of A94 to have done). But if the realism of this portrayal indicates that the artist had seen contemporary cavalrymen fighting thus equipped, it also helps to explain why the vast majority preferred to fight without such a shield. Its circular shape, large size, and no doubt considerable weight made it a clumsy and unwieldy shield for the rider, and it is not surprising that the evidence of the vase-paintings reveals that it was generally considered more trouble than it was worth (even by other-

FIG. 71
A Greek rider, unusually shown in action with a hoplite shield, clashes with a mounted Amazon on an Attic Bf amphora of the late sixth century (A95)

wise unprotected riders) for the limited protection which it gave, which was clearly only to the left side. Cavalry who do have shields tend to have the crescent-shaped pelta, as do the armoured riders of A97 who are charging two hoplites, or the Amazon rider of A98. But although this shield is not uncommonly carried by barbarians (both mounted and on foot), it is as yet rarely used by Greeks. (Perhaps the strange cavalrymen of A97 are Greek, possibly Northern Greek, but they could very well be Orientals.) Occasionally perhaps a small round shield was used. The cavalryman's shield on A52 (if it is genuine) is fairly small; and a very small shield is carried along with a lunate pelta by a rider who appears on one side of a sixth-century Attic gravestone, and who may be the squire of the aristocratic youth who appears on the other.[26] Fairly small shields are also held by the youthful javelineers who gallop along the famous terracotta revetment in Thasos of the same period: they are certainly not hoplite shields since they are held at arm's length, and Richter suggested that they were the crescent-shaped pelta, but they are perhaps more likely to be convex shields of round or oval shape shown in profile.[27] At any rate, the use of any round shield from horseback finds but few examples, and an attempt to estimate how Greek horsemen of the later Attic vase-paintings were likely to fight with their shields, whether as cavalry or on foot, must begin with a marked prejudice against the former possibility, although of the shield may be a relevant factor to take into account al the rest of their equipment.

To begin with the middle of the century, A99 depicts three riders galloping to the left one after another, and since they are equipped exactly like the hoplites running on foot on the other side, complete with the vast round shield, helmet, single lance and greaves, they are most probably mounted hoplites. And they look as though they could be taking part in a race for mounted hoplites in the same way that the other scene appears to be the hoplitodrome. 'Acamas' and 'Demophon', the two panoplied warriors leading their horses and carrying convex, round shields on their backs on A100, a vase of the 540s, may also be hoplites since they are fully equipped to fight in the phalanx. But the youth who stands on the far side of his horse on A101 (and has a largely obliterated counterpart on the other side of the vase) is more likely to have been a cavalryman. He carries a convex, apparently round shield on his back, which may well be fairly small and easily manageable (although only the top part is visible above the horse's back). He is bare-legged, wears only helmet and chlamys, and over his shoulder he carries two long and very thin lances from which little pennants are fluttering. The motif of a warrior standing on the far side of his horse and with a shield slung on his back is also found in the last quarter of the century, as on A102 and A103 for example. The former is a fanciful work and hard to make out, but it is possible to discern a helmet, chlamys, two spears and a shield either badly drawn or of strange shape, and the subject may perhaps be an Amazon. The other (A103) is a careful work. The shield on the warrior's back is convex and of Boeotian shape, and clearly fastened by straps which emerge horizontally from the scallops to join other straps which pass tightly round each shoulder, but he is otherwise unarmoured except for his helmet and appears to have no weapons. Now the shield is at least of a suitably small size to wear on the back while riding, and perhaps the artist had seen shields of that size fastened in the way he so carefully depicted. But if so, they were surely round or oval (since the little scallops of this shield can have served no useful purpose); and a shield so fastened at the beginning of a battle would have to stay on the back, since it could not be swung round or readily detached for manipulation.

Armoured horsemen holding round shields occur on A104, A105 and A106, of which the warriors of A104 ride like those of A99, while the others lead their horses. A104 shows two panoplied horsemen riding side by side, and since they are accoutred in every detail like the panoplied hoplite who walks behind them on foot in company with a Scythian archer, they may well have been mounted hoplites. A105 is a departure scene on which a woman is bidding farewell to a panoplied hoplite on foot, while a youth carrying two spears and leading a horse is walking towards an armoured warrior on the right who, unlike the other, has no greaves or weapons but only the helmet, round shield and chlamys. And if the youth is bringing the horse and spears to him, and if he is fully dressed, he may well have been a cavalryman since his bare legs and twin spears will contrast with the greaves and single lance of the hoplite. The panoplied warrior complete with round blazoned shield and greaves who stands with his horse on A106 also has two spears in contrast to the single lances of two other panoplied warriors, who have Boeotian shields and are without horses; but in this case his complete panoply tips the balance in favour of the mounted hoplite, and the second lance could well be the spare which we have so often observed being carried by a mounted squire on earlier vases. Another panoplied warrior standing with his horse appears on A107. He has a stilt-crested helmet, greaves and corslet, a sword slung at his side, and on his back a large, round, convex shield with a tripod blazon. He holds twin lances, and stands facing his horse's head as though preparing to mount. Finally, and unusually for this period, a mounted squire may be shown on A108. To the left a hoplite is marching away glancing back over his shoulder, while in the centre a mounted youth, wearing a Thracian cloak and carrying two spears, leads a second horse to the right towards an exactly similar hoplite, behind whom stands a Scythian archer. Now this brief analysis of armoured horsemen with shields, while necessary to complete a representative survey of the ceramic evidence for how the richer landed gentry of sixth-century Athens used their horses in war, is necessarily unsatisfactory and sometimes inconclusive. What is clear however is that while there probably were cavalrymen who used the hoplite shield from horseback, the vast majority did without shields altogether, and no doubt did better without them.

MOUNTED WARRIORS IN THE 6TH CENTURY

To return very briefly to Helbig and Alföldi, the evidence of the vase-paintings reveals how wrong they both were, the former in maintaining that there was no true cavalry in sixth-century Athens, the latter in insisting that there were no horsemen who were not true cavalry. They had made the common mistake of treating true cavalry and mounted hoplites as mutually exclusive. But two points from their arguments remain to be briefly mentioned, if only for the sake of completeness. When Helbig found representations of light horsemen actually fighting, he maintained that they were the squires of mounted hoplites. Now the much greater volume of evidence available to-day allows us to dismiss this explanation out of hand, but even his own evidence provided cases which his thesis could not explain. It was because he realized that the detachment of cavalry shown charging a hoplite force on A53 (*fig. 65*) could not be hoplites' mounted squires that he had to make them Thessalians, although they are dressed only in the usual chiton of his typical Athenian squire and have not the slightest Thessalian identification.[28] And there is a more fundamental objection, that a squire whose task it was to control two horses and keep them at hand was not likely to be able to engage in the battle himself, unless perhaps in the emergency of a rout, or perhaps in a pursuit in which his master had remounted; but I know of no painting which illustrates a joint pursuit by mounted hoplites and squires, and if it might be argued that the exhausted hoplite would stay behind and leave pursuit to his squire, there remain many examples of light cavalry operating while the hoplites are still engaged. This brings us to Alföldi's point, which concerns hoplites shown on foot with unarmoured riders who have either one or two horses. He maintained that the hoplites were ἄμιπποι, whose task was to protect and support the rider at close quarters against other hoplites.[29] Now in the case of those riders with two horses, little needs to be said except that only the blindest determination to refute Helbig's thesis at every point could have led him to cite the squired hoplites of A7 (*fig. 56*) as 'perfect Attic evidence'. Even if the youth could have managed two horses and fought at the same time, his lack of weapons could only make his contribution to the victory a singularly negative one. And in any case it is incredible that a panoplied hoplite could ever have been the ἄμιππος of a light horseman, even where the latter was armed and without a second horse. The hoplite's strength was with other hoplites in the phalanx, and he would have been both wastefully and ineffectively employed in trying to protect a horseman with whom he could never have kept up. A hoplite could not run for long under the weight of his armour, and when real ἄμιπποι are mentioned for the first time in Thucydides' description of the Boeotian army in 418 B.C., they are of course light-armed, as indeed were the ψιλοί who are described as combining with cavalry (though not actually called ἄμιπποι) in his account of Spartolus in 429 B.C.[30]

'Chalcidian'

The home of 'Chalcidian' pottery is uncertain. The alphabet and dialect of its painted inscriptions effectively limit the possibilities to Chalcis in Euboea, to some Chalcidian colony in the West, or to a colonial workshop in Etruria. The high quality of the work makes it hard to believe that the potters and painters were trained outside mainland Greece. And Chalcis itself has been explored only casually. But the distribution of the pottery, of which most has been found in Etruria and Southern Italy and none East of the Adriatic, combines with the absence of influence on the receptive schools of Eretria and Boeotia to favour the possibility that it was produced in the West by emigrant Greek artists.[31] At any rate, wherever its home, it was probably an area which was more suited to the rearing and use of horses than either Attica or Corinthia, and the pottery certainly bears witness to the use of the horse in war. If it was Chalcis in Euboea, the city was one in which Aristotle observed a connexion between early aristocratic constitutions and the martial supremacy of aristocratic knights;[32] and the Chalcidian aristocracy called themselves the *Hippobotae*, who were still in possession of their lands and perhaps also of the government in the last decade of the sixth century.[33] If it was a Chalcidian colony in the West, the warfare of the metropolis had most probably been transferred from that city along with its political institutions.[34] And if the 'Chalcidian' artists were working in Etruria, they were Greeks themselves, the warfare which they depicted looks Greek, and even if it was local, it was largely Greek at second hand since Etruria imported both hoplite equipment and tactics (along with pottery) from the Greek colonists.[35] The date of 'Chalcidian' at least is reasonably certain, and whatever contempor-

MOUNTED WARRIORS IN THE 6TH CENTURY

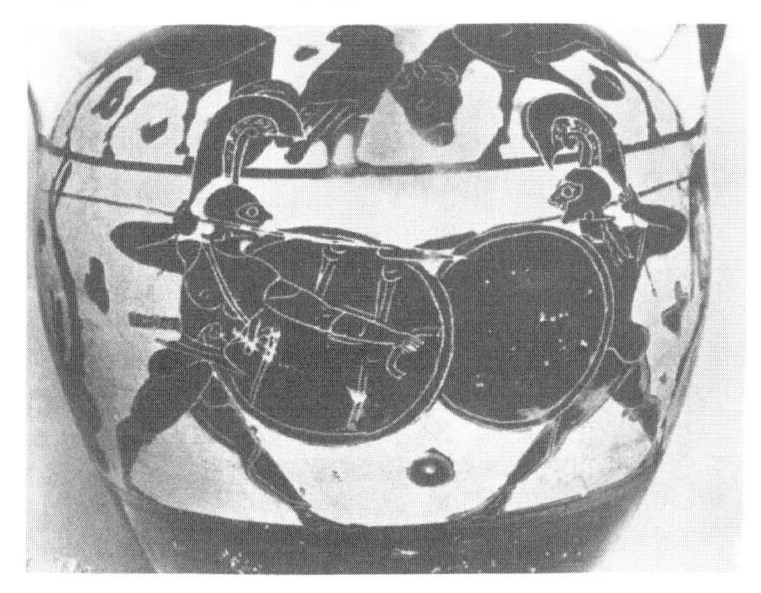

FIG. 72
Hoplite duel on a 'Chalcidian' vase of the second half of the sixth century (X7)

ary military evidence it provides will belong to the second half of the sixth century.

Armed horsemen both armoured and unarmoured appear frequently on the vases, but with the exception of an armoured mounted archer on X1, who looks contemporary (*fig. 76*), and an unarmoured Bellerophon who rides to attack the Chimaera with a lance as on X2, there are no scenes of fighting from horseback. There are however very many battles on foot between hoplites, often inscribed with heroic names (X3, X4, X5, X6), sometimes not (X7, X8, X9), and all equipped in the full panoply of Corinthian helmet, hoplite shield, bell-corslet and greaves, sometimes with a sheathed sword hanging at their side, and invariably using the single thrusting-spear (*fig. 72*). Their equipment and its method of use seldom give any indication of archaizing or heroizing, which seems to be confined to inscriptions, or to the presence of a goddess (X3, X4, X5), or very exceptionally there is a 'Boeotian' shield (X10). The majority of the warriors have the large, round, hoplite shield, accurately portrayed either from inside or out or in profile. Some however have a large oval shield, held vertically with the arm outstretched through the *porpax* and with the left hand clasping an *antilabe* at the lower edge

FIG. 73 'Chalcidian' mounted hoplites accompanied by their squires on vase X16

(X11, X12, X13, X14); and it is true that this type, unlike the round shield, could afford effective protection in battle only if held with the arm stiffened. But this is no adequate reason to reject it as heroic property: it is always shown so held, and indeed several warriors with vast round shields hold them with arm outstretched in the same way, which does not look unrealistic on X13 or X7 (*fig. 72*).[36]

With the exception of the mounted archer of X1 (*fig. 76*), the armoured horsemen are invariably complete with all the items of the hoplite panoply, and are attended by mounted, unarmed squires (*figs. 73, 74, 75*). Often the knight and his squire are shown riding side by side (X15, X16, X17, *figs. 73, 74*), but on X18 the knight ('Hector') is on foot taking leave of his wife ('Andromache') while his mounted squire ('Cebriones') holds his horse ready for him (*fig. 75*); and on X19 the knight is mounted and holding a second horse while the squire approaches saluting him. Some scenes are marked as heroic by inscriptions (X15, X18), while others have no heroic identification (X16, X17, X19). Most of the knights have round shields (X15, X16, X18, X19), usually blazoned, occasionally with a heavily bossed rim (X16, *fig. 73*). A few have the oval type (X17, *fig. 74*). And all carry two stout lances, except 'Hector' of X18, who

MOUNTED WARRIORS IN THE 6TH CENTURY

is still saying farewell and presumably has not yet taken his spears (*fig. 75*). Now the two lances would be more necessary to a cavalryman than to a hoplite, but one could easily be a spare for the squire to hold during battle. And the absence of any examples of fighting from horseback, coupled with the large number of battles on foot between hoplites identically equipped and the invariable presence of a mounted squire who could hold his master's horse and keep it at hand for him, suggests that these knights dismounted to fight. And if so, there is no reason to doubt that the vase-painters were reflecting an important aspect of contemporary warfare. However useful true cavalry might be, the hoplite phalanx was the backbone of the Greek army, whatever the terrain. And if a state had wide territories and broad plains, and if it had a rich, landed class of sufficient size to provide it, there would be great military advantage in a fully mounted hoplite force which was able to travel fast and arrive fresh to give battle wherever necessary. Of course these knights may also have fought as true cavalry on occasions, perhaps leaving their shields with their squires, but if so there is no ceramic evidence for it.

The mounted archer of X1 (*fig. 76*) is an interesting figure. He is

EARLY GREEK WARFARE

FIG. 74
A 'Chalcidian' departure scene showing a mounted hoplite with an oval shield (X17)

FIG. 75
'Hector', equipped as a hoplite, bids farewell to 'Andromache' while his mounted squire waits with the horses on 'Chalcidian' vase X18

being pursued by a hoplite on foot (wearing helmet, greaves, chiton and sword, and carrying a large, round shield), and as he gallops away he turns and aims a Parthian shot at his pursuer. Over a tunic with a flared skirt he wears a hoplite's bell-corslet, and he has two

140

MOUNTED WARRIORS IN THE 6TH CENTURY

FIG. 76
An armoured mounted archer aims a Parthian shot at a pursuing hoplite on 'Chalcidian' Vase X1

other pieces of the hoplite panoply in the form of greaves and a high-crested helmet. And slung at his left side on a shoulder strap is a large quiver. The ensemble is certainly unusual, but there is nothing impractical about it. On the contrary, it looks carefully contrived to give a cavalryman the most complete protection consistent with mobility. The position of the reins round the waist (leaving both hands free) adds to the realism of the portrayal, and it seems very probable that the artist was painting what he knew. Whether or not any Greek state either in Euboea or the West ever had such a force of armoured mounted archers must remain an open question, but if he was real, he could perhaps have been Etruscan, or a member of a Greek cavalry force which had borrowed the techniques of mounted archery from the Etruscans or their neighbours: a contemporary Etruscan Black Figure 'Pontic' vase gives evidence of mounted archers, and although they wear high-pointed caps and are unarmoured, their tactics and the way they manage the bridle are the same, as is the skirted tunic (which is also worn by the helmeted, mounted javelineers who pursue them).[37] Other mounted archers, this time unarmoured, occur along with squired mounted hoplites on X15, a vase liberally inscribed with heroic names but showing no sign of heroized or archaized equipment. A hoplite on foot, 'Demo-

141

docus', is greaving, while 'Hippolyte' holds his spear and his round shield, and his helmet stands on the ground beside him. To the left, a mounted hoplite rides side by side with his bearded squire. To the right, another panoplied hoplite is putting on his helmet. And further to the right a mounted archer, wearing only the chiton and with his bow and quiver slung on his back, sits holding a second horse while a similar archer on foot takes his leave. Besides chiton, bow and quiver the latter has ankle-boots with forward-curving tongues. Again, the realism of the scene suggests acquaintance with such warriors. Perhaps these too may be Etruscan, although if a Greek state formed a corps of mounted archers in an area in which they were common, they might well have taken advantage of items of native equipment just as the Etruscans borrowed hoplite armour and tactics.

Like Corinthian pottery of the first half of the century, the 'Chalcidian' of the second also favours the motif of chiton-clad youths riding either singly or in files, and carrying a long, single lance. And also like Corinthian, it fails to show them fighting from horseback (except for Bellerophon). The single rider of X20, or the riders galloping all round X21, X22, X23, X24 and X25, or the two galloping towards each other on X26, need not have any military significance at all, and even these last do not appear to be riding to attack each other since their lances are not poised for action. It is just possible however that they are light cavalrymen, and there may be some significance in the coincidence that the squires who accompany the panoplied knights are never armed whereas these riders, who have lances, are never shown leading a second horse. A military role may just possibly be suggested for the single rider of X20 by the hoplite battle raging on the other side. And X10 actually shows hoplites and two of these riders in the same scene. Two hoplites are fighting furiously in the centre, and from either side a tunic-clad rider (bearded this time) gallops up carrying a lance; and both are pulling up their horses with a jerk. Even here however there is no evidence of hostile intent, and the spear remains at the port (although it may be that the riders have only just seen each other, and are pausing to prepare for action). In conclusion, while light cavalry remain a probability, 'Chalcidian' vases clearly attest the use of the horse by only three types of warrior: much the commonest is the

MOUNTED WARRIORS IN THE 6TH CENTURY

panoplied knight who is accompanied by a mounted squire and almost certainly dismounts to fight as a hoplite in the phalanx; and there are the two types of mounted archer, the one heavily armoured, the other unarmoured. Bronze however may provide an armoured cavalryman like those of Corinthian vases C13 and C14 (*figs. 52, 53*). G. von Lücken and E. Langlotz have associated the mid-sixth century bronze rider from Grumentum with 'Chalcidian' artistry.[38] He wears only helmet and tunic, and his hands are pierced for reins, or perhaps he held a lance in his right hand and the bridle in his left.

East Greece

The local painters give scant evidence for contemporary East Greek warriors other than hoplites.[39] The vases depict riders, but except for Bellerophon they tend to be unarmed and are never shown in battle.[40] Contemporary warfare is better represented on the Clazomenian sarcophagi for the period *c.* 530 to *c.* 470 B.C., but again they attest only hoplite warfare in an area famous for its horses.

The head-piece of Borelli Painter no. 7, a sarcophagus from Clazomenae painted early in the last quarter of the sixth century, depicts a typical hoplite battle.[41] Fighting two against two they wear greaves, skirted tunics, and huge helmets with the characteristic sickle-shaped crest. They carry emblazoned hoplite shields equipped with aprons, and they are thrusting overarm with single lances. To left and right the battle-scene is flanked by a rider, apparently unarmed, who may perhaps represent mounted squires. Similar hoplite battles occur on the British Museum's famous sarcophagus of the first quarter of the fifth century.[42] The lowest of the three friezes on the left side of the lid is devoted to a full-scale battle between large numbers of hoplites, and it has no heroic indications, and no horses or chariots or squires.[43] On the top frieze a hoplite stands with a horse, but the rest of this heroized scene is devoted to the mounting of chariots by numerous hoplites, one of whom is dragging a woman into his chariot after him. On the right side of the lid the lower frieze is again a contemporary-looking battle, this time a cavalry charge against a hoplite force (*fig. 77*). Now the identity of the riders is uncertain, but they are clearly Asiatic barbarians, and most probably Persians. Their bows and quivers are clearly visible fastened at their sides and projecting backwards over their horses' rumps, and they

FIG. 77
Panel of a Clazomenian sarcophagus of the early fifth century showing East Greek hoplites being attacked with cutlasses by Persian cavalry who have bows and quivers strapped at their sides

wear some kind of soft headdress. Both these features are of course common to Scythians and Persians (although Scythians more often had pointed caps), but the distinctive Persian feature is the long cutlass with which five of the six cavalrymen are preparing to slash at the hoplites. This weapon never occurs in the hands of a Scythian to the best of my knowledge, whereas it is used by the Persians of several Attic vases of the earlier fifth century (after *c*. 490 B.C.).[44] The mounted Persian of an Attic Red Figure cup in Orvieto for example, with his characteristic headdress and his bow strapped to a large quiver fastened to a belt round his waist, would suit in every detail the silhouettes of the contemporary sarcophagus.[45] And the date certainly suits Persians rather than the once universally accepted Cimmerians, whose great invasion had ended about a century and a half earlier. A similar archer, this time unhorsed and being dispatched by two hoplites, provides the central motif of the top frieze of this panel, while three racing-bigae driven by single charioteers fill the greater part of the frieze on either side. But there is no evidence of Greek cavalry. The interior end-panels of the sarcophagus itself depict a panoplied hoplite on foot between two other hoplites, who are each holding a horse and are identically accoutred except that they have no shield or lance.[46] But it would be unwarranted to suggest that these are heavy cavalry. They are unarmed, and their purpose is clearly no more than to support the central motif in a purely decorative arrangement. If perhaps in doing so they signify the use of horses in war, they are more likely to have derived from mounted hoplites, and so too is the hoplite who stands with a horse among all the heroic war-chariots of the lid.

If it seems odd to find no representation of Greek cavalry, that deficiency may have been supplied by the head-piece of Borelli no. 8, an earlier sarcophagus than the last and painted perhaps between *c*. 525 and 510 B.C.[47] The subject is clearly an attack by two cavalry-

144

men on two hoplites, but the fragments show only the legs and rump of the horses and no trace of the riders is preserved. They could equally well have been barbarians like the cavalrymen attacking hoplites on Albertinum Group no. 19, which preserves the body of one rider and the legs of another.[48] It is not clear what weapons they are using, but their colourful costume with its elaborately embroidered trousers and upper garments identifies them generally as Asiatics, and probably as Persians. Finally there is an epigram concerning Magnesia in the Palatine Anthology which records the death in battle of a warrior called Hippaemon, who was buried with his horse Podargos, his dog Lethargos, and his squire Babes.[49] There is no reason to doubt that it is a genuine epitaph of the late Archaic period, and R. M. Cook has pointed out that it could well have belonged to an Archaic grave stele found at Dorylaeum, which gives an admirable illustration of the characters in the poem.[50] Hippaemon is shown riding his horse and looking back over his shoulder. Behind him is the outline of his squire, and under the horse there are traces of a dog. But unfortunately the stele is too worn to reveal any of Hippaemon's equipment besides the helmet discerned by Schede, and we cannot tell if he was likely to be a cavalryman or a mounted hoplite. The only certain conclusion that we can draw from the sadly inadequate evidence for East Greece is that the strength of armies was the strength of hoplites, and that the wealthy gentlemen who occupied the sarcophagi fought as hoplites and not as cavalrymen. If the reputation of East Greece combines with Borelli no. 7 and with the warriors holding horses on the British Museum's complete sarcophagus to suggest that they used horses in war, they were mounted hoplites. And if so, the value of a force of mounted hoplites, both strategically and personally, would have been as great on the broad plains of Asia Minor as in Euboea or the West.

VII
CONCLUSIONS

The reader will soon have realized that the full title of this book cannot be taken at face value any more than much of the poetic and artistic evidence which it studies, and the following remarks will be about the horsemen in early Greek warfare, not the chariots. Resubstituting the mounted horse for the heroic war-chariot of the Homeric poems revealed its role in the warfare of the Geometric Age communities in which Aristotle spoke of the military and political dominance of aristocratic horsemen. They were not cavalrymen, but heavy-armed footsoldiers who used their horses for transport, and they were accompanied by mounted squires who kept their horses and spare javelins for them while they fought, and were no doubt responsible for looking after armour and other spoils won during the battle. Before the hoplite reform revolutionized warfare in the seventh century, battles were the less organized affairs depicted in Homer and on the Late Geometric vase-paintings. Keeping the army together in unbroken lines was not fundamental to this earlier style of fighting, in which success depended far more on individual skill in arms, and warriors carried shields which protected their backs. After an initial charge the loosely ordered lines broke up into a number of smaller clashes, and these fluid engagements permitted the movement of mounted warriors and their squires through the battle. For mounted hoplites this was no longer possible. A hoplite could ride to battle but he could not use his horse to move about during the engagement between the phalanxes. Because the success of a phalanx depended on its cohesion, and victory went to the side which broke the ranks of the other while keeping its own intact, once a hoplite had taken his place in the line he had to keep it until one side was routed. But if horse-owning hoplites could not use their horses

CONCLUSIONS

during the main engagement, they still rode to war accompanied by their mounted squires.

Corinthian and Attic vases depict mounted hoplites throughout the seventh and sixth centuries (or at least until the middle of the sixth century in the case of Corinth, whose ceramic evidence then disappears). The evidence for the warfare of other states is much poorer, but what there is attests mounted hoplites elsewhere both in Old Greece and in the colonies of the East and West. For Sparta there is at least one representation which suggests that the name of the royal bodyguard of classical times derived from *Hippeis* who were mounted hoplites in the seventh century. In seventh-century Euboea, our reconstruction of the warfare of the Eretrian *Hippeis* and the Chalcidian *Hippobotae* indicates that they rode to battle and fought on foot, probably in hoplite panoply and close formation but relying on the sword rather than the thrusting-spear at close quarters. For a state which was most probably a Greek colony in the West, the 'Chalcidian' pottery attests mounted hoplites in the second half of the sixth century, and it may also reflect a style of warfare which colonists had taken to the West from Euboea. For East Greece the evidence is not so explicit, but it is clear that the wealthy occupants of the painted sarcophagi fought as hoplites, and there are indications that they rode to war. The personal advantages of riding to war accompanied by a mounted squire are not limited to those who intend to fight from horseback. And there are obvious strategical advantages for states with a class of horse-owning gentry sufficiently large to mount a whole phalanx.

For reasons inherent in the nature of hoplite equipment I suggested that the same military innovation which restricted the traditional role of the war-horse on the battlefield might also have encouraged the development of true cavalry. Although a cavalry charge could rarely hope for success in a head-on clash with an ordered phalanx of hoplites, the phalanx was vulnerable in the rear and on the flanks, and Thucydides' narrative of the Athenian expedition to Sicily in the later fifth century revealed how troublesome a cavalry force could be to a hoplite army without its own cavalry support in open country. But if it is *a priori* not unlikely that the cavalrymen who appear on sixth-century Attic and Corinthian vase-paintings had precursors in the seventh, there are no certain representations of them, and all battles are fought on foot. Helmeted spearmen are shown riding into battle on Corinthian vases of the first half of the sixth century, and Corinth probably had unarmoured cavalry too, although the representations are not so decisive. On Attic vases cavalry appears both armoured and unarmoured from the early sixth century, though armoured cavalrymen become common only in the last quarter. With the exception of the rare archer, they all fight with spears, which are used both as javelins and lances. Occasionally a squadron of cavalrymen is shown making a frontal attack on a phalanx, but generally they are stationed on the wings, engaging other cavalry, or helping in the rout of a broken phalanx. Our only other certain illustrations of Greek cavalry were provided by the 'Chalcidian' vases of the second half of the sixth century. The majority of their military horsemen are mounted hoplites accompanied by squires, but there are mounted youths with spears who could have been light cavalry, and there were certainly mounted archers. Now the bow was an uncommon cavalry weapon in Greek armies, and I suggested that the mounted warrior of *fig. 76*, equipped with the helmet, corslet and greaves of the hoplite panoply but using a bow, may reflect the borrowing of the techniques of mounted archery from the natives who inhabited the region of a Western Greek colony. When Greeks tried to settle or make war in a country dominated by cavalry, it is likely that they soon learned to support their phalanxes with cavalry squadrons of their own (and for this reason it seems hard to believe that Greek armies in Asia Minor were unsupported by cavalry in the seventh and sixth centuries despite the lack of evidence). The Attic vase of the second quarter of the sixth century which shows Greek mounted javelineers charging a force of barbarian horse-archers may illustrate how Athenians adapted to warfare in the Hellespontine regions in which they were beginning to take a close interest. And it is possible that experience gained in foreign adventures contributed to the development of Athenian cavalry reflected on the sixth-century vases, and to the discomfiture of the hoplite forces of neighbours nearer home. Another contributory factor may have been the influence of Thessaly. Successful intervention by Thessalian horsemen on the side of Chalcis in the Euboean war of which we hear in the seventh century, and their subsequent activities in the so-called First Sacred War, may well have

CONCLUSIONS

FIG. 78 Thessalian (right) and Scythian cavalrymen administering the *coup de grâce* to a fallen hoplite on an Attic Bf vase of the late sixth century

opened the eyes of states with hoplite armies to the value of a cavalry force even on less perfect terrain than the broad plains of the Peneus.[1] And it is interesting to find both Thessalian cavalrymen and mounted Scythian spearmen on Attic vase-paintings of the later sixth century, the former as allies of the Pisistratids, the latter probably as mercenaries like the many Scythian foot-archers.[2]

The mention of Thessaly introduces the one region of Greece where we can be certain there was Greek cavalry throughout the Archaic period. We can be equally certain that there were no mounted hoplites, because Thessaly never seems to have had much in the way of effective infantry, and we hear of no hoplites at all. When Thessalian horsemen appear on Attic vases of the last quarter of the sixth century, they were probably a familiar sight in Attica as a result of their alliance with the Pisistratids whom they helped against the successive Spartan invasions under Anchimolius and Cleomenes, though less effectively the second time than the first.[3] In contrast to many Athenian cavalrymen of the time who wore armour, the Thessalians appear to have fought without it. Their standard dress was the tunic, the characteristic broad-brimmed hat, and sometimes

149

a short riding-cape; and in battle they had a sword slung at their side, and fought with a pair of long, heavy lances (*fig. 78*).[4] Thessaly was a conservative land, and there is little reason to suppose that her horsemen had changed much through the seventh and sixth centuries. Militarily and constitutionally as well as geographically she remained apart from the world of the Greek city-states and the mainstream of their development in the Archaic period. Her three thousand square miles of alluvial plains enclosed by mountains were loosely governed by feuding aristocratic families who held large estates worked by serfs, and it is revealing of their scale of life to hear of a single nobleman, Meno of Pharsalus, who in 477 B.C. took twelve talents of silver and a private army of two or three hundred cavalry raised from his own serfs to reinforce the Athenians against Eion.[5] On their own terrain the Thessalian cavalry were formidable opponents, and in 455 B.C. Athenian troops got a foretaste of the difficulties they were to experience in Sicily when the expedition to restore Orestes failed to make any headway in open country against the Thessalian mounted defence.[6] But it is also true that Thessaly lacked effective infantry, and without it her attempts at southward expansion in the Archaic period were unlikely to succeed against major hoplite resistance even if her aristocratic families had been able to maintain their unity for long enough to establish an empire.

To return finally to Aristotle's theory that the hoplite reform was connected with the trend to more democratic constitutions because it removed military supremacy from the horse-owning aristocracy,[7] it is certainly true that the sociology of its armed forces can affect a state's constitution. When in the fifth century the Athenian hoplite force in its turn took second place in military importance to the city's fleet, it was the importance of the fleet which maintained the universal thetic suffrage and doomed from the outset the oligarchic plans to restrict the franchise in the later phase of the Peloponnesian War. But how much and how quickly did the hoplite reform change the sociology of warfare in the seventh century, and in what circumstances is it likely to have produced political consequences? Snodgrass has pointed out that hoplite warfare was adopted in Etruria apparently without producing the far-reaching social and political consequences which have so often been claimed for it in Greece.[8] The Etruscans combined hoplite tactics with an aristocratic system of

CONCLUSIONS

nobles and clients. And it was after the Roman adoption of hoplite warfare that the Fabii went to war as a *gens* with their clients against the Veientes at Cremera in 477 B.C.[9] Clearly then there is no fundamental reason why hoplite phalanxes could not have been organized on gentilitial lines in early Greece, and very probably the civil wars in which Alcaeus and his aristocratic friends fought at Mytilene in the late seventh and early sixth centuries provide an example.[10] Now it is true that the greater numbers required by phalanx warfare and the smaller degree of skill and training meant that the military class often needed to be socially less exclusive than before. But there are two points which need to be stressed. In the first place the hoplite panoply remained expensive. Very occasionally the state may have equipped its hoplite force, as may have been the case at Sparta.[11] Sometimes perhaps nobles may have armed their retainers, and an extreme example is provided by Meno of Thessaly and his private army of mounted serfs. But generally the traditional Greek conception of οἱ ὅπλα παρεχόμενοι underlies the sociology of hoplite armies, and the cost of procuring the equipment will have restricted the extension of the warrior class to the well-to-do farmers and lesser gentry. The second point is that the hoplite class was not a separate socio-economic entity between the aristocracy and the peasantry who were too poor to equip themselves. The aristocrats themselves fought as hoplites. If they used horses in war, some fought as cavalry, especially the younger men. Many more however were hoplites who rode to war accompanied by mounted squires. Some great horse-rearing states probably had a large enough class of horse-owners to furnish a fully mobilized hoplite force, but in most cities mounted hoplites were only a proportion of the army; and on Attic vase-paintings for example, those who were rich enough to afford the luxury of a war-horse are shown dismounting to join the phalanx with the less wealthy hoplites who had marched to battle (see above, p. 112, *fig.* 56). Now it is true that the independence of the Geometric Age warrior was replaced by the interdependence of the members of the phalanx, and the possible cohesive effects of hoplite warfare, psychological, social and even political, are not to be discounted. But if early hoplite warfare was organized on gentilitial lines, the example of Etruria requires us to ask how the non-aristocratic hoplites were likely to have become a self-conscious political force, and a sufficiently revolutionary one to have contributed, as is commonly maintained, to the rise of tyranny.

That hoplite warfare had been so organized is difficult to doubt. In Attica for example, the various regions were dominated by the local aristocratic families, the Alcmaeonidae, Pisistratidae and the rest,[12] and the co-operation of these families will have been as important to the maintenance of the Athenian army as to the maintenance of the Athenian republic. The regional influence and loyalty enjoyed as a hereditary benefit by the heads of these families were strong, and the incentive to break them down and to develop total devotion to the concept of the state was not so compelling in communities which did not have the Spartan hoplites' peculiar problem of holding in subjection a discontented (and largely nationalistic) servile population which vastly outnumbered them. Just as the Athenian republic required the continuing agreement of the great aristocrats to take turns in ruling and being ruled – or at least of a sufficiently powerful group to cow the others into submission – so too the Athenian army required them to agree to bring their clients, dependents and lesser neighbours to fight in unison under the polemarch and not against each other. And if Athenian politics were the perpetual grouping and regrouping of aristocratic houses to further their own influence and to secure for their own members the great offices of state, their local influence meant that forces were ready to challenge other groups in arms if political manoeuvring failed, or if a nobleman wished to assert the individual supremacy of his family against the aristocratic equalitarianism of the republic, or against exclusion from the politically privileged circle which in some states formally embraced only part of the nobility. To do so was of course to take a grave risk since the coalition of the prospective tyrant's opponents will usually have been more powerful than his own; and for this reason it was valuable to secure military reinforcements of mercenaries or of a powerful foreign ally, usually a marriage connexion and often a tyrant himself, who both provided an example and was keen to promote his own influence. So it was that in the later seventh century, at a time when the Alcmaeonids seem to have been monopolizing the Athenian government, Cylon tried to make himself master of Athens with the support of troops from his father-in-law, the tyrant Theagenes of Megara;[13] and in the sixth, when Pisistratus

CONCLUSIONS

finally succeeded where Cylon had failed, he was joined by a rich and ambitious Naxian aristocrat who brought money and troops, and he enjoyed the support of a thousand Argives thanks to a diplomatic marriage with the daughter of an Argive nobleman.[14] Elsewhere civil war was probably a completely internal affair, as it seems to have been in Mytilene, a city which produced a spate of tyrants in the later seventh century before Pittacus in the early sixth relinquished after ten years his popular autocracy, to which he may have given a degree of constitutional legality by formal election as single plenipotentiary magistrate.[15] Sometimes a civil war against stronger forces was avoided by a plan to assassinate entrenched political opponents, and this is what Aristodemus did in Cumae in the late sixth century,[16] and it was probably what Cypselus had done in mid-seventh century Corinth.[17] Occasionally too a tyrant gained power by the purely diplomatic means of playing off other aristocratic factions against each other, as Pisistratus did briefly at Athens.[18] But when the aristocratic groups mobilized their factions against each other, there is no reason to suppose that they fought differently from when they fought together as the army of the state, and that the battles in Alcaeus' Mytilene or the Pisistratid engagement at Pallene were not hoplite battles between rival *gentes* and their pyramids of supporters.

If non-aristocratic hoplites became unified into a self-conscious political force, the process will surely have required time and a loosening of the hereditary bonds of loyalty to local aristocratic houses. And this in turn is more likely to have followed the establishment of a tyranny than to have preceded it. It is of course dangerous to generalize about tyrants in the Archaic period, but there is little evidence to suggest that they came to power as the champions of unified hoplites. In the case of Pheidon of Argos in the early seventh century, if his military successes suggest that he may have organized the first Argive phalanxes, he is unlikely to have done so before he had converted his hereditary 'constitutional' monarchy into an autocracy.[19] There is a story that Cypselus in the middle of the century came to power through holding the office of polemarch, but it is incredible that the son of an outcast mother and a non-Bacchiad father could have held so important an office under a régime as exclusive as that of the Bacchiads, and in any case the account mentions no military functions attaching to the position.[20] And there was no general rush of hoplites to support Cylon's attempt to seize power at Athens about 630 B.C.[21] At the beginning of the sixth century Solon wrote of the dangers of a revolution and his fears that a prospective tyrant might mobilize the widespread discontent of the poor to his own advantage,[22] but it is far from certain that those farmers who were sufficiently well off to fight as hoplites were the sufferers from aristocratic oppression and debt-slavery. What he feared is more likely to have been a street-fighting revolution of debt-ridden peasants and *hektemoroi* with pitchforks and clubs. At any rate, when Pisistratus sought the tyranny it was simply a bodyguard of club-bearers that first installed him in power, and an aristocratic coalition the second time. If he had been the champion of a united hoplite class, it would hardly have been possible for Megacles and Lycurgus to expel him as easily as they did, and when he finally established himself he needed large foreign forces to supplement the local support which no doubt joined him when he landed in the vicinity of his ancestral estates on the Marathon–Brauron plain.[23] The crowds had shouted approval for Pittacus (much to Alcaeus' disgust) when he came to the top in the Mytilenaean power struggles at the beginning of the century,[24] but this cannot be taken to mean that he had been backed by the whole Mytilenaean hoplite army, and certainly he made no constitutional innovation to suggest the reward of a politically aggressive middle class for its support.[25] On the other hand, once a tyrant was in power, he may have helped towards the unity of a hoplite class. When he mustered the citizen army to fight for the state, they were commanded by a perpetual commander-in-chief, and he will often have sought to usurp the local patronage and loyalty formerly enjoyed by the nobles who had opposed him. And the extent to which he did this will have depended upon the duration of his tyranny, his popularity, and his relations with rest of the nobles (the numbers he won over and the numbers he killed and exiled). Perhaps also a tyrant may have created new hoplites by benefaction or compulsion. By a helpful economic policy Pisistratus and others probably increased the number of farmers able to equip themselves. And there may have been earlier tyrants who did what Dionysius of Syracuse was to do, and equipped armies from their own treasuries.[26] At any rate, when Archaic tyrannies were replaced

CONCLUSIONS

by republican government again, the constitutions seem generally, though not invariably, to have been less exclusive than what had gone before, or to have become so. And perhaps a larger and more unified hoplite class was partly responsible. But certain examples of hoplite franchises are few, and the problem of the many factors which combined to produce politically conscious lower classes demanding more or less democratic constitutions is not solved by a simple military equation.

Appendix
THE HISTORICAL BASIS OF THE HOMERIC BACKGROUND PICTURE

My thesis about the historical reality behind the Homeric picture of chariot-warfare maintained that the poems show no real conception of the Mycenaean world of their ostensible period, but present a disguised picture of conditions in the very different and much simpler communities of the Dark Ages which emerged after the Mycenaean collapse. If this is true of chariot-warfare, it should also be true of the other aspects of the Homeric background picture, and this appendix is designed to give a brief outline of the evidence. To begin with, a primary distinction can be drawn between the story-line itself and the background picture of society, institutions, material culture, and ideology. For example, the numerous genealogies can be dismissed as the annals of specific princely families, but we may keep their general significance, that pride of birth was important in the society, and that noble houses liked to claim divine descent. The specific decisions and actions of specific kings, nobles or commoners may be disregarded, but we may usefully study the way that decisions were taken and the structure of society, as being at least based on historical foundations. The countless individual battles can be discounted as historical battles, but generally they are relevant to the history of the art of war. Then once this primary distinction has been drawn, the background picture itself can be analyzed in connexion with archaeological and other literary evidence to determine the likely historical basis of its main aspects, and to explain its inherent inconsistencies. These inconsistencies and incongruities indicate how little the Homeric poets knew about the realities of life in Bronze Age Greece, and by considering them carefully it is possible to distinguish two sides in the Homeric picture: the one is a consistent, basic picture essentially belonging to the Dark Ages; and

APPENDIX

the other, which the Dark Age historian should discard, is its disguise. And the disguise has two aspects. First there are some Mycenaean Age survivals, mainly places and things, some of which may well have been transmitted to our Homeric epics in formulae derived from Mycenaean poetry. But for the most part the disguise takes the form of a deliberate archaizing and heroizing veneer, applied by the bards to bring their picture into line with what little was known or could be conjectured about the Mycenaean Age, and achieved by the suppression or simple alteration of some Dark Age features, the exaggeration of others, and a good deal of invention, which was sometimes purely imaginative and sometimes inspired by the few general facts known about the Mycenaean world. This veneer is thickly applied, but still sufficiently transparent for us to recognise it for what it is; and what lies beneath it is a consistent and historical Dark Age picture whose pivotal date is most probably the ninth century B.C.

The Homeric picture presents an amalgam of material culture spanning both the Bronze Age and the Dark Ages down into the eighth century at least, but the bulk of the picture belongs to neither of these extremes. From the earlier extreme there are Mycenaean survivals, both specific and general; but the former are few, and the latter both few and even greater sources of confusion and inconsistency. Of the specific survivals we may cite for example the descriptions of some arms and pieces of armour. The most notable of these is the famous boar's-tusk helmet, whose description is much the best account of any Mycenaean object in Homer.[1] But here it is important to qualify what is meant by survival, for although this account could be based on an earlier, traditional account, G. S. Kirk has rightly pointed out that it could equally well be based on the observation of an heirloom or antique which had survived into post-Mycenaean times. And the same qualification applies to Nestor's dove-cup, which was very probably of Mycenaean Age manufacture whatever its rather dubious relationship to the cup of Shaft Grave 4 at Mycenae.[2] Another Bronze Age relic is Ajax's 'tower-shield', convincingly identified with the Mycenaean–Minoan curved, rectangular body-shield current in the sixteenth century but unrepresented after the twelfth, and in this case it appears that we have a Mycenaean survival in the fuller sense.[3] D. L. Page has convincingly argued that the formula in which the tower-shield appears, always with Ajax's name, is a relic of Mycenaean poetry: Ajax appears on a Linear B tablet,[4] and the confusion about the Ajaxes in Homer indicates that the dual Αἴαντε (like the only other example in the epic, Μολίονε) is a very ancient term used to mean Ajax and his brother, but clearly misunderstood by the Homeric bard who intruded Ajax son of Oileus into incongruous situations in order to bring the conventional Αἴαντε into line with modern usage.[5] The body-shields of Hector and Periphetes may also be Mycenaean relics, since although their shape is not indicated (as it is in the case of Ajax's shield), their enormous size and the fact that Hector's shield is described as hanging by a telamon suggest the Mycenaean body-shield, either of the 'tower' or 'figure-of-eight' type, rather than a Geometric Age shield.[6] Page has argued that the epithets 'bronze-corsleted' (χαλκοχιτώνων) and 'well-greaved' (εὐκνήμιδες), Hector's 'bronze-helmeted' or 'glittering-helmeted' (χαλκοκορυστής, κορυθαίολος), or the epithet 'ashen-speared' (εὐμμελίης) are examples of inherited formulae of Mycenaean pedigree; and Kirk added the 'silver-studded sword' (φάσγανον ἀργυρόηλον), but also noted how very scarce these possible cases of identifiable poetical survival seem to be.[7] And in the case of an epithet like 'bronze-corsleted', it is important to remember that there are two possible origins besides poetical survival: with or without the aid of a few antiques (and it is hard to believe that none survived), the fact that Mycenaean warriors wore bronze corslets might have been remembered or even conjectured; and the eighth-century Argos corslet has made it even more uncertain that such things were unknown in the ninth century or even a bit earlier, at any rate in an age when, if a very rich nobleman possessed one, he would hardly have been allowed to waste it by taking it to the grave with him. Now the most important of the detailed Mycenaean survivals seem to be some elements of the political geography which appears in the Achaean Catalogue.[8] But even apart from the fact that the incompatibility of the Catalogue (especially its Boeotian emphasis) with the rest of the *Iliad* indicates that it developed separately and was added purely mechanically at a late stage in the composition of the whole, there are some more important reasons why we should not overrate the significance of the appearance of a number of names which fit Achaean sites that were apparently gone in post-

APPENDIX

Mycenaean times and were unknown to the Greeks of the historical period. In the first place, a collection including such place-names is hardly conclusive evidence for a historical coalition against Troy, or for any historical coalition at all. Moreover, as Kirk has stressed, the specific nature of the epithets of such place-names need not indicate direct experience of those places, because it would be unwise to underestimate the possible element of fiction and arbitrary invention.[9] And finally it is far from necessary even to agree with Kirk in restricting the memory of such places to a couple of generations after the Mycenaean collapse: he may be right that 'most children know something about their grandfathers, almost nothing about their great-grandfathers',[10] but it is also true that when a family has been uprooted and has migrated, the name of its original town is very likely to be handed down for a good many more generations than that. At any rate, if there are these and one or two other specific Mycenaean survivals,[11] either in the sense of memories of things and places which disappeared with the Mycenaean collapse (some perhaps preserving, in noun–epithet formulae, actual fragments of Mycenaean poetry, and even the names of historical Mycenaean Age kings), or in the sense of descriptions of Mycenaean objects which did survive as heirlooms or antiques, it becomes abundantly clear from the more general Mycenaean 'survivals' how very little was known about the Mycenaean world. By general survivals, I mean such features as the exclusiveness of bronze as the metal for arms and armour, and of the war-chariot as the warrior's means of locomotion. I have argued that these are Mycenaean survivals only in the sense that they reveal the knowledge of two simple facts about the Mycenaean world: that it was the Bronze Age, and that the war-chariot was a distinctive feature of its battles. In the detailed descriptions of fighting with spears and 'chariots' the language of contemporary experience reveals the essentially Geometric Age basis of the military picture beneath the simple, general archaizations. I shall now examine other aspects of the Homeric background picture, whose few Mycenaean survivals similarly fail to conceal how little knowledge survived the Mycenaean collapse to be incorporated in the epics.

To begin with the economy, the Homeric bards knew that Bronze Age kings were richer than those they knew in the Dark

Ages, but the size of Odysseus' household illustrates how far their heroic exaggerations fell short of the true scale of Mycenaean wealth. When Odysseus is given fifty women slaves, he is given a household far bigger than any that is likely to have existed even in eighth-century Ionia, but it is very much smaller than the royal household of thirteenth-century Pylos, where Webster has counted no less than 347 women, 240 girls, and 159 boys, and all just in Pylos itself.[12] Similarly M. I. Finley has contrasted Eumaeus' easily memorized inventory of the livestock of Odysseus, who is supposed to be much richer than most, so rich in fact that 'not twenty men together have such wealth', with the incomparably vaster and more specialized agricultural and manufacturing operations of the Mycenaean palace-administration, which required a hierarchy of officials and supervisors, and the careful, highly detailed, written records and catalogues of the Linear B tablets.[13] Not only is there no evidence of knowledge of the art of writing or of scribes in Homer, but there is no need for them in the simpler conditions of life. Moreover there is nothing in Homer even to suggest the varied and complicated feudal system of tenure which has been deduced from the tablets.[14] Land in Homer is in private ownership: even the suitor Antinous concedes that both Odysseus' estate and kingship are Telemachus' patrimony, and that he will be left with the former (or what may be left of it after the suitors' depredations) when someone else has succeeded to the latter.[15] And nothing indicates that Homeric social relations and obligations are of a feudal nature (in the proper sense of relations based on a land tenure system in which estates are fiefs held on conditions of allegiance and service to a superior lord). So complete an absence of tenurial and operational references is of course inconceivable if they were a feature of the world known to the Homeric bards, and it is in marked contrast to other epics, such as *Beowulf* or the *Song of Roland*. The Homeric social terminology is similarly post-Mycenaean.[16] As many as six apparently important 'leadership' words known from the tablets fail to turn up even once in the twenty-eight thousand lines of the Homeric poems, which produce instead their own words; and four of these are apparently not new words, beginning their history with the poems, but archaic words with no further life outside Greek poetry. Moreover the two words which are common to the tablets and to Homer, *anax* and *basileus*, em-

APPENDIX

phasize beyond question the difference between the societies; for whereas the Mycenaean Age *wanax* was the Great King of the palace-state and the *pa₂-si-re-u* merely a local dignitary of clearly very inferior status (whatever the more exact nature of the position), in Homer these terms are interchangeable, usually according to purely metrical considerations.[17] Similarly contrasting are the types of polity which these different patterns of social terminology underline. The Mycenaean palace-states were absolute monarchies, whose kings were set on an altogether higher plain from the rest of society. The Homeric states are monarchies too, but the king is very much in the nature of *primus inter pares*.

If then the Homeric picture is no guide to the world of the Linear B tablets, we can turn to assess how accurate a guide it is likely to be to the Dark Age communities, the very different and much humbler societies which emerged from the chaos of the Mycenaean collapse. Archaeology has shown much of the material culture of the Homeric picture to be Dark Age, and even in minor ways a tell-tale object often points to the Dark Age background despite the thickest veneer of heroizing. An interesting example is provided by Agememnon's catalogue of the presents which he is prepared to give Achilles by way of amends.[18] The list certainly approaches a Mycenaean Age scale, especially where it includes several cities, but it actually begins with the inevitable tripods and glittering cauldrons, which are constantly mentioned as important valuables in the Homeric poems,[19] and which are extremely uncommon objects until the Geometric period, when they appear in large numbers at a variety of sites.[20] And this Dark Age indication is fully confirmed by Strasburger's point about the Dark Age 'peasant mentality' which shows through in Agamemnon's mention of the work capacity not only of the seven Lesbian captive women but even of his own wife, the queen of Mycenae no less, when he is comparing her unfavourably with Chryseis.[21] A more significant Dark Age indication is the knowledge of the working of iron. Iron appears not only in similes but in descriptions of articles in common use among the heroes (except of course for weapons, whose special significance was discussed in Chapter III). As Miss Lorimer noted, the epithet πολιός clearly indicates the grey of steel, and πολύκμητος implies a knowledge of the new method of mild steel production with its day-long hammering.[22] And the simile in which the hissing of Polyphemus' eye pierced by the red-hot stake is likened to the noise of an axe or adze being dipped into cold water by the blacksmith to temper it, 'for therefrom comes the strength of iron',[23] fortifies Achilles' allusion to the use of iron for farm implements in the *Iliad*, when he says what the lump of iron will mean for its winner at the funeral games, that no matter how extensive his fields, his shepherd or cowherd will not have to be sent into town for iron for full five years.[24] In the Mycenaean world however, articles of iron are never mentioned in the tablets;[25] and the few artifacts revealed by archaeology fall mainly into the category of 'soft iron', decorative articles, mainly rings and other iron jewellery, which are completely unknown in the Protogeometric period, as indeed in Homer.[26]

Similarly post-Mycenaean is cremation, the exclusive Homeric method of disposal of the dead, which is in contrast to the usual Mycenaean method of (usually multiple) inhumation. Bronze Age cremation is very exceptional indeed, and no weight can be attached to the one or two possible examples.[27] It became common in Attica about 1025 B.C., and then it spread from mainland Greece to the Ionian settlements in Asia Minor, where it was retained, in Colophon at least, until the end of the ninth century.[28] And whatever Mylonas might say to try to reconcile Homeric and Mycenaean burial customs, the basic difference of method remains.[29] He argued that Homeric cremation reflects Achaean borrowing of that practice from the Trojans of Troy VI, and suggests that the Achaeans reverted to inhumation again at home under the influence of 'ancient sepulchres' and 'limited supply of wood'! Even if we forget that what applied to Troy VI need not have applied to VIIa, it is clearly perverse to prefer such a far-fetched explanation of Homeric practice instead of seeing it as a reflection of the almost universal Greek Geometric Age custom, and especially so since Colophon (who incidentally laid a very strong claim to Homer) attests cremation for an Ionian city.[30] Moreover the fact remains that although references to burials at home are few, they all treat cremation as the normal method of disposal. In the *Odyssey*, Anticleia speaks of the 'appointed way with mortals when one dies: for the sinews no longer hold the flesh, but the strong might of blazing fire destroys them'.[31] Or in the *Iliad*, the Calydonian boar is described as having

APPENDIX

brought many men to the pyre.[32] And although some expressions may at first sight appear to indicate inhumation, it is clear that they refer to the interring of the ashes after cremation as an essential preliminary. For example, concerning the disposal of the dead suitors we are only told that they were carried out of Odysseus' palace and 'buried' by their friends.[33] But θάπτειν, far from contrasting with cremation, clearly implies it. Patroclus pleads to Achilles, 'Bury me (θάπτε με) as quickly as possible'; and of course his corpse is cremated.[34] Or again, Elpenor begs not to be left unburied (ἄθαπτον), 'but cremate me';[35] and later, when Odysseus 'buries him' (θάπτει), the description makes it clear that preliminary cremation is automatically involved.[36] Miss Lorimer's conclusions remain sound on this subject.[37] The Homeric picture reflects the Dark Age practice of cremation, adopted in the transition from sub-Mycenaean to Protogeometric, and resulting from some profound emotional disturbance: cremation created the language of its own ritual, and there was no impulse to translate it back into the idiom of the Bronze Age (even if the fact of Mycenaean inhumation was known). And in case any should doubt the fact, the resilience of so important a ritual to 'limited supply of wood' is eloquently attested by the cremation-burials of Geometric Age Thera, an island singularly devoid of combustible materials.[38] Finally, if I agree with Mylonas that the rather unimpressive Protogeometric cremations could hardly have inspired the magnificent description of Patroclus' funeral, I also agree with Miss Lorimer that 'Homer's experience is, with perhaps a slight time-lag, exactly what that of an eighth-century Athenian would have been';[39] and certainly funeral games for rich noblemen were common in Hesiod's day.[40] And if the time-lag allows us to place the historical basis of the (exaggerated and heroized) Homeric descriptions of funerals in the ninth century, we shall see that this fits in well enough with the linguistic dating of the bulk of the formular system which survives in our texts.

In Scheria most obviously of all we are not in the Mycenaean world but in the Geometric period after the migrations and colonization of Ionia which began at the beginning of the tenth century, or perhaps just a little before. We are told that the Phaeacians had migrated there under the leadership of Nausithous, who 'drew a wall about the city, built houses and made temples for the gods, and divided up the ploughland'.[41] And the description of the city, with boats drawn up on either side of a causeway and with an embattled wall-circuit shielding the approach onto the peninsula, provides a guide-book description of the typical migration settlement on the seaboard of Asia Minor as revealed by the excavations of the site of Old Smyrna.[42] It may be that Alcinous' palace has certain Bronze Age features, some apparently Egyptian and derived perhaps from the legend of fourteenth-century Thebes,[43] and its wealth and splendour are of course vastly greater than any Geometric Age residence could have boasted; but in contrast to a true Mycenaean palace, it is only the 'best house' of a city through which the stranger must be directed to find it.[44] And with its situation on a promontory, with a short land frontier and a safe anchorage, with its temple to Poseidon, its agora, and the controlling power of the nobles recognised by the king, the city clearly suggests all the conditions of an early Ionian settlement.[45] In fact, J. M. Cook noted that the strong claim to Homer which Colophon made in historical times supports the Smyrnaean claim.[46] And if what excavation has revealed of Smyrna's condition in the ninth and eighth centuries seems unworthy of the descriptions of cities and material conditions in the *Odyssey*, which would be better satisfied by the more spacious residences and the temple with its ἀγάλματα πολλὰ καὶ ἐσθλά of the seventh, it must be remembered that other, greater, ninth- and eighth-century cities of Ionia no doubt advanced much more quickly than little Smyrna. Elsewhere than in Scheria there are further Homeric parallels with the architecture of Old Smyrna. In the *Iliad*, there are Achilles' barrack and the temple that the priest of Apollo roofed at Chryse, which Cook compared with the early, single-room, mud-brick, oval cottage of Smyrna Level I, dating from the end of the tenth century.[47] The later, eighth-century houses of similar construction (though sometimes with an open porch), jostling each other uncomfortably in Old Smyrna, reminded him of the Homeric simile of a sudden conflagration sweeping through a town.[48] Or for another example from the *Odyssey*, the domed building round whose peak Telemachus is pictured slinging his line to hang the shameless maidservants suggests Old Smyrna's sunken granaries.[49] Now the picture of Scheria, so patently based on Dark Age communities planted in Asia Minor, was disguised, heroized, and elevated to a less mundane

APPENDIX

plain by the Homeric poets in various ways. The splendour of Alcinous' palace we have already mentioned. It is not a Mycenaean palace, nor even any sort of palace known to have existed. It is an invented palace, made suitably heroic by a few Bronze Age antiques and a general indication of great wealth and grandeur. Another disguise is the magical, supernatural veneer, of ships that navigate themselves as well as the usual personal intervention of particular gods and goddesses in the story-line.[50] But beneath the disguise, the historical communities of Geometric Age Ionia are revealed by the social and political conditions of Scheria no less clearly than by the architectural features of the town. And likewise the heroic veneer does not manage to disguise completely the way of thought engendered by the comparatively humble, 'peasant' conditions of even the highest level of Dark Age life, so very different from the Mycenaean world. As Strasburger observed, it is somewhat incongruous with the splendour of Alcinous' palace to find his daughter, the princess Nausicaa, asking her father if she may borrow a cart to take the laundry down to the river, in order that he may have clean linen to wear when attending councils of state. And later we find the king himself insisting that the other great nobles chip in with him to provide parting gifts for Odysseus, 'since it is hard for one man to foot the expense alone'.[51]

Strasburger's examples are clearly remote from the way of thought of a Mycenaean Age king, but what of the general heroic ethos – the violent, personal drive for honour, the challenges and insults, the exultation and arrogance in victory in battle and games alike? Kirk has suggested that it was derived indirectly from the Bronze Age, or at least from a highly glamourized view of the Bronze Age which gained currency in its imaginative but depressed successor.[52] But it is important to distinguish between these two possible sources. I agree with Kirk that the early Iron Age is unlikely to have produced much in the way of exotic and formalized military behaviour. But since the treatment of weapons and chariots indicates that little description of Bronze Age battles is likely to have survived the Mycenaean collapse, I suggest that the heroic ethos is more likely to be the result of invention (owing much to pure imagination perhaps, but something to aristocratic ethos generated in the settled Dark Age communities which, by the ninth century at least, could hardly be called 'depressed') than to have been a tradition transmitted from the Bronze Age. Kirk inclines to the opposite view. He argues that while the heroic ethos seems to run contrary to the length and patience of the siege of Troy, it joins the three basic types of Homeric war as reflecting more accurately conditions in the Bronze Age, and deriving from Bronze Age tradition.[53] His three basic types of Homeric war are the smaller, localized wars and raids, the civil war into which Ithaca was plunged, and the large-scale but short-lived siege. But all three types could equally well be based on Geometric Age conditions, and they are surely more likely to be so. To take siege-warfare first, there is no reason to doubt that Geometric Age cities like Old Smyrna, whose excavation reflects so clearly the Homeric description of Phaeacia, were sometimes put under siege. They had battlements on which women and elders no doubt watched their army fighting before the walls exactly as Priam's Trojans do;[54] and the 'large scale' of a siege can be a simple heroizing exaggeration. Localized wars and cattle-raiding expeditions like those of Nestor's reminiscences are of course timeless;[55] but perhaps the mention of the chariot-contest at Elis in Nestor's explanation of the quarrel between Elis and Pylos reflects the Geometric Age rather than a possible Bronze Age survival.[56] Civil strife is timeless too. Kirk suggested that the Ithacan civil strife, which culminated in a massacre and nearly started a war between the small states of the North-West Peloponnese, is strongly redolent of conditions as they must have been in an age of disintegration. But civil strife is also appropriate to the Geometric Age communities, especially at the time when they were ripe for the disappearance of kingship, as the Homeric states often seem to be: after all, Ithaca was apparently perfectly able to manage without a king for twenty years. And surely the Ithacan civil strife is more likely to belong with the Ithacan social and political conditions, which are so clearly not Mycenaean. The Homeric kings are not Mycenaean monarchs, but *primi inter pares*. There is no mention of the migrations and colonization except where it is treated as a past event (in Scheria). And the fact that Ithaca can manage without a king for twenty years and her nobles share the same title as the king himself suggests to me that her civil strife may reflect noble power-struggles in the Geometric Age communities, when individual nobles, perhaps excluded from

APPENDIX

charmed circles, sometimes led their friends in adventures abroad (as did the restless Cretan of Odysseus' story[57]), but often stayed at home to trouble the peace: certainly we have ample testimony for a long history of such noble power-struggles in early Greek states, as in Mytilene to judge from the notices of Aristotle and the allusions in the poems of Alcaeus.

The subject whose treatment is the most important source of inconsistencies and difficulty in Homer is the Panachaean theme itself. Now it is strictly irrelevant to my purpose whether or not there ever was a Panachaean coalition led by the *wanax* of Mycenae against Troy, although it is worth noting that archaeology can tell us for certain only that Troy was destroyed by an enemy, and the Homeric epic reveals for certain only that Bronze Age Greeks had something to do with it.[58] The feasibility of joint operations in the Achaean world is difficult to assess, and even Kirk's cautious suggestions require strong reservations. He suggested that the homogeneity of Achaean material culture, especially in the thirteenth century, might imply a degree of political as well as cultural unity;[59] but the evidence is mainly ceramic, and cultural homogeneity is not the same as political unity. He also suggested that the geographical proximity of Argos, Tiryns and Midea to Mycenae seems to entail that they must somehow have been allied to Mycenae; but if this is probable enough – although it could perhaps be argued that the close proximity of these fortified casbahs is suggestive rather of an uneasy and mistrustful co-existence – it is certainly no evidence that the overlordship of the Mycenaean *wanax* was any more extensive, let alone 'Panachaean'. And Finley has rightly stressed how other national epics have exaggerated and distorted a country's share in a war beyond recognition.[60] At any rate, whether or not a large-scale Panachaean expedition for whatever purpose was, or could have been, organized under the leadership of the Great King of Mycenae, it is clear that such an expedition is alien to the social and political framework of the Homeric picture, which shows no real conception of the Mycenaean world to which, if anywhere, the Panachaean expedition must belong. This is the reason why its treatment is beset with such obvious difficulties and confusions in Homer. What for instance was the relationship of the other kings to Agamemnon and Menelaus? It is not even the case that the title *anax* is reserved for

Agamemnon, whilst the other kings are mere *basilēes*, as Kirk made out. Later legend rationalized the expedition with the story of an oath of support taken by all the suitors of Helen;[61] but apart from a vague reference to unspecified promises, the Homeric epic leaves vague the relations between the other kings and Agamemnon, and the reason why he takes such a large cut of all the spoils, even those won by the private expeditions of other kings like Achilles.[62] Other obvious difficulties posed by the narrative of the War are the ignorance of the proper (or even reasonable) use of chariots in battle, and indeed the whole confusion of the Homeric battle-pieces, in which vast numbers of common warriors, 'bronze-corsleted' and 'well-greaved', clearly well equipped with arms and armour, are mentioned from time to time, but are treated in the narrative exactly as Odysseus refers to them, as 'not counting in battle'.[63] And the supremacy of the aristocracy in the Homeric battles, along with the spear-type and the role of the war-chariot, is another pointer to the Geometric Age communities, which were so very different from the vast and highly organized palace-states of the Bronze Age that were capable of the mass production of vast numbers of chariotry, and that clearly had a feudal system which could explain the obligations of lesser rulers to an overlord. If then the theme of a Panachaean coalition is incongruous with the social, political, economic and military conditions depicted in the poems, the Dark Age historian must suspect the Panachaean situations when he is fitting an ideology to those conditions. And this brings us back to the heroic ethos. It is always maintained that the community principle is lacking in the ideology of the Homeric world, and the lack of expressions of patriotic duty and pride are contrasted with the sentiments of Tyrtaeus in the seventh-century Spartan city-state.[64] M. I. Finley expressed the general view when he said that the Homeric hero had no responsibility other than familial, and that his sole obligation was to his own prowess and his drive to victory and power.[65] This certainly is the impression we get from the poems as a whole, but it is not a valid judgement if we concentrate our attention on the single-state situations. In the situation of a single state under attack, Hector voices the obligations of patriotism no less strongly than Tyrtaeus.[66] This is in sharp contrast to the lack of corresponding appeals to Panachaean responsibility on the Greek side, and the contrast is not accidental. It is instructive to

APPENDIX

look at the one instance of such an appeal, which Odysseus makes after listing the magnificent gifts which Agamemnon is prepared to give Achilles to induce him to swallow his injured pride and rejoin the fighting.[67] Achilles completely ignores this point in his reply, and the speech of Phoenix reveals why. Phoenix retails an anecdote about the Aetolian Meleager, another indispensable hero who was similarly in a great anger and refusing to fight. Meleager too was offered gifts of recompense, but he remained implacable until the eleventh hour, when he was moved to save his city by his wife's patriotic plea.[68] But Phoenix tells Achilles that he would not be urging him to relent, however badly the expedition needed him, except for the honourable recompense promised by Agamemnon, and the fact that Agamemnon had sent a deputation of the very noblest men to offer his amends.[69] The situations of Meleager and Achilles are different: Meleager was defending his own city, and the patriotic plea which counts more than injured personal feelings in the case of a single city under attack, whether Meleager's Calydon or Hector's Troy, is meaningless in the Panachaean situation, which itself was conceptually and practically alien to the world of the bards. And when Hector and Ajax are encouraging their respective sides in the battle for the ships, Hector calls for patriotic sacrifice, Ajax for the necessity of saving the ships so that each man can get back to his own separate homeland.[70] We find the same contrast when we look at the games. In the Panachaean games, there is not the slightest evidence of patriotic sentiment, but in the single-state situation of Scheria we find King Alcinous proudly laying on displays and entertainments for Odysseus with the expressed intention of showing his visitor the Phaeacian excellence in the various activities.[71] The indications are that much of the heroic ethos with its intensely personal and familial emphasis belongs with the Panachaean theme as part of the heroizing 'disguise' of the basic Dark Age world, in which the strength of the community principle must not be assessed according to the infrequency of patriotic expressions in the poems as a whole, but according to their much more significant expression in only the single-state situations.[72]

We have noticed how little conception the Homeric poems reveal of the very different, vaster and more complex conditions of the Mycenaean world as it has been disclosed by archaeology, and especially by the Linear B tablets. And once we have discarded the few incompatible specific features at either end of the time-scale, whether three mentions of Bronze Age body-shields or the one or two possible 'hoplite' allusions,[73] and have removed, or at least allowed for, what has been found to be a thick but transparent veneer of heroizing and archaizing, whether of bronze as the military metal or of battalions of well armed commoners who do not count in battle, or of war-chariots which are really disguised Geometric cavalry, or of straight exaggeration either of wealth or of aristocratic behaviour, we may finally summarize the indications of date for our consistent remainder, the Dark Age basic background picture of society, institutions, warfare and ideology, and in particular the stage of political development reached by the basic Homeric community. Kirk has argued that the essential contraction and the ignored digamma provide something approaching proof that the bulk of the formular system which survives in our texts was developed at least two or three hundred years after the fall of Troy.[74] And if this is so, a pivotal date of the ninth century (overlapping the late tenth and early eighth) suits very well the rest of the evidence. In the first place the background picture belongs firmly to the age of iron and cremation, and these aspects cannot be earlier than the late eleventh century; and a considerably later date for it is indicated by the fact that the period of chaos and migrations which followed the Mycenaean collapse are clearly in the past. There is no suggestion that the Homeric picture belongs to a period of great upheavals and migrations. The only reference to colonization treats it as a past event, and Scheria so clearly attests familiarity with the communities planted in Asia Minor in the great period of migration which began not earlier than the close of the eleventh century. Sufficient time must have elapsed since the period of chaos and initial resettlement for the establishment of hereditary, landed aristocracies so sharply distinct from the rest of society, which unquestioningly accepts the superiority and privilege of noble birth; and for this we must allow several generations. Throwing-spears, tripods, separate temples all point to the ninth century at the earliest, and so too does the Homeric war-chariot if my thesis is sound. And however much allowance we make for the imagination and poetic exaggeration of the heroizing bards, the familiarity with such expensive noble sports as chariot-

APPENDIX

races, with funeral games (and their tripod prizes), or with the general architectural and town-planning features, suggests a basic inspiration from a later and more advanced level of material culture than archaeology has revealed for the Protogeometric period, and brings the picture nearer to Hesiod's time. But if the basic picture belongs to the post-migration Geometric Age, and if societies have had time to develop a dominant hereditary nobility, it is important to stress that the Homeric communities are not yet 'city-states'. We have seen that the community can inspire responsibility, duty and pride, but it has no corporate power, and contains no formal apparatus of government. The organs of government characteristic of the city-state proper are present in embryo, in the council of noble elders and in the popular assembly; but although the king shares the same titles with the other heads of the noble houses and often seems little more than *primus inter pares*, the Homeric government is still a hereditary monarchy in which final decision rests with the king; and the popular assembly, in the manner of the Roman *contio* rather than the *comitia*, neither votes nor decides nor elects, but merely listens inarticulate to information and directions or to discussions of the nobles. The birth of the city-state is perhaps not too far distant in the future; but the first city-states were aristocratic republics, and there is nothing of this in the Homeric world. The significance of the interchangeable titles for king and nobles is not that kingship was unfamiliar to the Homeric bards who deliberately reintroduced it for the purpose of archaizing, but that it was of a *primus inter pares* nature. And that this really was the nature of Geometric Age kingship is clear from the fact that its disappearance was such a vanishing act: in complete contrast to the disappearance of kingship at Rome, it was so little convulsive that it failed to leave any reliable, historical tradition, and we have to make do with myths or the schematic reconstructions of learned antiquarians like Aristotle. The Homeric community has not yet reached the stage of political development which embodied the fundamental principle of the city-state, which Aristotle so neatly expressed as the principle of equals taking turns in ruling and being ruled, and which was of course the negation of the principle of kingship.[75] The transition from kingship to the phase of aristocratic republicanism, though not convulsive, was nonetheless momentous, and if the Homeric state sometimes seems ripe for it, it is clear that it has not yet occurred. But it had occurred in most Greek communities by the time they emerged from the Dark Ages into the clearer light of history in the late eighth and the seventh centuries.

NOTES

Chapter I
The Chariot in Homer

1 *Iliad* 5.192–204.
2 A. M. Snodgrass, *Early Greek Armour and Weapons* (Edinburgh, 1964), p. 260, n. 26.
3 M. Detienne, 'Remarques sur le char en Grèce', *Problèmes de la Guerre en Grèce Ancienne*, ed. J-P. Vernant (Paris, 1968), p. 315.
4 M. S. F. Hood, 'A Mycenaean Cavalryman', *BSA*, 48 (1953), 84f; E. Cassin, 'A propos du char de guerre en Mésopotamie', *Problèmes*, pp. 297f; G. Garbini, *The Ancient World* (London, 1966), pl. 14.
5 H. L. Lorimer, *Homer and the Monuments* (London, 1950), pp. 324–5, 256, n. 4; M. G. Amadasi, *L'iconografia del carro da guerra in Siria e Palestina* (Studi Semitici 17, Rome, 1965).
6 W. MacQuitty, *Abu Simbel* (London, 1965), pl. 110; W. Stevenson Smith, *Interconnections in the Ancient Near East* (New Haven and London, 1965), fig. 120; W. Wreszinski, *Atlas zur altaegyptischen Kulturgeschichte* (Leipzig, 1914–40), vol. 2, p. 170.
7 T. G. E. Powell, 'Some Implications of Chariotry', *Essays in honour of Sir Cyril Fox*, ed. Foster and Alcock (London, 1963), pp. 165–6.
8 F. Studniczka, 'Der Rennwagen im syrisch-phönikischen Gebiet', *JdI*, 22 (1907), 149, fig. 2; Lorimer, *HM*, p. 313, fig. 42.
9 Evidence summarized by Lorimer, *HM*, pp. 309f.
10 M. Lejeune, 'La Civilization Mycénienne et la Guerre', *Problèmes*, p. 49.
11 Lorimer, *HM*, pp. 322–3; D. L. Page, *History and the Homeric Iliad* (Berkeley, 1959), pp. 11f.
12 Lorimer, *HM*, p. 256; see also G. S. Kirk, 'The Homeric Poems as History', *Cambridge Ancient History* (Cambridge, 1964), vol. 2, ch. 39(b), p. 21.
13 G. Karo, *Die Schachtgräber von Mykenai* (Munich, 1930), p. 206.
14 Karo, pl. 4; Lorimer, *HM*, pl. 24.
15 *AE*, 1889, pl. 10i; Lorimer, *HM*, p. 311, fig. 39; *JHS*, 45 (1925), 35, fig. 36; A. J. Evans, *The Palace of Minos* (4 vols., London, 1921–36), vol. 4, p. 820, fig. 799; W. Reichel, *Homerische Waffen* (Vienna, 1901), p. 139, fig. 88. A sherd from Tiryns also appears to show a chariot-borne lancer: H. Schliemann, *Tiryns* (London, 1886), p. 354, fig. 155.
16 Lorimer, *HM*, p. 311, fig. 38 (LM Ib).
17 Lejeune, *Problèmes*, pp. 41, 47ff.
18 Lorimer, *HM*, p. 325; Amadasi, *L'iconografia del carro da guerra*, esp. figs. 16.1, 17.1; E. A. W. Budge, *Assyrian Sculptures in the British Museum in the reign of Ashur-nasir-pal, 885– 860B.C.* (London, 1914), for many examples of ninth-century Assyrian chariot-warfare. Contrast Homer and Geometric art, in which archery from the chariot is completely unknown – a strange fact if Greek contacts with the East were really as strong as they are often claimed to have been. Even the great bowman Pandarus exchanges his bow for the javelin when he mounts Aeneas' chariot to go after Diomedes (*Iliad* 5.238, 280); and his speech to Aeneas makes it clear that the bow is used only on foot, and that the chariot-borne warrior is a spearsman (180).
19 G. S. Kirk, *The Songs of Homer* (Cambridge, 1962), pp. 123–4.
20 Cassin, *Problèmes*, pp. 300ff.
21 Snodgrass, *EGAW*, pp. 161, 255, n. 12.
22 The single exception is a confrontation of chariots on one side of a Boeotian fibula illustrated and discussed by J. Charbonneaux, 'Deux Grandes Fibules Géométriques', *Préhistoire*, 1 (1932), 191ff, fig. 2. But the extraordinary width of the plate indicates that both these fibulae are forgeries; and the remarkable correspond-

173

NOTES

ence between the sea-battle scenes indicates that the second fibula (fig. 4) is specifically a forgery of the design of the 'Aristonothos' vase of about 650 B.C.: Rome, Mus. Cap. 172; Lorimer, *HM*, pl. 17.1; Charbonneaux, fig. 21; *CVA* Italy (Rome 2), pl. 1741. Moreover, even if the fibulae had been genuine, Charbonneaux rightly explained that the combatants had to remain in their chariots because the limited space available on a fibula cannot easily fit the usual epic duel by dismounted warriors whose chariots frame the scene; hence the curiously elongated spears.

23 J. K. Anderson, 'Homeric, British and Cyrenaic Chariots', *AJA*, 69 (1965), 349–52.
24 Kirk, *The Songs of Homer*, p. 124.
25 Caesar, *BG*, 4.24.
26 See also T. G. E. Powell, *The Celts* (London, 1958), pp. 108–9.
27 Diodorus, 5.21.5.
28 Caesar, *BG*, 4.33.
29 Tacitus, *Agricola*, 12.1.
30 Xenophon, *Cyropaedia*, 6.27.
31 *Ibid.* 28.
32 Snodgrass, *EGAW*, p. 160 and n. 6.
33 *Ibid.* p. 162.

Chapter II
The Chariot in Geometric Art

1 Lorimer, *HM*, p. 307.
2 Snodgrass, *EGAW*, pp. 159–60.
3 Lorimer, *HM*, p. 317, pl. 25.1; Snodgrass, *EGAW*, p. 161.
4 This explanation is supported by the fact that the G3c representations show only a single profile horse; to indicate a pair would require 'overlapping'.
5 R. C. Bronson, 'Chariot Racing in Etruria', *Studi in onore di L. Banti* (Rome, 1965), p. 90. His two PC aryballoi are one in Syracuse, Johansen, *VS*, p. 98, no. 4, pl. 34.1, and the other in Berlin, *ibid.* pl. 32.
6 As T. J. Dunbabin, *The Greeks and their Eastern Neighbours* (London, 1957), p. 20. Bronson objects that the warriors on foot between the chariots suggest rather a processional scene. But the impression of speed given by the forelegs raised in the gallop, and by the robed, single charioteer who leans backwards while the one in the next chariot leans forwards, is surely suggestive of a race; and perhaps the running warriors indicate that the panoplied foot-race at the athletic festivals in classical times was precedented in the Geometric period.

7 Three-horse teams on Attic LG vases: (LG Ib) nos. **7, 42, 43**; (LG IIb) nos. **18, 19, 38**. Four-horse teams: (LG Ib) no. **5**; (LG IIb) nos. **16, 39, 40, 41**.
8 Three-horse pyxis-lids: Agora P5060, P5061 (Attic LG Ia, 760–750 B.C.), *GGP*. pls. 9f, m; Agora P4784 (LG Ib), *GPP*, pl. 6; *GGP*, pl. 10k. Four horses: *Kerameikos*, vol. 5.1, pls. 67, 60, inv. 1310 (Attic LG Ia); for a Boeotian LG example, see *Prähistorische Zeitschrift*, 1 (1909), pl. 13.1; *GGP*, p. 203, n. 6. Pairs of horses on pyxis-lids are found earlier still, in Attic MG II: see *GGP*, p. 23.
9 R. A. Higgins, *Greek Terracottas* (London, 1967), p. 22, pl. 8b.
10 R. S. Young, 'Late Geometric Graves', *Hesperia*, Supp. 2 (1939), pp. 65–6, fig. 42 (from grave 12). Such chariot groups continue from the eighth into the seventh century: see Higgins, p. 43; also D. Burr, *Hesperia*, 2 (1933), 615, no. 299, fig. 82, and no. 300 (fragmentary similar group), from a Protoattic votive deposit.
11 Pausanias, 5.8.7.
12 Bronson, 'Chariot Racing in Etruria', pp. 100ff.
13 Budge, *Assyrian Sculptures*, pls. 14, 15 (bottom), 16 (bottom), 17 (bottom), 18 (top), 24 (bottom).
14 *Iliad* 23.326ff.
15 Athens 4082; *AE*, 1896, pl. 3; S. D. Markman, *The Horse in Greek Art* (Baltimore, 1943), p. 30, fig 15. (Markman's date of 775–750 B.C. is as usual much too early, and Miss Lorimer more reasonably assigned it to the fifth century, *HM*, p. 167, n. 2.) The warrior is a hoplite whose double-grip shield is clearly shown. Note the four horses, of which only the centre two are yoked. The form of the chariot is that of contemporary racing-chariots, and chariots looking like this were the models of the LG vase-painters of type G3.
16 J. Boardman, *The Greeks Overseas* (Penguin, Harmondsworth, 1964), pl. 17; D. E. Strong, *The Classical World* (London, 1965), pls. 41, 42.
17 Lorimer, *HM*, p. 311, fig. 38 (no indication of yoke or shaft).
18 *Ibid.* p. 313, fig. 41; Evans, *P of M*, vol. 4, p. 816, fig. 795.
19 (1) *fig. 23*: *HM*, fig. 40; *P of M*, vol. 4, p. 823, fig. 803; *JHS*, 45 (1925), 36, fig. 37; (2) sealing from Hagia Triadha, *P of M*, vol. 4, p. 828, fig. 808; (3) the Tiryns boar-hunt fresco, *HM*, p. 315, fig. 44; (4) the Maroni crater (Cyprus, c. 1350 B.C.), *HM*, p. 315, fig. 45; Strong, *The Classical World*, p. 32, pl. 21.
20 E. von Mercklin, *Der Rennwagen in*

Griechenland (Leipzig, 1909); Lorimer, *HM*, p. 316.

21 Lorimer noted that the flaps would be an obstacle for anyone running up at the side to seek shelter in his chariot in the Homeric manner; but this of course does not apply if the chariot is used effectively and fought from at speed.

22 From Mycenae (LH IIIc, *c.* 1200 B.C.): (1) *fig. 24*, Athens 1272, *HM*, pl. 2.3; Furtwängler and Loeschcke, *Mykenische Vasen*, pl. 41, no. 427; (2) Nauplia 8357, *EGAW*, pl. 20. From Tiryns: Schliemann, *Tiryns*, p. 354, fig. 155; pl. 15.

23 Olympia, inv. 9080; Curtius u. Adler, *Olympia*, vol. 4 (Berlin, 1890), no. 253, pl. 15; Lorimer, *HM*, p. 318, fig. 46.

24 Schliemann, *Tiryns*, pl. 15c (bottom right).

25 Bronson, 'Chariot Racing in Etruria', p. 100, discounts the representations of a single yoked horse pulling a chariot as unlikely: 'if the horse moved faster than a walk, the chariot would move sideways'. Note also that some painters who showed only one profile horse indicated two by the reins, e.g. nos. **28, 29, 30.**

26 This is not invariably done of course. In **16** the single profile wheel is kept, and the hoops are clumsily splayed out to accommodate two occupants.

27 Nos. **42** and **43** are fragmentary: the chariot-bodies are lost but the teams of three horses remain. The chariots were probably of the G1 type since the vases are by the same early hand as nos. **4** and **5,** which both portray G1 chariots (the latter the most cart-like of them): Dipylon Workshop, (iii) Villiard's Group, LG Ib: see Coldstream, *GGP*, pp. 31–2.

28 *Iliad* 23.264, 513 etc.

29 *Iliad* 11.709, 750: Nestor describes his battle with the Molione; *Iliad* 23.638: they perform as a single competitor in a chariot-race. J. M. Cook, 'Protoattic Pottery', *BSA*, 35 (1934–5), 206, argued that the twins are nothing more than the creation of artists faced with the difficulty of filling a space too broad for a single figure and too narrow for two. Kirk agreed, *BSA*, 44 (1949), 93ff, and added that the double figure appears three times in one frieze on a crater in New York, *AJA*, 19 (1915), pls. 21–3. But there is ample space for two figures on vase **10;** and there is only a single figure in each of the other chariots on this vase, even the elongated version on the right with two profile wheels (*fig. 3*). Repetition of a motif is not a fatal objection to its identification, although Webster's parallel of repeated lion-slayers is not necessarily valid, *BSA*, 50 (1955), 41. It is far from certain that the lion-slayer motif yet enjoyed the specific identity of Heracles: as Buschor showed, the human-horse hybrids were not definitely pinned down to 'Centaurs' before the 670s B.C.

30 Hesiod, *Works and Days*, 654.

31 See n. 10, above.

32 For boxing matches and musical or poetic contests, see Dunbabin, *The Greeks and their Eastern Neighbours*, p. 20, pl. 2 (note bronze tripods and other prizes standing by). Wrestling, boxing and a prize cauldron on a stand appear on no. **41.** A panoplied foot-race perhaps on no. **9** (*fig. 18*; see above, n. 6).

33 Three horses: *Iliad* 16.466–75 (allusion in battle scene); *Odyssey* 4.590 (a three-horsed chariot offered as a gift by Menelaus to Telemachus). Four horses: *Iliad* 8.185ff. (Hector calls encouragement to his four horses in battle: passage athetized by Aristarchus); *Iliad* 11.699 (a quadriga destined for the games at Elis 'to run for a tripod' has been seized by King Augeias); *Odyssey* 13.81 (a simile).

34 Bronson, 'Chariot Racing in Etruria', pp. 89–90.

35 V. Karageorghis, 'A Mycenaean Horse Rider', *Bulletin van de Vereeniging tot bevordering der Kennis van de antieke beschaving*, 33 (1958), 41: the number is usually two, but three and even four are found on late vases. A single occupant appears in the war-chariot of Shaft-Grave 5, but a war-chariot whose driver has to fight is clearly impossible; and in this case the material hardly allows the depiction of a second occupant, besides the fact that the stele is honouring only one deceased nobleman.

36 M. I. Finley, *Early Greece: The Bronze and Archaic Ages* (London, 1970), p. 83.

37 *Iliad* 21.37–8.

38 *Iliad* 11.535; 20.500; 21.38.

39 *Iliad* 5.262, 322.

40 *Iliad* 10.475 (hapax).

41 *Iliad* 5.727–8.

42 *Iliad* 23.335; 436.

43 *Iliad* 6.40; 16.371.

44 *Iliad* 24.265–74. I follow W. Leaf in identifying the nine cubits long *zygodesmon* with the 'pole-end support' of Greek Geometric and Archaic racing-chariot representations: *JHS*, 5 (1884), 187ff.

45 Lorimer, *HM*, p. 326.

46 *Ibid.* p. 319.

47 *Iliad* 4.226; 10.322, 393; 23.503; Lorimer, *HM*, p. 327.

48 *Iliad* 10.438, 505.

49 E. Delebecque, *Le Cheval dans l'Iliade* (Paris, 1951), pp. 169ff (lexique).

NOTES

50 *Iliad* 23.132; Delebecque, pp. 90–1.
51 Note that where the LG artists put two occupants into a chariot they had to elongate it: sometimes it appears clumsily stretched over one wheel, and often a second wheel was added for 'balance' (see above, p. 34, n. 26). And even the fine painters of Archaic pottery, who were well able to depict two occupants side by side in perspective without elongating the chariot (e.g. Middle Corinthian vases in Payne, *NC*, pls. 32.4, 42.1), nevertheless preferred to show only one man in a warchariot, the robed charioteer, while the noble warrior was shown on foot; and this was so even in the scenes of Achilles dragging Hector's body (e.g. nos. **47**, **48**: the robed charioteer of **48** also has a helmet!).

Chapter III
The Homeric *Hippēes*

1 *Iliad* 2.202.
2 Lorimer, *HM*, p. 257; Snodgrass, *EGAW*, p. 137, n. 43.
3 A. M. Snodgrass, 'Barbarian Europe and Early Iron Age Greece', *Prehistoric Society Proceedings*, 31 (1965), 231.
4 Snodgrass, *EGAW*, p. 174; D. H. F. Gray, 'Metal Working in Homer', *JHS*, 74 (1954), 5.
5 Aristotle, *Politics*, 1297b.16–19.
6 Ibid. 1289b.33ff.
7 Heraclides Ponticus, *Politics*, 22.
8 J. M. Cook, 'Old Smyrna', *BSA*, 53–4 (1958–9), esp. 12ff, 20f.
9 Cassin, *Problèmes*, pp. 300f.
10 Cassin quotes the letter from Hattusil III (c. 1275 B.C.) to the Cassite King of Babylon, Kadasman-Enlil.
11 Hood, 'A Mycenaean Cavalryman', pp. 86–7. They appear mainly on the Syrian and Hittite side. A Karnak relief of c. 1300 B.C. depicts a mounted warrior with rectangular shield fleeing transfixed by an arrow from Pharaoh's bow (Seti I storming Jenoam in Syria: Wreszinski, vol. 2, no. 36). Another shows Seti in battle with mounted Hittite archers with plumed helmets (*ibid.* nos. 45–6). Riding figures appear on the Egyptian side on the Kadesh battle-reliefs of Ramses II, both at Luxor (*ibid.* no. 64a) and Abu Simbel (nos. 169–78).
12 C. F. A. Schaeffer, *Ugaritica*, (3 vols, 1939–56), vol. 1, p. 103, fig. 96E; vol. 2, p. 158, fig. 61C. Date 1350–1200 B.C.
13 Hood, 'A Mycenaean Cavalryman', p. 92. For Tell Halaf reliefs, Von Oppenheim, *Tell Halaf* (English translation,

London, 1931), pp. 149ff, pl. 18b. For Maras, Sencliri, Charchemish, Tell Ahmar, see *Der Alte Orient*, 38 (1939), 70.
14 Hood, 'A Mycenaean Cavalryman', figs. 47, 48.
15 C. W. Blegen, *Prosymna* (Cambridge, 1937), no. 760, fig. 615.
16 Snodgrass, *EGAW*, p. 163, n. 18.
17 Lorimer, *HM*, p. 504, n. 2.
18 Allard Pierson Museum, Amsterdam, no. 1856; Karageorghis, 'A Mycenaean Horse Rider', pp. 38–42 and three figs.; *CVA* Pays-Bas 1 (Mus. Scheurleer 1), pl. 12.7.
19 Evans, *P of M*, vol. 4, p. 787, fig. 763 (i) = *Scripta Minoa*, vol. 2, no. 222 (cf. no. 227).
20 Athens 4691; Lorimer, *HM*, pl. 12.1.
21 *AE*, 1904, pl. 3; Lorimer, *HM*, pp. 153–4, fig. 10 ('protogeometric'); Snodgrass, *EGAW*, p. 163 ('Geometric'). V. R. d'A. Desborough, *Protogeometric Pottery* (Oxford, 1952), p. 269, argues convincingly for a geometric date from both ceramic and external evidence. It is assigned to late LM IIIb by A. Furumark, *Opuscula Archaeologica*, 3 (1944), 226, and to LM IIIc by Coldstream, *GGP*, p. 259, n. 10.
22 E. H. Hall, *Excavations in Eastern Crete: Vrokastro* (Philadelphia, 1914), fig. 53F; Coldstream, *GGP*, p. 258, n. 4.
23 *Tiryns*, vol. 1, pl. 15.5; *Argive Heraeum*, vol. 2, pl. 57.4; *BCH*, 78 (1954), 413, fig. 4. For unarmed men with single horses on Argive LG, see Nauplia 1984, 1973, and *Asine*, fig. 223.
24 *JHS*, 74 (1954), 153, pl. 8.3.
25 Unarmed: (1) *Kerameikos*, vol. 5.1, inv. 1306, grave 50, pl. 141; (2) *Arch. Hom.*, pl. F6. Armed: (1) vase **14**; (2) *Kerameikos*, vol. 5.1, inv. 268, grave 28, pl. 87; (3) Copenhagen 1628, Dunbabin, *The Greeks and their Eastern Neighbours*, pl. 3.2; *GGP*, p. 76. Panoplied 'Dipylon' warriors: (1) *Kerameikos*, vol. 5.1, pl. 87 (huge Dipylon shield and 3 spears); (2) Bowl from Thera, Athens 13038, *GGP*, p. 67; *AM*, 28 (1903), pl. 3, H.1.19.
26 *Kerameikos*, vol. 5.1, inv. 2159, pls. 111, 141.
27 E.g. amphora, Athens market, *GGP*, p. 66 (early LG IIb).
28 *BSA*, 35 (1934–5), pl. 35, no. 29.
29 Oxford; K. Schefold, *Frühgriechische Sagenbilder* (Munich, 1964), p. 39, figs. 9, 10; *Arch. Hom.*, p. F123, fig. 24a.
30 *Hesperia*, 2 (1933), 593, fig. 58; *Arch. Hom.*, p. F119, n. 400; pl. W10a; p. F115, fig. 20g.
31 On the shape of the bell-corslet, see Snodgrass, *EGAW*, p. 73.

32 Nauplia 4268, 4274; *GGP*, p. 143, n. 16.
33 *Kerameikos*, vol. 5.1, inv. 850, grave 85, pls. 141, 37 (*c.* 740 B.C.); *Arch. Hom.*, p. F115, fig. 20d.
34 Stuttgart KAS 10; *CVA* Deutsch. 26 (Stuttgart 1), pls. 1218.1, 1222.4.
35 Athens 738; *AM*, 18 (1893), pl. 8.2 (from grave 9).
36 Toronto 925.28.7 (C 861); Robinson-Harcum–Iliffe, *Greek Vases in Toronto* (Toronto, 1930), no. 120, pl. 19. I am indebted to Dr J. W. Hayes of the Royal Ontario Museum for his authoritative report on this vase.
37 Athens 12341 and Berlin 8396; R. Hampe, *Frühe Griechische Sagenbilder in Böotien* (Athens, 1936), pl. 15 and p. 12, fig. 1, no. 60; *Arch. Hom.*, p. F122, figs. 23a and b.
38 F. Willemsen, *Olympische Forschungen* (Berlin, 1957), vol. 3, pl. 46, no. B1665, and pp. 148ff, fig. 18.
39 Schefold, *Frühgriechische Sagenbilder*, p. 38, fig. 8; *Arch. Hom.*, p. F112, fig. 23c.
40 C. Frödin and A. W. Persson, *Asine: Results of the Swedish Excavations, 1922–30*, p. 310, fig. 213.4.
41 *Ibid.* pp. 333–4, fig. 225.6, 7.
42 Hood, 'A Mycenaean Cavalryman', p. 92; Snodgrass, *EGAW*, p. 163, n. 22.
43 C. Waldstein, *The Argive Heraeum* (Boston, 1902–5), vol. 2, p. 40, nos. 244, 245, 246, pl. 48.2, 4, 3; note also no. 247.
44 P. Jamot, 'Terres cuites archaïques de Tanagre', *BCH*, 14 (1890), 219, figs. 7 (armed with round shield) and 6 (unarmed) = Markman, *The Horse in Greek Art*, p. 31, fig. 16 and p. 29, fig. 14; *Tiryns*, vol. 1, p. 83, fig. 20, no. 141 (Nauplia 1867: round shield and large helmet, 7th century); *Perachora*, vol. 1, p. 228, pl. 100, nos. 166 (helmet and round shield), 167; J. Martha, *Figurines en Terre Cuite du Musée de la Soc. Arch. d'Athènes* (Paris, 1880), nos. 602 (helmet and shield), 603.
45 J. M. Cook, 'The Agamemnoneion', *BSA*, 48 (1953), 64, pl. 23, esp. no. I.19.
46 *Arch. Hom.*, p. F120, n. 403.
47 J. K. Anderson, *Ancient Greek Horsemanship* (Berkeley and Los Angeles, 1961), p. 11.
48 T. B. L. Webster, 'Homer and Attic Geometric Vases', *BSA*, 50 (1955), 43ff; Coldstream, *GGP*, p. 351.
49 A. Alföldi, 'Die Herrschaft der Reiterei in Griechenland und Rom nach dem Sturz der Könige', *Gestalt und Geschichte: Festschrift K. Schefold* (Berne, 1967), p. 24, says that κελητίζειν here means 'jump from one horse to another'. But it means nothing more than 'to ride' as distinct from 'to drive' a horse. Odysseus sitting astride his single plank is likened to a man riding a κέλης ἵππος. At Herodotus, 7.86, κέλητας are simply riding-horses as distinct from ἅρματα. And there is nothing of Alföldi's significance in Aristophanes' obscene use of κελητίζειν at *Wasps*, 501.
50 Delebecque, *Le Cheval dans l'Iliade*, pp. 90–1.
51 *Iliad* 5.263–4, 323–4; also perhaps 10.330.
52 Snodgrass, *EGAW*, p. 175.
53 Delebecque, *Le Cheval dans l'Iliade*, pp. 162, 166.
54 Lorimer, *HM*, p. 325; Snodgrass, *EGAW*, p. 175.
55 Delebecque, p. 80. At *Iliad* 10.530, μάστιξεν δ'ἵππους, τὼ δ'οὐκ ἀέκοντε πετέσθην is a formula used for chariots (e.g. 5.768, 11.519), and similar to the expressions at 5.366, 8.45, 22.400. Similarly, ἵππων ἐπεβήσετο (10.513) and ἐπεβήσετο δ'ἵππων (10.529) are usually employed of mounting chariots, but here signify mounting horses. Moreover, here presumably Diomedes is mounting only one horse – Odysseus is on the other.
56 See also Delebecque's list of verbs, *Le Cheval*, p. 81.
57 *Odyssey* 3.477–4.3, etc. (Compare the tragedians.)
58 Xenophon, *De Re Equestri*, 7.5, 8.10; *Hipparchus*, 1.21. Prize amphoras of the early fourth century depict the contest for mounted javelineers, see J. D. Beazley, *The Development of Attic Black-Figure* (Berkeley, 1951), pp. 96–7. Anderson, *Ancient Greek Horsemanship*, p. 151, is wrong in saying that the lance replaced the javelin in the Macedonian cavalry, whose main weapons throughout the Macedonian period were the javelin and xyston: see W. W. Tarn, *Hellenistic Military and Naval Developments* (Cambridge, 1930), p. 72.
59 Compare *Iliad* 17.699, where the duty of Laodocus, the ἡνίοχος for Antilochus, is described thus: Λαοδόκῳ, ὅς οἱ σχεδὸν ἔστρεφε μώνυχας ἵππους.
60 W. Helbig, 'Les Ἱππεῖς Athéniens', *Mémoires de l'Institut National de France* 37/1 (1904), 157ff; Aristotle, *Politics*, 1297b.16-24.
61 Athens 992; *AE*, 1970, pls. 37a, 38a.
62 Helbig, 'Les Ἱππεῖς Athéniens', pp. 180f, 166f; H. Metzger and D. van Berchem, 'Hippeis', *Gestalt und Geschichte: Festschrift K. Schefold* (Berne, 1967), p. 156; Alföldi, 'Die Herrschaft der Reiterei', pp. 17ff; J. Wiesner, *Arch. Hom.*, p. F136.
63 Polybius, 3.115.1–3.

NOTES

64 T. G. E. Powell, *The Celts* (Lodnon, 1958), pp. 108–9.
65 Plutarch, *Eumenes*, 7.7ff.

Chapter IV
Dipylon Warrior, Hoplite and Cavalryman

1 Snodgrass, *EGAW*, p. 196; contrast 'The Hoplite Reform and History', *JHS*, 85 (1965), 112.
2 T. B. L. Webster, 'Homer and Attic Geometric Vases', *BSA*, 50 (1955), 41ff; Snodgrass, *EGAW*, pp. 58ff.
3 *BCH*, 85 (1961), 770, fig. 20; Snodgrass, *EGAW*, p. 58.
4 Lorimer, *HM*, p. 157; G. Ahlberg, 'Fighting on Land and Sea in Greek Geometric Art', *Acta Instituti Atheniensis Regni Sueciae*, Series in 4°, 16 (1971), 60 (and many illustrations).
5 As A. J. Evans, 'A Mykenaean Treasure from Aegina', *JHS*, 13 (1892–3), 216 (although I do not agree that the Dipylon shield had anything to do with the apparently wicker Bronze Age shield of the Hittites, *fig. 1*: note that the two shields which appear of similar size in his figs. 25 and 26 are really not comparable at all).
6 For examples in the *Iliad*, Ajax clearly has his shield slung on his back at 14.402–6, when Hector hurls his spear at Ajax's chest and the latter is saved from injury only because the spear-point struck the spot where the shield's telamon crosses that of the sword, and the two thicknesses of belt prevented it from penetrating the flesh. And at 11.545ff Ajax's steady retreat under Trojan pressure reveals the value of a shield on the back: 'they hung on the heels of the great Ajax, pricking the centre of his shield with their spears' (563–5). Note also Diomedes' reproachful words to Odysseus at 8.94.
7 London 1971. 11–18.1; Lorimer, *HM*, pl. 7.2–4.
8 *Fig. 40*: Copenhagen 1628 (Attic LG IIa); Lorimer, *HM*, p. 157, fig. 13; Perrot and Chipiez, *Histoire de l'Art*, vol. 7, p. 179, fig. 63; Dunbabin, *The Greeks and their Eastern Neighbours*, pl. 3.2; G. S. Kirk, 'Ships on Attic Geometric Vases', *BSA*, 44 (1949), 111, fig. 3. *Fig. 41*: Nauplia, votive clay shield from the Geometric Heraeum at Tiryns; Lorimer, *HM*, p. 170, pl. 9.1.
9 *Fig. 42*: Nauplia, clay votive shield found with *fig. 41*; Lorimer, *HM*, pl. 10.1. Note also that these votive shields themselves are equipped with central handles but are perfectly flat, unlike the clay model of the Dipylon shield, *fig. 39*.
10 Corinth; Snodgrass, *EGAW*, pl. 15b.
11 *Fig. 43* is the earliest known representation of the inside of the hoplite shield, but no doubt some earlier representations of the outsides of large round shields were hoplite too, e.g. see above, p. 58, *fig. 37*.
12 Lorimer, 'The Hoplite Phalanx', *BSA*, 42 (1947), 76ff; Detienne, 'La Phalange: Problèmes et Controverses', *Problèmes*, esp. pp. 133ff; R. Nierhaus, 'Eine frühgriechische Kampfform', *JdI*, 53 (1938), 90ff; Snodgrass, 'The Hoplite Reform and History', *JHS*, 85 (1965), 110–22.
13 E.g. the 'Aristonothos' vase, Rome, Mus. Cap. 172; Lorimer, *HM*, pl. 17.1; *CVA* Italy (Rome 2), pl. 1741.
14 E.g. Florence 3776; A. Rumpf, *Chalkidische Vasen* (Berlin and Leipzig, 1927), fig. 15; Inghirami, *Vasi fittili*, vol. 3, pl. 278.
15 Paris E796, *fig. 72*.
16 Berlin (Pergamonmuseum) A41; *CVA* Deutschland 2 (Berlin 1), pls. 76, 80.
17 Thucydides, 5.71.
18 A. Andrewes, *The Greek Tyrants* (London, 1962), p. 32; W. G. Forrest, *The Emergence of Greek Democracy* (London, 1966), p. 90.
19 See below, pp. 108n 17, 130n 25, 134.
20 Snodgrass, *EGAW*, pl. 33, illustrates an alabastron in Berlin of the second half of the seventh century which gives a 'still life' arrangement of the panoply excluding the shield. It depicts two spears, one longer and thicker, the other shorter and slimmer and equipped with a throwing-loop. Perhaps the second spear shown in the left hand of many Protocorinthian hoplites was a javelin, e.g. on the McMillan and Chigi vases (see below, n. 21).
21 The earliest is an aryballos in Berlin, c. 675 B.C. Next come the Chigi vase in Rome, Villa Giulia, and the McMillan aryballos in London (89.4–18.1), c. 650 B.C.: see K. F. Johansen, *Les Vases Sicyoniens* (Copenhagen, 1923), pls. 32, 39, 31; Lorimer, 'The Hoplite Phalanx', figs. 3, 2, 10.
22 Aristotle, *Politics*, 1297b.22–24.
23 F. E. Adcock, *The Greek and Macedonian Art of War* (Berkeley and Los Angeles, 1957), p. 4.
24 Snodgrass, 'The Hoplite Reform and History', p. 114.
25 M. I. Finley, 'Sparta', *Problèmes*, p. 149.
26 Detienne, 'La Phalange', *Problèmes*, p. 129, n. 56.
27 Aristotle, *Politics*, 1289b.30–32, 1305b.33.

NOTES TO PAGES 61–90

Compare in the fifth century the Xenophontine *Ath. Pol.*, 1.2, where οἱ ὁπλῖται are classified with οἱ γενναῖοι and οἱ χρηστοί in contrast with ὁ δῆμος.
28 Aristotle, *Politics*, 1289b.33–36.
29 Alföldi, 'Die Herrschaft der Reiterei', p. 13.
30 Aristotle, *Politics*, 1297b. 18–22.
31 *Ibid.* 1289b.38.
32 Alföldi, p. 14.
33 Alföldi simply accepts it as a fact without mentioning that the only source is Pollux 8.108. On the problem of the naucraries, see C. Hignett, *A History of the Athenian Constitution* (Oxford, 1952), p. 68.
34 Achilles boasts about such raids at *Iliad* 10.328; G. S. Kirk, 'Ships on Attic Geometric Vases'.
35 *Odyssey* 14.256ff (265–8 and 271–2 quoted). Admittedly this is Egypt, but the Homeric poems treat the Trojans exactly as Greeks, and the same is no doubt true of the Egyptians.
36 Theophrastus, *Characters*, 21.
37 The difficulties of fighting bareback have been greatly overrated, e.g. by Adcock, *The Greek and Macedonian Art of War*, pp. 49–50, who took too seriously Xenophon's extemporized picture of the precariously poised trooper 'as much afraid of falling off himself as he is of the enemy' – a picture designed to allay the Ten Thousand's very real fears of the Persian cavalry, whose reputation did not terrify them for no reason (Xenophon, *Anabasis*, 2.2.18–19).
38 W. W. Tarn, *Hellenistic Military and Naval Developments* (Cambridge, 1930), pp. 73–6.
39 E.g. Thucydides, 7.6.
40 Herodotus, 5.63.
41 *Ibid.* 5.64.
42 M. W. Frederiksen, 'The Campanian Cavalry', *Dialoghi di Archeologia*, 2 (1968), 9, 11.
43 Thucydides, 7.11–13 (Nicias' letter); also 6.71, 93.
44 *Ibid.* 6.66. For a similar example, see 7.5, where the nature of the position immobilizes the Syracusan cavalry. Compare the next battle which the Syracusans win on open ground (7.6).
45 *Ibid.* 6.70.
46 *Ibid.* 6.68.
47 *Ibid.* 7.4, 44.
48 *Ibid.* 8.78ff.
49 Herodotus, 5.63.
50 Xenophon recommended that horses' hoofs should be hardened by inducing them to stamp on a pavement of cobblestones that matched the size of the hoofs (*Hipparchus*, 1.16; *De Re Equestri*, 4.3–4).
51 For the adoption of hoplite equipment and phalanx tactics by the Etruscans, see Snodgrass, 'The Hoplite Reform and History', pp. 116–19.
52 *Ath. Pol.*, 7.3–4.

Chapter V
Mounted Warriors in the Seventh Century

1 E.g. Johansen, *VS*, nos. 5, 11, 44; Payne, *PV*, pl. 10.
2 E.g. Johansen, *VS*, nos. 50, 56, pls. 31, 35.
3 E.g. *ibid.*, pls. 23.2b, 30.2, 30.3; Payne, *PV*, pls. 20.2–4, 17.1.
4 Helbig, 'Les ἱππεῖς Athéniens', p. 175, and n. 1 (where he gives this interpretation of vase A18).
5 *Ibid.*, p. 175, fig. 5.
6 Contrast this advanced artistry with that of the 'single-horse' squire of C1. Here not only is the artist happy to show a second outline, but he depicts the pairs overlapping each other.
7 For an emergency in which mounted hoplites fight from horseback, see the ambush scene on an Etruscan Bf vase, Würzburg 799: E. Langlotz, *Griechische Vasen in Würzburg* (Munich, 1932), pls. 232–4.
8 Friezes of unarmed riders: Boston 03.782, Davison, fig. 58 (EPA); Private collection, Davison, fig. 70a–b (EPA); Berlin A42, Kübler, *Altattische Malerei* (Tübingen, 1950), pl. 48 (MPA); D. Burr, *Hesperia*, 2 (1933), 593, fig. 58. Horsemen breaking into chariot processions: Munich 1351, J. M. Cook, 'Protoattic Pottery', *BSA*, 35 (1934–5), pl. 41; Ceramicus 1271, Kübler, *AM*, pl. 34. For two horses racing neck and neck: Agora P754, Burr, *ibid.*, p. 592, no. 210, fig. 58.
9 Most notable besides the knight of A2 is the EPA Sunium plaque of a penteconter full of warriors, similarly equipped with helmets, large round shields and twin spears: Athens 3588; J. M. Cook, 'Protoattic Pottery', pl. 40b.
10 Athens 4437 (in the same case with vase A1).
11 Athens 1002; *ABV*, p. 4; R. M. Cook, *Greek Painted Pottery* (London, 1960), pl. 17.
12 Paris E874; *ABV*, p. 8 (Gorgon Painter no. 1).
13 Apollodorus gives his *floruit* as 664–663 B.C. Against Blakeway's eighth-century date, see F. Jacoby, 'The Date of Archilochus', *CQ*, 35 (1941), 97–109, who puts Archilochus' activities in the period 680–640 B.C.

179

NOTES

14 Archilochus, frag. 6 (Diehl, 1925).
15 *Ibid.* frag. 51.
16 *Ibid.* frag. 3 (*ap.* Plutarch, *Theseus*, 5).
17 Aristotle, *Politics*, 1289b.36–40: see above, p. 42.
18 The only mounted swordsmen known to me from Greek painting are the Persian cavalrymen who are preparing to slash with long cutlasses at Greek hoplites on the British Museum's complete Clazomenian sarcophagus, see below, p. 144, fig. 77. But even here the sword is not the primary weapon; the riders clearly have bows and quivers strapped to their sides, and the cutlass was resorted to only for close quarters after the arrows had been expended. It was probably less effective a cavalry weapon than a lance or javelins, but it had the advantage for an archer that it could be carried conveniently in a scabbard, which left both hands free for shooting. (Swords are used from horseback on an Etruscan Bf vase, Würzburg 799, but these horsemen are mounted hoplites who have been ambushed by hoplites on foot and foot-archers, who attacked them from each side before they could dismount: see above, n. 7.)
19 W. G. Forrest, 'Colonization and the Rise of Delphi', *Historia*, 6 (1957), 163–4.
20 *Iliad* 2.542–4.
21 *AE*, 1903, 14, fig. 7; J. Boardman, 'Early Euboean Pottery and History', *BSA*, 52 (1957), 27–9.
22 Strabo, 10.1.12, p. 448.
23 Herodotus, 5.99; Thucydides, 1.15.
24 For many illustrations, see M. F. Vos, *Scythian Archers in Archaic Attic Vase-Painting* (Archaeologica Traiectina, 6, Groningen, 1963), pp. 12ff, pls. 5, 6b, 7, 8, 13.
25 Tyrtaeus speaks of light-armed men with stones and javelins, and apparently they kept close behind the hoplites to benefit from the cover afforded by their shields (frag. 8.35–8, Diehl, 1925). For a slinger operating from behind a hoplite, see a later pithos-fragment from Sparta, *Artemis Orthia*, pls. 15, 16. For archers in hoplite battles, see above, p. 70, fig. 43; Johansen, *VS*, pl. 33a, f; *Perachora*, vol. 2, no. 27, pl. 57; Lorimer, 'The Hoplite Phalanx', pp. 93, 100, figs. 7, 9d. And archers had of course been common in the pre-hoplite warfare of LG art, e.g. see above, p. 67, fig. 40. See further, Snodgrass, *EGAW*, pp. 181f, 203f; Lorimer, 'The Hoplite Phalanx', pp. 115–16.
26 To deal with the superior Syracusan cavalry Nicias stressed that Athens would need to send large forces of archers and slingers on the proposed Sicilian expedition in 415 B.C.: Thucydides, 6.22.
27 It is hard to know if Strabo was right to assume that the τηλεβόλα of the stele included javelins as well as the longer-range weapons, the bow and the sling. At any rate, it is only bows and slings that Archilochus mentions as being out of favour. If the horses were used only for transport and not perhaps plunged into the thick of battle, they would be less likely to be harmed by javelins aimed at each other by opposing ranks of heavy-armed warriors before they closed with the sword; and the javelins would have been spent before the conflict began to be decided and the squires had to take their horses in close at their masters' need when the lines had broken up. Moreover, in view of Nicias' emphasis on the effectiveness of bows and slings against horsemen (see above, n. 26), we have an added indication that the spear-famed lords were mounted infanteers, since if they were all cavalry and one side was weaker in what was the main arm, it would be pushing chivalry very far to forgo so effective a defence.
28 Plutarch, *Moralia*, 760E–F.
29 For the fame of 'Chalcidian blades', see e.g. Alcaeus, frag. Z34.7 (Lobel-Page).
30 Callinus, frag. 1.5, 9–11 (Diehl, 1925).
31 Snodgrass, *EGAW*, p. 180.
32 Mimnermus, frag. 13 (Diehl, 1925).
33 Alcaeus, frag. Z34 (Lobel-Page).
34 D. L. Page, *Sappho and Alcaeus* (Oxford, 1955), p. 222.
35 Herodotus, 5.95; Strabo, p. 600.
36 Page, *Sappho and Alcaeus*, p. 211; Snodgrass, *EGAW*, p. 183.
37 Fragments of Tyrtaeus give a perfect description of the hoplite shield and spear, and the close order of the phalanx formation (fragments 1A.18–19; 6–7.15; 8.11, 21–6, 29–34; Diehl, 1925). Snodgrass, *EGAW*, pp. 181–2, is puzzled by the possibility that a hoplite could hang back out of range of the missiles (fragment 8.28). But what Tyrtaeus says is not that a man could *fight* out of range of the missiles: the point of his exhortation is that to fight at all a hoplite must brave them. As for the shield-epithet 'bossed' in fragment 9.25, I fail to see why bosses, even if they are all round a shield as on vase A2, fig. 35, should be incompatible with a double grip inside; and for a later example, see the shields of the mounted hoplites on Chalcidian vases, X16 and X18, figs. 73, 75.
38 Tyrtaeus, fragment 8.35–8 (Diehl, 1925).
39 Tyrtaeus, fragment 1B.12 (Diehl, 1925).

NOTES TO PAGES 90–132

40 Thucydides, 5.72 (418 B.C.). Perhaps the three hundred troops specially picked by King Leonidas to go to Thermopylae were the *Hippeis* too (Herodotus, 7.205). See further, Detienne, 'La Phalange', *Problèmes*, pp. 134ff.
41 Athens 15.355; *Artemis Orthia*, p. 206, pl. 92.3; E. L. I. Marangou, *Lakonische Elfenbein- und Beinschnitzereien* (Tübingen, 1969), pp. 82–3, pl. 63.
42 Helbig, 'Les Ἱππεῖς Athéniens', p. 160.
43 *Artemis Orthia*, pl. 191, shows several models of crouching bowmen among the many lead figures of hoplites (all probably from the end of the seventh century).
44 *Artemis Orthia*, p. 212, pl. 104.1.

Chapter VI
Mounted Warriors in the Sixth Century

1 Helbig, 'Les Ἱππεῖς Athéniens', pp. 246–7.
2 Alföldi, 'Die Herrschaft der Reiterei', p. 19.
3 I have not seen these fragments and rely on the verbal description in *Perachora*, vol. 2, p. 255, no. 2473.
4 For an archaic bronze greave, see Olympia, inv. B63; Snodgrass, *EGAW*, p. 88.
5 See above, pp. 78–9.
6 For an Attic example, see A105, on which a horseman's two spears and bare legs contrast with the single spear and greaves of a hoplite.
7 But even the corslet was heavy, and the armoured Corinthian cavalrymen of C13 and C14 wore only a tunic and a helmet (which was probably worn in battle to increase stature and present a terrifying aspect as to protect the head).
8 East Greek horsemen also had 'saddle-cloths' (though no saddles of course): see below, n. 41.
9 Livy, 35.28.8. Alföldi's other references, p. 26, nn. 113, 114 – all those in Diodorus and Polybius – only mention 'Tarentines', not how they fought or whether they had second horses or not; and the lexicon references of n. 115 are similarly inconsequential.
10 Arrian, *Tactica*, 4.5. (The only conceivable suggestion that ἀμφίπποι fought in battle comes in 2.3; but even so they are not equated with the 'Tarentines', whose definition depended on their use of javelins, and more properly in connexion with certain tactics.)
11 Pollux, 1.13.
12 Alföldi, p. 25, pl. 7.2; A. E. Newhall, *AJA*, 35 (1931), 27ff, pl. 2.

13 Both are by the 'C' Painter: Beazley, *ABV*, pp. 55, 58. (A37 = no. 91; A7 = no. 119). Note also the similar motif on A16, a vase allied to the 'C' Painter (*ABV*, p. 227, where it is mentioned under no. 17), and on a later vase, A49.
14 Vase A14 (clearly a heroic duel since a goddess stands behind each of the duellists and holds a spare spear for her favourite).
15 On C23 even the shield decoration is identical for the hoplites on foot on the one side and the panoplied rider on the other.
16 Anderson, *Ancient Greek Horsemanship*, p. 147.
17 As the heavy-armed Amazon riders do on two later sixth-century Attic vases, A91 and A92. But neither Greeks nor Amazons are shown fighting from horseback with the round hoplite shield hanging on the back.
18 The first 50 pages of *ABV* provide scarcely any military scenes, and only a very occasional 'horseman'.
19 Anderson, *Ancient Greek Horsemanship*, pp. 145–6.
20 See above, n. 13.
21 A39 is one of the rare examples: the mounted ephebes flanking the duel are unarmed, and no second horse is shown (c. 540 B.C.).
22 G. M. A. Richter, *CVA* U.S.A. 11 (Metropolitan Museum 2), p. 6.
23 M. F. Vos, *Scythian Archers*, pp. 12ff, pls. 10, 11, 12a. Also the rider poising his lance and wearing the high-pointed cap on a sherd of c. 500 B.C., Acropolis 722a, Graef, *AcrV.*, pl. 40.
24 Helbig, p. 221, makes the cavalryman of A77 a Thessalian, depicted at a time when Athens admired the bravery of her Thessalian allies against the Spartan expedition under Anchimolius. But the casting of Penthesilea as a Spartan seems curious even if the prince of Phthia is appropriate for a Thessalian; and certainly he is not dressed in the characteristic Thessalian manner of Helbig's figs. 25 and 26, and pl. 2.1. I believe he is an Athenian cavalryman like the similar riders of my other, uninscribed examples (unknown to Helbig).
25 For mounted Amazons with large, convex, round shields slung from their shoulders, see A91, A92, A93: all wear helmets and swords and carry lances, and on A93 they are fully equipped as hoplites right down to the greaves (an unusual feature for Amazons).
26 Athens 41; G. M. A. Richter, *The Archaic Gravestones of Attica* (London, 1961), no. 20, fig. 68 (given as 575–545 B.C.).

NOTES

27 Thasos museum; G. M. A. Richter, *Archaic Greek Art* (New York and Oxford, 1949), p. 95, fig. 161. With shields these horsemen are clearly not hunting hares, as Richter maintains! The presence of hares and other animals as decorative motifs in military scenes is common enough (e.g. *fig. 36*), and here the subjects of war and hunting are combined.
28 Helbig, p. 221.
29 Alföldi, p. 19.
30 Thucydides, 5.57; 2.79.
31 R. M. Cook, *Greek Painted Pottery*, pp. 157f; J. Boardman, 'Early Euboean Pottery and History', pp. 12–14.
32 Aristotle, *Politics*, 1289b.39; see above, pp. 42, 90–3.
33 Herodotus, 5.77.
34 Frederiksen, 'The Campanian Cavalry', p. 22, suggests that the choice of site was often influenced by its suitability for 'cavalry' and therefore for 'cavalry institutions'.
35 Compare the hoplites on the Etruscan sarcophagus from Caere, A. S. Murray, *Terracotta Sarcophagi in the British Museum* (London, 1898), pl. 9, with the identical ones on 'Chalcidian' vases like X4. Note also the mounted hoplites being ambushed by hoplites on foot on Würzburg 799, an Etruscan Bf vase of *c.* 470 B.C.: Beazley, *EVP*, p. 17; Langlotz, *G.V. in Würz*., pls. 232–4; Gerhard, *AV*, pl. 194; Helbig, p. 255, fig. 37.
36 Note that this is not the impossible position to which I objected in Chapter IV (see above, p. 72). That position was the more usual hoplite hold with the elbow bent and the fore-arm horizontal (parallel to the ground), but with the elbow thrust out in front and kept sufficiently far to the left to make the left side of the shield project in front of the right side of the man on the left. The 'Chalcidian' position in contrast cannot give frontal protection to anyone but the user. The elbow is not bent, the whole arm is held stiffened, and all lateral movement to parry blows aimed at side or front is provided by the shoulder.
37 Vatican 231 (Etruscan Bf, *c.* 550–530 B.C.); Ducati, *Pontische Vasen*, pls. 8a, 9a; Beazley, *EVP*, pl. 1; Helbig, p. 256, fig. 38.
38 London 1904.7-3.1; H. B. Walters, *Select Bronzes in the British Museum* (London, 1915), pl. 1; G. von Lücken, 'Archaische griechische Vasenmalerei und Plastik', *AM*, 44 (1919), 66, figs. 1, 2; E. Langlotz, *The Art of Magna Graecia* (London, 1965), p. 259, no. 26.
39 *CVA* Great Britain 13 (British Museum 8), pls. 584.3, 591.2, for hoplites on Clazomenian Bf vases of 550–525 B.C. The former depicts hoplites fighting, and an Asiatic archer wearing a high cap. On the latter the naked, mounted youth preceding a hoplite may be a mounted squire: perhaps the scene was derived from the pursuit of Troilus, but if so the significance had been forgotten since there is no sign of pursuit.
40 *Ibid*., pls. 600.1, 593.1, 588.6, 587.19, 588.4, 595, 606.2 (Clazomenian, East Greek and Rhodian Bf vases, 550–500 B.C.).
41 Istanbul 1427 (71) + London 86.3–26.1 (A672); Johansen, *Acta Archaeologica*, 13 (1942), figs. 19 (Istanbul), 20 (London fragment, also *CVA* G.B. 13, pl. 614.1). Perhaps mounted squires also on Munich 8774, *CVA* Deutschland (Munich 6), pl. 1379.
42 London 96.6–15.1; *CVA* G.B. 13, pl. 610; Murray, *Terracotta Sarcophagi*, pp. 1–13, pls. 1–7.
43 Murray, *Terracotta Sarcophagi*, p. 10, fig. 3.
44 Vos, *Scythian Archers*, p. 45, finds no Scythian with a sword. See Vos also on the Scythian preference for the pointed cap. For Persians using the cutlass on Attic vases, see (1) Bf lecythos, *AJA*, 36 (1932), 27, fig. 1; (2) Rf cup, *ARV*, p. 417, no. 4; Gerhard, *AV*, pl. 166; (3) Rf amphora, New York 06.1021.117; *ARV*, p. 1656; Richter and Hall, *Red Figured Athenian Vases in the M.M.A.*, no. 35, pl. 34; *JdI*, 26 (1911), 285, fig. 4.
45 Orvieto, Faiana 65; Vos, *Scythian Archers*, pl. 14b.
46 *CVA* G.B. 13, pl. 610. 1; Murray, *Terracotta Sarcophagi*, pls. 4, 5.
47 *Antike Denkmäler*, vol. 1, pl. 46.1 (once in Smyrna).
48 Paris CA244; *BCH*, 16 (1892), 240ff, figs. 1, 2.
49 *Anth. Pal.* VII, 304.
50 Istanbul 526; R. M. Cook, 'Dogs in Battle', *Festschrift Andreas Rumpf* (Cologne, 1950), pp. 38–42; M. Schede, *Meisterwerke der Turkischen Museen zu Konstantinopel* (Berlin and Leipzig, 1928), vol. 1, pl. 3.

Chapter VII
Conclusions

1 The scattered sources for Thessalian activities in the Archaic period are collected by W. G. Forrest, 'The First Sacred War', *BCH*, 80 (1956), 42. See also A. R. Burn, *The Lyric Age of Greece* (London,

1960), pp. 201–4 (although his reconstruction is not always warranted by the nature of the sources).
2 For Thessalians, see Helbig, 'Les Ἱππεῖς Athéniens', figs. 25, 26, pl. 2. For Scythian foot-archers and mounted spearmen, see Vos, *Scythian Archers*: mounted spearmen on his pls. 10, 11, 12a, and my vases A79 and A94.
3 Herodotus, 5.63–4.
4 Munich 1500; Helbig, pl. 2.1 (facing p. 220).
5 Demosthenes, 13.23, 23.119.
6 Thucydides, 1.111.
7 Aristotle, *Politics*, 1297b.16–28.
8 Snodgrass, 'The Hoplite Reform and History', pp. 116–19; A. D. Momigliano, 'An Interim Report on the Origins of Rome', *JRS*, 53 (1963), 119–21.
9 Livy, 2.48–50; Snodgrass, *ibid.*, p. 120.
10 Snodgrass makes a distinction between men in hoplite equipment and members of a phalanx, but I believe that the invention of the double-grip shield was responsible for the phalanx formation; and in any case phalanx tactics were well established by Alcaeus' day, and certainly by the time Cremera was fought in 477 B.C.!
11 See above, p. 74, n. 25.
12 R. Sealey, 'Regionalism in Archaic Athens', *Historia*, 9 (1960), 155ff.
13 Herodotus, 5.71; Thucydides, 1.126.
14 *Ath. Pol.*, 15.2, 17.3; Herodotus, 1.61.
15 Page, *Sappho and Alcaeus*, pp. 150ff; Aristotle, *Politics*, 1285a.35.
16 Dionysius of Halicarnassus, 7.3ff.
17 Neither Nicholas of Damascus (Jacoby, 90F57) nor Herodotus (5.92) mentions any fighting: Nicholas says simply that Cypselus killed the last reigning Bacchiad; Herodotus that he exiled many, deprived many of their goods and many more of their lives.
18 *Ath. Pol.*, 14.4.
19 Herodotus, 6.127; Ephorus, 70F115 (Jacoby); Pausanias, 2.24.7; Aristotle, *Politics*, 1310b.26; Andrewes, *The Greek Tyrants*, pp. 40–4.
20 Nicholas, 90F57. It is incredible that a polemarch was not what the word implies in the seventh century; and since Nicholas mentions only civil functions attaching to Cypselus' office, the story is clearly a reconstruction deriving from fourth-century Athens and probably attributable to Ephorus: see Andrewes, *The Greek Tyrants*, p. 46.
21 According to Thucydides, 1.126, the very opposite occurred, and the Alcmaeonid archons were rapidly reinforced by local farmers who came in from the fields.
22 Solon, frags. 3.17–20, 24.20–7, 25.6–7 (Diehl, 1925).
23 *Ath. Pol.*, 13–15; Herodotus, 5.62 (landing at Marathon). For the Pisistratid estates at Brauron, see Plato, *Hipparchus*, 228b; Plutarch, *Solon*, 10.
24 Alcaeus, frag. Z24 (Lobel-Page).
25 Aristotle, *Politics*, 1274b.18–19, specifically maintains that Pittacus was a law-giver but not the author of a constitution.
26 Diodorus, 14.43.2–3.

Appendix
The Historical Basis of the Homeric Background Picture

1 *Iliad* 10.261–5; Lorimer, *HM*, pp. 212–19, pl. 15; D. L. Page, *History and the Homeric Iliad* (Berkeley, 1959), p. 218; G. S. Kirk, *ODC*, p. 176 (191).
2 *Iliad* 11.632ff.
3 *Iliad* 7.219; 11.485; 17.128: φέρων σάκος ἠΰτε πύργον. Lorimer, *HM*, pp. 182, 134ff, figs. 1, 2, 3, 7, 8. Ajax's shield is slung over his left shoulder by a telamon, is obviously very heavy, and is used in the 'stationary fight' in which he is said to be Achilles' equal, and for which the body-shield is adapted (*Iliad* 14.402; 16.106; 13.324–5).
4 KN Np 973: 'Ai–wa'.
5 Page, *HHI*, pp. 233–8.
6 *Iliad* 6.116 (the rim of Hector's shield bangs against his neck and ankles as he walks); 15.646 (Periphetes trips over the bottom rim of his shield). Page, *HHI*, p. 234; Kirk, *SH*, p. 181.
7 Page, *HHI*, pp. 238ff; Kirk, *SH*, p. 111, n. 3; p. 115, n. 1; *HPH*, pp. 15–16, 19; *ODC*, pp. 185–6 (200–1).
8 Page, *HHI*, ch. 4.
9 Kirk, *ODC*, p. 185 (200).
10 Kirk, *HPH*, p. 15.
11 Kirk, *ODC*, p. 176 (191), suggests the technique of metal inlay 'described with some probable contamination in *Iliad* 18'; also the hundred broad gates of Egyptian Thebes (*Iliad* 9.381–4). He rightly refuses to add the plan of Odysseus' palace, despite D. H. F. Gray, 'Houses in the Odyssey', *CQ* (New Series), 5 (1955), 7ff. No amount of scholarly draughtsmanship can alter the fact that the Homeric palaces are not Mycenaean palaces or any known ones: see Finley, *Early Greece*, p. 83.
12 T. B. L. Webster, *CH*, p. 460. But he draws the opposite and incredible conclusion, that the true Mycenaean scale was known but 'deliberately reduced to make the past credible'!
13 *Odyssey* 14.96ff; M. I. Finley, *The*

NOTES

World of Odysseus, p. 166; *HMPT*, pp. 192–3 (134–5).
14 Finley, *HMPT*.
15 *Odyssey* 1.387.
16 See Finley's comparative table, *HMPT*, p. 199(141).
17 M. Parry, *L'Epithète traditionnelle dans Homère* (Paris, 1928), esp. pp. 113, 185–6; M. Ventris and J. Chadwick, *Documents in Mycenaean Greek* (Cambridge, 1956), pp. 121–2.
18 *Iliad* 9.121ff.
19 E.g. *Iliad* 18.373ff; 23.259, 513 etc.; *Odyssey* 4.129; 13.13.
20 Finley, *Early Greece*, p. 83; S. Benton, 'Excavations in Ithaca III' and 'The Evolution of the Tripod-Lebes', *BSA*, 35 (1934–5), 52ff, for many examples of bronze tripod-cauldrons of the ninth and eighth centuries. The earliest known ornamental tripod-lebes is of Protogeometric date (*AA*, 1935, 286, fig. 15). See also Kirk, *ODC*, p. 178 (193).
21 *Iliad* 9.128 (the Lesbians); 1.115 (Clytaemnestra compared with Chryseis); H. Strasburger, 'Der Soziologische Aspekt der homerischen Epen', *Gymnasium*, 60 (1953), 107ff.
22 E.g. *Iliad* 6.48; 10.379; 11.133; *Odyssey* 14.324; 21.10; Lorimer, *HM*, pp. 118–19.
23 *Odyssey* 9.391–3.
24 *Iliad* 23.834–5.
25 J. Chadwick, *The Decipherment of Linear B* (Pelican, Harmondsworth, 1958), p. 116.
26 Lorimer, *HM*, pp. 111–12.
27 The only verified case seems to be Tomb 41 at Prosymna: see Blegen, *Prosymna*, pp. 143, 242.
28 Lorimer, *HM*, pp. 103–10. Kirk, *ODC*, p. 178 (193), says that 'the rare assumptions in Homer that cremation is the normal means of disposal of the dead must be Protogeometric or Geometric in origin'. They deserve credit for more significance than that – how many allusions can Kirk find to inhumation as the normal method?
29 Mylonas, *CH*, pp. 481ff.
30 Lorimer, *HM*, p. 105. Colophon admittedly gives us our only evidence of Geometric Age sepulture in Ionia, but its cremation deposits are unmixed.
31 *Odyssey* 11.218ff.
32 *Iliad* 9.546.
33 *Odyssey* 24.417.
34 *Iliad* 23.71.
35 *Odyssey* 11.72–6.
36 *Ibid.* 12.13.
37 Lorimer, *HM*, p. 120.
38 E. Pfuhl, 'Der archaische Friedhof am Stadtberge von Thera', *AM*, 28 (1903), 1ff.
39 Mylonas, *CH*, p. 486; Lorimer, *HM*, p. 110.
40 Hesiod, *Works and Days*, 654.
41 *Odyssey* 6.7–10.
42 J. M. Cook, 'Old Smyrna', *BSA*, 53–4 (1958–9), 12. For other typical peninsular sites in Ionia, see his *The Greeks in Ionia and the East* (London, 1962), pp. 30ff and pls. 5, 6 (photographs of Lebedos and Myonnesus).
43 Lorimer, *HM*, p. 97.
44 *Odyssey* 7.22ff.
45 *Ibid.* 6.262ff; Lorimer, *HM*, p. 429; C. A. Roebuck, *Ionian Trade and Colonization* (New York, 1959), p. 40; E. Akurgal, 'The Early Period and Golden Age of Ionia', *AJA*, 66 (1962), 369ff. On the separate temple as a post-Mycenaean development, see Kirk, *ODC*, p. 179 (194): the only probable exception is a small temple at Delos, described by G. de Santerre, *Délos Primitive et Archaïque* (Paris, 1958), pp. 89ff; otherwise the earliest separate roofed temples belong to the later ninth century, the temple of Hera Akraia at Perachora being the firmest example.
46 J. M. Cook, 'Old Smyrna', p. 20f.
47 *Iliad* 24.448–56; 1.39.
48 *Ibid.* 18.737–9.
49 *Odyssey* 22.465–7.
50 *Ibid.* 8.556–62. Note also the mysterious reference to long voyages covered in supernaturally quick time and without fatigue (7.325–6), and the fact that the Phaeacians are remote from other mortal men, very dear to the gods, and never to be attacked by enemies (6.201ff).
51 *Odyssey* 6.57–65; 13.15; Strasburger, 'Der Soziologische Aspekt', p. 106. Note also *Odyssey* 7.20ff, where the daughter of a nobleman whose house stood near the king's is found carrying a pitcher through the streets (Athene in disguise).
52 G. S. Kirk, 'War and the Warrior in the Homeric Poems', *Problèmes*, pp. 101–2, 104.
53 *Ibid.* pp. 113, 115ff.
54 J. M. Cook, 'Old Smyrna', p. 12, for the ninth-century embattled wall-circuit (note reconstruction, also reproduced in his *The Greeks in Ionia and the East*, p. 31, fig. 4). Akurgal, 'The Early Period and Golden Age of Ionia', pp. 369ff, notes that Smyrna Level II was perhaps destroyed after a siege, and he suggests a connexion with Colophon's conquest of Aeolian Smyrna, an event recorded by Mimnermus, frag. 12 (Diehl, 1925), and by Herodotus, 1.50, although the latter attributes it to treachery.
55 *Iliad* 7.132ff; 11.670ff.

56 Note also that there are no Bronze Age representations of chariot-races, and hardly any of chariots with a single occupant.
57 *Odyssey* 14.199ff.
58 Four different views of the nature of the Bronze Age Greek participation in the destruction of Troy are presented by M. I. Finley, J. L. Caskey, G. S. Kirk, and D. L. Page, in 'The Trojan War', *JHS*, 84 (1964), 1–20.
59 Kirk, *Problèmes*, p. 99; V. R. d'A. Desborough, *The Last Mycenaeans and their Successors* (Oxford, 1964), p. 219.
60 Finley, 'The Trojan War', pp. 2ff.
61 E.g. Hesiod, frag. 96.40–9 (Rzach).
62 *Iliad* 2.286 (Odysseus scorns the assembled Achaeans as 'not fulfilling the promises they made to Agamemnon' by wanting to be off home); *Iliad* 1.163–71 (Agamemnon's large cut of all spoils); *Iliad* 9.328–33 (Achilles claims to have himself sacked twelve cities by sea and eleven by land, and to have brought all the spoils to Agamemnon, who kept most for himself and distributed only a small part).
63 *Iliad* 2.202.
64 E.g. C. M. Bowra, *Early Greek Elegists* (London, 1938), p. 65; A. W. H. Adkins, *Merit and Responsibility* (Oxford, 1960), p. 40, who argues that the agonal instincts of the Homeric nobles are so strong that the co-operative excellences must always take second place to them.
65 Finley, *The World of Odysseus*, p. 33.
66 E.g. *Iliad* 12.243; 3.50; compare 6.403; 22.56.
67 *Iliad* 9.300–3.
68 *Ibid.* 590–6.
69 *Ibid.* 515–23, 600–5.
70 *Iliad* 15.496–9, 502–5. Compare *Odyssey* 8.523–5.
71 *Odyssey* 8.101–3, 250–3.
72 See further P. A. L. Greenhalgh, 'Patriotism in the Homeric World', *Historia*, 21 (1972), 528–37.
73 Kirk, *ODC*, p. 179 (194), accepts only three clear references to hoplite warfare: *Iliad* 12.105; 13.130ff; 16.212ff. I think we must add 13.340–3.
74 Kirk, *HPH*, p. 14.
75 Aristotle, *Politics*, 1287a.16–18.

List of numbered vase-paintings in Chapters I–III (bold numbers)

Vase	Chariot type	Style and date		
1	G1	LG Ia (760–750)	Paris A517; *GGP*, pl. 7a; Davison, fig. 3.	
2	G1	LG Ia	Athens 802; *GGP*, p. 31, n. 18; Davison, fig. 10c.	
3	G1	LG Ia	Paris A523; *GGP*, p. 30; Davison, fig. 14.	
4	G1	LG Ia	Paris A522; *GGP*, p. 30; Davison, fig. 15a–b.	
5	G1	LG Ib (750–735)	Paris A547; *GGP*, p. 31; Davison, fig. 22. (Note four-horse team.)	
6	G1	LG Ib	Athens 990; *GGP*, pl. 8b; Davison, fig. 25; Reichel, *Homerische Waffen*, p. 124, fig. 64.	figs. 7, 26
7	G1	LG Ib	New York 14.130.14; *GGP*, p. 42; Davison, fig. 26. (Note three-horse team.)	
8	G2	LG	*Ann. dell'Inst.*, 1872, pl. i2; *Préhistoire*, 1 (1932), 247, fig. 26; Reichel, *Homerische Waffen*, p. 125, fig. 67.	fig. 6
9	G3a	LG Ia–b (c. 750)	Athens 806; *GGP*, p. 46; *AJA*, 44 (1940), pl. 25; Ahlberg, fig. 53. (Earliest charioteer to wear the long robe.)	fig. 18
10	G3a	LG IIa (735–720)	Athens, Agora P4885; *GGP*, p. 55; *HM*, pl. 26.3; *EGAW*, pl. 2; Ahlberg, fig. 2; Davison, fig. 97. (The 'Molione' in battle with their chariot.)	fig. 3
11	G3a	LG IIa	Eleusis 454; *GGP*, p. 55; Davison, fig. 99.	
12	G3a	LG IIa	Athens 14763; *GGP*, p. 55; *BSA*, 47 (1952), pl. 3a; Davison, fig. 101.	
13	G3a	LG IIa	London 1899.2–19.1; *JHS*, 19 (1899), 198–201, pl. 8; *GGP*, p. 55; Davison, fig. 98. (A naked rider with two horses, the second indicated by the two pairs of reins, is in a procession of chariots with single, robed charioteers.)	fig. 8
14	G3a	LG IIb (720–700)	New York 10.210.7; *GGP*, pp. 81–2; Davison, fig. 51. (On the neck are antithetical horses whose bridles are held by a plumed-helmeted warrior with round shield.)	

LISTS OF VASE-PAINTINGS

Vase	Chariot type	Style and date	
15	G3*a*	LG IIb	Athens, Stathatou collection 222; *GGP*, p. 59, pl. 11g; Davison, fig. 115.
16	G3*a*	LG IIb	Athens 894; *GGP*, p. 58; Davison, fig. 33. (A four-horse chariot of an elongated G3*a* type with two warriors aboard precedes a two-horse chariot of the same type with a single occupant.)
17	G3*a*	LG IIb	Oxford 1916.55; *GGP*, p. 55; Davison, fig. 111a–b.
18	G3*a*	LG IIb	Athens, Agora P4990; *GGP*, p. 58; Davison, fig. 36; *Hesperia*, Supp. 2 (1939), 55–7, figs. 37–8. (Race of chariots with single, robed occupants and three-horse teams.)
19	G3*a*	LG IIb	Baltimore 48.2231; *GGP*, p. 58; Davison, fig. 35. (Note the three-horse teams.)
20	G3*b*	LG IIb	Cleveland 1927.27.6; *GGP*, p. 58; Davison, fig. 34.
21	G3*b*	LG IIb	Athens 184; *GGP*, p. 55; Davison, fig. 96.
22	G3*b*	LG IIb	Toronto 929.22.10 (C951); *GGP*, p. 59; Davison, *fig. 9* fig. 119. (Solitary rider in a procession of chariots.)
23	G3*c*	LG IIa	Leiden I.1909/1.1; *GGP*, p. 55, pl. 11a–b; *fig. 10* Davison, fig. 94.
24	G3*c*	LG IIa	Paris, Musée Rodin; *GGP*, p. 55; Davison, fig. 95.
25	G3*c*	LG IIa	London 1914.4–13.1; *GGP*, p. 67; Davison, fig. 102.
26	G3*c/f*	LG IIa	Erlangen I.458; *GGP*, p. 67; Davison, fig. 77a–c. *fig. 15*
27	G3*d*	LG IIb	Athens 17935; *GGP*, pp. 58, 61, pl. 11c.
28	G3*d*	LG IIb	Berlin 3203; *GGP*, pp. 57–8; Davison, fig. 48a–b. *fig. 11*
29	G3*d*	LG IIb	Philadelphia MS5464; *GGP*, pp. 57–8; Davison, fig. 49.
30	G3*d*	Latest LG IIb (*c.* 700)	Oxford 1935.19; *GGP*, p. 145, n. 5; Davison, fig. 59; *BSA*, 35 (1934–5), pl. 38a.
31	G3*d*	EPA	Munich 1351; *BSA*, 35 (1934–5), pl. 41; *GPP*, pl. 14b; Strong, *The Classical World*, pl. 27; *Arch. Hom.*, p. F115, fig. 20i (detail); Anderson, *Ancient Greek Horsemanship*, pl. 2c. (Solitary rider in a procession of chariots with single, robed occupants.)
32	G3*e*	Sub-G	Rome, Villa Giulia 1212; *GGP*, p. 60; Davison, *fig. 12* fig. 126a–b (poor illustration, not showing rider); *AJA*, 68 (1964), 174ff, pls. 57–8; *Arch. Hom.*, p. F115, fig. 20f. (A solitary rider, whose two pairs of reins indicate a second horse, appears in a procession of alternate two-horse chariots and warriors on foot armed with round shield and twin spears. The chariots show both side-rails.)

LISTS OF VASE-PAINTINGS

Vase	Chariot type	Style and date		
33	G3e	EPA	New York 10.210.8; *GGP*, p. 206; *BSA*, 35 (1934–5), pl. 47; Davison, fig. 69a–b. (Mourners on the neck. Procession of alternate naked riders and robed charioteers round the belly. Both side-rails shown as on **32**.)	*fig. 13*
34	G3*f*	LG Ib	London, Baring collection; *GGP*, p. 32; Davison, fig. 93.	
35	G3*f*	EPA	Oxford 1935.18; *BSA*, 35 (1934–5), 182, fig. 5; Davison, fig. 54.	
36	G3*f*	EPA	London 1936.10–17.1; Davison, fig. 55.	
37	G3*f*	EPA	New York 21.88.18; *BSA*, 35 (1934–5), pl. 50; Davison, fig. 57.	*fig. 14*
38	G3*d*?	LG IIb	Buffalo C12847; *GGP*, p. 59; Alföldi, p. 24, n. 94, pl. 7.1; *Arch. Hom.*, p. F119, n. 397, pl. F IVa. (A rider, perhaps with bell-corslet, appears brandishing a javelin and leading a second horse in a procession of three-horse chariots containing a driver and a warrior armed with two spears.)	
39		Early LG IIb	London 1927.4–11.1; *GGP*, p. 73; Davison, fig. 136; Forrest, *The Emergence of Greek Democracy*, p. 57 (plate). (Four-horse chariots of type G3*f* but elongated and given two profile wheels to accommodate two warriors.)	
40		LG IIb	Borowski amphora, on loan in Berlin in 1960, now in the Folkwangmuseum, Essen. (Four-horse chariots, as on **39**.)	*fig. 27*
41		Late LG IIb	Athens 810; *GGP*, p. 60; Davison, fig. 38; *AM*, 17 (1892), 226, fig. 10; *HM*, p. 231, fig. 28; Helbig, p. 166, fig. 1; *Arch. Hom.*, p. F119, n. 397, fig. 20c. (The fragments show a helmeted rider on a rearing horse, four-horse chariots, and warriors on foot with round shields and twin spears.)	*fig. 32*
42	(G1)	LG Ib	Sydney 46.41; *GGP*, p. 31; Davison, fig. 21. (Fragment showing three-horse team – the chariot itself is missing.)	
43	(G1)	LG Ib	Paris A541; *GGP*, p. 32; Davison, fig. 23; *CVA* France 1 (Louvre 1), pl. 13.1–19, 14.1–3.	
44	G3*f*	EPA	Athens 3820–2; *BSA*, 35 (1934–5), pl. 48.	
45		Boeotian Sub-G	Munich 2234; *GGP*, p. 205; *BSA*, 42 (1947), 123, fig. 12; *HM*, pl. 6.2; Ahlberg, fig. 46; G. Lippold, *Münchener Archäologische Studien* (1909), 451, fig. 21. (Battle-scene with chariot of type similar to G3*e* but elongated and with two profile wheels. Robed driver and warrior with rectangular shield on chariot. Ajax (?) on foot, with his great thrusting-spear.)	*fig. 4*

LISTS OF VASE-PAINTINGS

Vase	Chariot type	Style and date		
46		Attic Bf	London B304; *JHS*, 5 (1884), 192; Anderson, *Ancient Greek Horsemanship*, pl. 16; Johansen, *The Iliad in Early Greek Art*, fig. 39 (harnessing of racing-chariot on belly), 52 (battle-scene on shoulder).	*figs. 16, 17*
47		Attic Bf	Cracow 1245; *ABV*, p. 380; Johansen, *The Iliad in Early Greek Art*, p. 148, fig. 54; *CVA* Pologne 2, pl. 6.2a–b.	
48		Attic Bf	Boston 63.473; Johansen, *The Iliad in Early Greek Art*, p. 149, fig. 55. (Like **47**, this vase depicts Achilles dragging Hector's body. Achilles himself is on foot while the chariot, a four-horsed contemporary racing-type, is driven by a robed charioteer.)	

Lists of numbered vase-paintings in Chapters V and VI

(The vases are numbered in order of first mention in the relevant sections of the text of Chapters V and VI.)

LIST OF CORINTHIAN VASE-PAINTINGS ('C' NUMBERS)

C1	London 1969.12-15.1; *BMQ*, 36 (1971-2), 42ff.	*fig. 37*
C2	Athens 341; Payne, *NC*, p. 287, no. 482; Alföldi, p. 14, fig. 1; *Arch. Hom.*, p. F120, fig. 22.	*fig. 36*
C3	*Perachora*, vol. 2, no. 1571, pl. 61.	*fig. 45*
C4	Rome, Villa Giulia 22679 (the 'Chigi' vase); Payne, *PV*, pls. 27-9; Johansen, *VS*, pl. 39; *CVA* Italy 1 (Villa Giulia 1), pl. 1; *BSA*, 42 (1947), 81, fig. 2 (hoplite battle only).	
C5	*AE*, 1970, 86-113, pl. 34.	
C6	*Perachora*, vol. 2, no. 2434, pl. 97.	*fig. 46*
C7	*Perachora*, vol. 2, no. 1556, pl. 61.	*fig. 47*
C8	*Perachora*, vol. 2, no. 1590, pl. 61.	*fig. 48*
C9	Brussels; Payne, *NC*, no. 986, pl. 34.8; A. Furtwängler, *Sammlung Somzée* (1897), p. 77, pl. 43; Helbig, p. 246, fig. 32.	*fig. 50*
C10	Athens 330; Payne, *NC*, no. 991, pl. 32.2.	*fig. 51*
C11	Brussels; Payne, *NC*, no. 996; Alföldi, pl. 4.2-3.	
C12	London B39 (84.8-4.7); Payne, *NC*, no. 1399, pl. 39.1, 3.	
C13	London 1814.7-4.491 (OC421); Payne, *NC*, no. 1090.	*fig. 52*
C14	Brunswick (AT) 235; *CVA* Deutschland 4 (Braunschweig), pls. 149-50.	*fig. 53*
C15	Copenhagen 3259; *CVA* Danemark 2 (Copenhague 2), pl. 93.4a-b.	
C16	Paris E628; Payne, *NC*, no. 1169; Pottier, pl. 45.	
C17	Paris E629; Payne, *NC*, no. 1186; Pottier, pl. 46.	
C18	Paris E630; Payne, *NC*, no. 1181d; Pottier, pl. 46.	
C19	Brussels A710; Payne, *NC*, no. 1181c; *CVA* Belgium 1 (Brussels 1), pl. 10.4a.	
C20	California 8/361; *CVA* U.S.A. 5 (California 1), pl. 188.1b.	*fig. 54*
C21	Orvieto 2727; Payne, *NC*, pp. 109, 318, no. 1197; *CVA* Italy 41 (Orvieto 1), pls. 1859.2, 1862.1.	
C22	Riehen, private collection; Alföldi, pl. 6.2.	
C23	Naples H683; Payne, *NC*, no. 1172; Gerhard, *AV*, pl. 220.	
C24	Leipzig T4849; Payne, *NC*, no. 1483; *CVA* Deutschland 14 (Leipzig 1), pl. 688.	*fig. 55*

LISTS OF VASE-PAINTINGS

- C25 *Perachora*, vol. 2, p. 255, no. 2473.
- C26 Paris E637; Payne, *NC*, no. 1475, fig. 19a (but this drawing fails to show the outline of the second horse); Pottier, vol. 2, p. 57.
- C27 Paris A437; Pottier, pl. 14; *CVA* France 12 (Louvre 8), pl. 493.2.
- C28 Brussels A1011; *CVA* Belgium 1 (Brussels 1), pl. 10.1a.
- C29 Paris E646; Payne, *NC*, no. 1423; Pottier, pl. 51.
- C30 Syracuse; Payne, *NC*, no. 1168; *Mon. Ant.*, 19 (1908), 90ff, pls. 1–2.
- C31 Paris E647; Pottier, pl. 51.
- C32 London B38.
- C33 Paris E636; Payne, *NC*, no. 1456, pl. 41.4; Pottier, pl. 49.
- C34 Paris E638; Payne, *NC*, no. 1474; Pottier, pl. 50.
- C35 Madrid 10840; Payne, *NC*, no. 1482; *CVA* Espagne 1 (Madrid 1), pl. 15.
- C36 Paris L49 (CA4); Payne, *NC*, no. 1405a (given as L176 instead of L49); *CVA* France 9 (Louvre 6), pl. 391.13.
- C37 Rome, Mus. Cap. 28; Payne, *NC*, no. 1479; *CVA* Italy 36 (Rome, Mus. Cap. 1), pl. 1606.
- C38 Brussels A1035; Payne, *NC*, no. 891; *CVA* Belgium 1 (Brussels 1), pl. 8.2.
- C39 New York 12.2299; Payne, *NC*, no. 1195, pls. 34.7, 33.6.
- C40 Bucharest 18801; *CVA* Rumania 2 (Bucharest 2), pl. 52.1, 6.
- C41 Heidelberg 84; *CVA* Deutschland 10 (Heidelberg 1), pl. 446.6–8.
- C42 Paris E639; Payne, *NC*, no. 1461; *JdI*, 1886, pl. 10.1a.
- C43 Paris E621; Payne, *NC*, no. 1481; Pottier, pl. 44.
- C44 London 1933.10-26.1.
- C45 Paris E633; Pottier, pl. 47.
- C46 Leipzig; Payne, *NC*, no. 1454; *AA*, 1923-4, 71, fig. 12.

LIST OF ATTIC VASE-PAINTINGS ('A' NUMBERS)

A1	Athens 15.995.	*fig. 34*
A2	Berlin 31006 (Pergamonmuseum); *BSA*, 35 (1934–5), 179; *CVA* Deutschland 2 (Berlin 1), pls. 88.4, 87.2.	*fig. 35*
A3	Berlin 31.573.141 or A41 (Pergamonmuseum); *CVA* Deutschland 2 (Berlin 1), pls. 76, 80.2; *BSA*, 42 (1947),90, fig. 6.	*fig. 44*
A4	Berlin F56; *BSA*, 35 (1934–5), 188, 192, 202; *CVA* Deutschland 2 (Berlin 1), pl. 90; *BSA*, 42 (1947), 86, fig. 4.	
A5	Athens, Acropolis 553; Graef, *AcrV.*, pl. 25.	
A6	Athens, Acropolis 466; Graef, *AcrV.*, pl. 22f.	
A7	Naples; *ABV*, p. 58, no. 119; *Mon. Ant.*, 22 (1913), pl. 57; Beazley, *MMS*, 5 (1934), no. 82, fig. 20; Anderson, *AGH*, pl. 29; Metzger-Berchem, pl. 57.4.	*fig. 56*
A8	Gotha Z.V. 2477; *ABV*, p. 101; *CVA* Deutschland 24 (Gotha 1), pl. 1150.2.	
A9	Athens 531; *ABV*, p. 55; Beazley, *MMS*, 5 (1934), no. 65, figs. 16, 17.	
A10	Würzburg 451; *ABV*, p. 57; Beazley, *MMS*, 5 (1934), no. 80, figs. 18, 19; Langlotz, *G.V. in Würz.*, pls. 126.2, 117.6, 127.	
A11	Athens, Agora P24946 (ΣA3055).	
A12	Athens, Acropolis 590; Graef, *AcrV.*, pls. 27a, d; Beazley, *AJA* 54 (1950), 310; Brommer, *Vasenlisten*, vol. 2, p. 350.	
A13	Berlin 4823; *ABV*, p. 81 (Painter of Acropolis 606, no. 4); Beazley, *Attic Black-Figure, A Sketch*, pls. 2.3, 3.2; Metzger-Berchem, pl. 56.3.	

LISTS OF VASE-PAINTINGS

A14 London B379; *ABV*, p. 60; Helbig, fig. 3.
A15 Athens 15.261.
A16 Vatican 369; *Mus. Greg.*, vol. 2, pl. 68; Albizzati, pp. 153-4, figs. 93, 94; *ABV*, p. 227; Beazley, *MMS*, 5 (1934), 114.
A17 Taranto; *CVA* Italy 18 (Taranto 2), pl. 869.1, 3. *fig. 57*
A18 Paris E870; *ABV*, p. 105; Pottier, pl. 60.
A19 Paris, inv. Campana 259; *CVA* France 1 (Louvre 1), pl. 35.12.
A20 Paris E857 (inv. Campana 285); Pottier, p. 79; *CVA* France 1 (Louvre 1), pl. 35.16.
A21 London B381; *ABV*, p. 61; *CVA* G.B. 2 (B.M. 2), pl. 67.2c; Helbig, fig. 8.
A22 Tarquinia 617; *CVA* Italy 26 (Tarquinia 2), pl. 1174.1.
A23 Tarquinia 1550; *CVA* Italy 26 (Tarquinia 2), pl. 1172.1.
A24 Marseilles, Mus. Borély 3000; *ABV*, p. 51; Beazley, *MMS*, 5 (1934), 105, no. 3, fig. 14.
A25 Athens 532; *ABV*, p. 52; Beazley, *MMS*, 5 (1934), 103, no. 12, fig. 13.
A26 Mainz 89; *CVA* Deutschland 15 (Mainz 1), pl. 734.3-4.
A27 Paris F65; *ABV*, p. 52; Pottier, pl. 68; Beazley, *MMS*, 5 (1934), 104, no. 11; *CVA* France 12 (Louvre 8), pl. 509.9.
A28 Laon 371015; *ABV*, p. 681; *CVA* France 20 (Laon 1), pl. 892.1, 3.
A29 Munich 86000; *CVA* Deutschland 9 (Munich 3), pl. 420.3 (also drawing of figured zone, p. 34).
A30 Athens 15.116, formerly Acropolis 606; *ABV*, p. 81; Graef, *AcrV.*, pl. 31; *fig. 58* Anderson, *AGH*, pl. 30a.
A31 Orvieto.
A32 Leipzig T314; *CVA* Deutschland 14 (Leipzig 1), pl. 679.2, 4. *fig. 59*
A33 Paris, inv. Campana 256; *CVA* France 1 (Louvre 1), pl. 34.12.
A34 Copenhagen 13536; *ABV*, p. 714; *CVA* Danemark 8 (Copenhague 8), pls. 322-4.
A35 Warsaw 138536; *ABV*, p. 61; *CVA* Pologne 4 (Varsovie 1), pl. 163.2, 164.1; Metzger-Berchem, pl. 57.3.
A36 London B76; *ABV*, p. 85.
A37 London B380; *ABV*, p. 55; *CVA* G.B. 2 (B.M. 2), pl. 66.1b; Alföldi, *fig. 60* pl. 5.2; Helbig, fig. 4.
A38 Laon 371017; *CVA* France 20 (Laon 1), pl. 875.2-3.
A39 Florence 3799; *CVA* Italy 42 (Firenze 5), pl. 1873.1.
A40 California 8/60; *CVA* U.S.A. 5 (California 1), pl. 200.2b, d.
A41 New York 01.8.6 (G.R. 521); Beazley, *MMS*, 5 (1934), 95, no. 4, figs. 2, 3; *CVA* U.S.A. 11 (Metropolitan Museum 2), pl. 2.2a.
A42 Paris E876; *ABV*, pp. 90, 683; Pottier, p. 83, pl. 62; *CVA* France 2 (Louvre 2), pl. 71.4.
A43 London B49; *ABV*, pp. 326, 715; *CVA* G.B. 4 (B.M. 3), pl. 155.2b.
A44 London B400; *ABV*, p. 163.
A45 Naples 81292; *ABV*, p. 109 (given as Naples 2770); *CVA* Italy 20 *fig. 61* (Naples 1), pl. 950; Metzger-Berchem, pl. 50.1.
A46 Vandoeuvres (Geneva); Metzger-Berchem, pls. 55, 56.2.
A47 Athens, Ceramicus HS227.
A48 London B191; *ABV*, pp. 152, 325, 687; *CVA* G.B. 4 (B.M. 3), pl. 164.5b. *fig. 62*
A49 New York 25.78.4; *ABV*, pp. 119, 685; Beazley, *MMS*, 5 (1934), 114, no. 82; *CVA* U.S.A. 11 (Metropolitan Museum 2), pl. 10.12b.

LISTS OF VASE-PAINTINGS

A50	Warsaw 142320, formerly Goluchów 20; *ABV*, p. 300; *CVA* Pologne 1 (Goluchów), pl. 10.2a–b.	*fig. 63*
A51	Paris E804; *ABV*, p. 108; Rumpf, *Sakonides*, pl. 12b.	
A52	Paris F72; Pottier, pl. 69; *CVA* France 14 (Louvre 9), pl. 621.	*fig. 64*
A53	Berlin 1797; *ABV*, p. 227; Helbig, pl. 2.2 (facing p. 220).	*fig. 65*
A54	Tarquinia RC1886; *CVA* Italy 25 (Tarquinia 1), pl. 1151.1.	
A55	Paris F306; *ABV*, p. 263; *CVA* France 2 (Louvre 2), pl. 75.7.	
A56	Athens, Ceramicus HS583.	
A57	Paris F75; *ABV*, pp. 156, 688; Pottier, pl. 69; Karouzou, *The Amasis Painter*, no. 62, pl. 14.1–2; *CVA* France 14 (Louvre 9), pl. 622.3–10.	
A58	Cambridge N132; *CVA* G.B. 11 (Cambridge 2), pl. 500.29.	
A59	Roman Market (Basseggio), formerly Depoletti; *ABV*, p. 675 ('Stroibos Kalos' no. 4); Gerhard, *AV*, pl. 190.3–4.	
A60	Munich 2242 (J. 971); Bothmer, ch. 4, no. 121, pl. 56.	
A61	Paris F217; *ABV*, p. 298; Pottier, pl. 79; *CVA* France 5 (Louvre 4), pl. 206.1, 3.	
A62	Brunswick AT239; *ABV*, p. 307; *CVA* Deutschland 4 (Braunschweig), pl. 153.3–4.	
A63	London B213; *ABV*, p. 143. (*CVA* fails to show relevant scene on shoulder.)	
A64	London B375.	*fig. 66*
A65	New York 41.162.116, formerly Gallatin collection; *CVA* U.S.A. 8 (Fogg and Gallatin), pl. 389.5a–b.	*fig. 67*
A66	Paris, inv. Campana 11290; *CVA* France 19 (Louvre 12), pls. 863.1, 864.1–4.	
A67	Mannheim 43; *ABV*, p. 517; *CVA* Deutschland 13 (Mannheim 1), pl. 604.1–2.	
A68	New York, Gallatin collection; *CVA* U.S.A. 1 (Gallatin), pl. 25.2.	
A69	Bologna C254 (Pellegrini 35); *ABV*, p. 341; *CVA* Italy 7 (Bologna 2), pl. 317.4.	
A70	Capua 145; *ABV*, p. 694; *CVA* Italy 23 (Mus. Campano 2), pls. 1065.2, 1066.1.	
A71	Brussels A2135; *ABV*, p. 505; *CVA* Belgium 2 (Brussels 2), pl. 62.6.	
A72	Athens, Acropolis 1957.Αα498.	*fig. 68*
A73	Laon 37.910; *ABV*, p. 499; *CVA* France 20 (Laon 1), pl. 887.8–9.	
A74	Paris C10354; *CVA* France 17 (Louvre 10), pl. 735.1.	*fig. 69*
A75	Bologna, Coll. Palagi 1432 (Pellegrini PU194); *ABV*, p. 288; *CVA* Italy 7 (Bologna 2), pl. 310.	
A76	Würzburg 206; *ABV*, p. 282; Langlotz, *G.V. in Würz.*, no. 206, pl. 52.	*fig. 70*
A77	Munich 1502a (478); *ABV*, p. 321; Gerhard, *AV*, pl. 205.1–2; Bothmer, ch. 4, no. 105, pl. 55.4.	
A78	Havana, Lagunillas; Bothmer, ch. 4, no. 97, pl. 55.2.	
A79	Cambridge G.50; *ABV*, p. 270; Vos, p. 30, no. 313; *CVA* G.B. 6 (Cambridge 1), pl. 250.1.	
A80	London B249; *CVA* G.B. 5 (B.M. 4), pl. 206.1a–b; Bothmer, ch. 4, no. 98, pl. 55.3.	
A81	Bologna, Coll. Palagi 1436 (Pellegrini PU195); *ABV*, p. 288; Brommer, *Vasenlisten*, p. 136, no. 31; *CVA* Italy 7 (Bologna 2), pl. 314.2–3.	
A82	Brussels A2295; *CVA* Belgium 2 (Brussels 2), pl. 62.5a–b.	
A83	Naples 81144; *CVA* Italy 20 (Naples 1), pl. 973.5–6.	

LISTS OF VASE-PAINTINGS

A84 Karlsruhe B25; *CVA* Deutschland 7 (Karlsruhe 1), pl. 306.4.
A85 London E136; *ARV*, p. 50; Pfuhl, pl. 94, fig. 328.
A86 Orvieto 2604; *ABV*, pp. 652, 643-4; *CVA* Italy 41 (Orvieto 1), pl. 1847.1, 3.
A87 London 1949.2-17.1; Bothmer, ch. 6, no. 9, pl. 65.3.
A88 Bologna D.L. 58 (Pellegrini 21); *CVA* Italy 7 (Bologna 2), pl. 311.2.
A89 Paris, Musée Rodin TC152; *ABV*, p. 498; *CVA* France 16 (Mus. Rodin), pl. 705.12; Bothmer, ch. 5, no. 147.
A90 Laon 37972; *CVA* France 20 (Laon 1), pl. 882.6; Bothmer, ch. 5. no. 137.
A91 London B158; *ABV*, p. 368; *CVA* G.B. 4 (B.M. 3), pl. 147.2b; Bothmer, ch. 5, no. 111, pl. 63.1.
A92 London 99.7-21.3; *ABV*, p. 330; Gerhard, *AV*, pl. 199; Bothmer, ch. 5, no. 112, pl. 63.2.
A93 Honolulu 3594; *ABV*, p. 699; Bothmer, ch. 5, no. 141, pl. 63.7.
A94 Paris A481 (MNC 672); Pottier, pl. 18; Vos, p. 30, no. 295.
A95 Brussels R300; *ABV*, p. 288; *CVA* Belgium 3 (Brussels 3), pl. 117.2b; Bothmer, ch. 4, no. 96, pl. 55.1. *fig. 71*
A96 Paris F211; *ABV*, p. 368; *CVA* France 4 (Louvre 3), pl. 163.1, 3.
A97 Paris F206 (inv. Campana 166); *ABV*, p. 145; Technau, *Exekias*, pl. 22; *CVA* France 4 (Louvre 3), pl. 158.4.
A98 Paris, Petit Palais 311; *ABV*, pp. 337, 692; *CVA* France 15 (Petit Palais), pl. 647.2; Bothmer, ch. 4, no. 95.
A99 Bologna, Coll. Palagi 1437 (Pellegrini PU191); *CVA* Italy 7 (Bologna 2), pl. 302.3.
A100 Berlin 1720; *ABV*, p. 143; Technau, *Exekias*, pl. 2; Helbig, p. 184, fig. 10.
A101 Altenburg 214; *CVA* Deutschland 17 (Altenburg 1), pls. 803, 804.1, 805.1.
A102 Orvieto 2599; *CVA* Italy 41 (Orvieto 1), pl. 1839.
A103 Cambridge GR.13.1937.
A104 Tarquinia RC3454; *CVA* Italy 25 (Tarquinia 1), pl. 1141.2.
A105 Capua 144; *ABV*, p. 686; *CVA* Italy 23 (Mus. Campana 2), pls. 1069.2, 1070.1.
A106 Tarquinia RC5652; *CVA* Italy 26 (Tarquinia 2), pl. 1190.2.
A107 Athens, Ceramicus; *ABV*, p. 339; *AA*, 1933, 267, fig. 4.
A108 New York 41.85; *ABV*, p. 384; *CVA* U.S.A. 12 (Metropolitan Museum 3), pl. 553.2.

LIST OF 'CHALCIDIAN' VASE-PAINTINGS ('X' NUMBERS)

X1 Leningrad, Hermitage 1479; Rumpf, no. 104, pl. 109. *fig. 76*
X2 Bonn 464A; Rumpf, no. 150, pls. 135, 137.
X3 Florence 4210; Rumpf, no. 1, pl. 1.
X4 Pembroke-Hope; Rumpf, no. 5, pl. 12; Lorimer, *HM*, pl. 21.2.
X5 London B155; Rumpf, no. 6, pls. 13, 14, and fig. 1.
X6 London B75; Rumpf, no. 9, pl. 19.
X7 Paris E796; Rumpf, no. 34, pl. 68. *fig. 72*
X8 Leningrad, Hermitage 1312; Rumpf, no. 49, pl. 88.
X9 Naples market; Rumpf, no. 153, pl. 147.

LISTS OF VASE-PAINTINGS

X10 Baltimore, Robinson collection; *CVA* U.S.A. 4 (Baltimore, Robinson collection 1), pls. 150.1a, 151.1.
X11 Paris E797; Rumpf, no. 35, pl. 69.
X12 Tarquinia RC5655; Rumpf, no. 152, pl. 146.
X13 Orvieto; Rumpf, no. 151, pls. 139, 142.
X14 Florence 3776; Rumpf, no. 1, p. 184, fig. 15.
X15 Paris, Cabinet des Médailles 203; Rumpf, no. 4, pls. 10, 11; *CVA* France 7 (Paris, Bibl. Nat. 1), pl. 310.
X16 Würzburg L. 162; Rumpf, no. 25, pls. 49, 51. *fig. 73*
X17 Paris E802; Rumpf, no. 105, pl. 112. *fig. 74*
X18 Würzburg 160 (given by Rumpf as 315 and 457); Rumpf, no. 14, pls. 31, 32; Alföldi, pl. 2.1; Langlotz, *G.V. in Würz.*, pls. 23, 24. *fig. 75*
X19 Formerly Feoli-Magnoncour; Gerhard, *AV*, pl. 205.3-4; Rumpf, p. 182, fig. 12.
X20 Munich 592; Rumpf, no. 7, pl. 16.
X21 Würzburg 147; Rumpf, no. 114, pl. 129.
X22 Paris E798; Rumpf, no. VII, pl. 206.
X23 Vienna 1041; Rumpf, no VIII, pl. 209.
X24 Paris E812; Rumpf, no. XIV, pl. 215.
X25 Leningrad, Hermitage 2; Rumpf, no. XXVI, pls. 221-2.
X26 Tarquinia; Rumpf, no. XV, pl. 216.

INDEX OF COLLECTIONS

(This index contains only the vases referred to by numbers in the text. Details of publication can be found in the appropriate List of Vase-Paintings. The bold numbers are the mainly Geometric vases referred to in Chapters I – III. The 'C', 'A' and 'X' numbers refer to the Corinthian, Attic and Chalcidian vases discussed in Chapters V and VI, and they are numbered in order of first mention in the relevant sections of those chapters.)

ALTENBURG
Staatliches Lindenau-Museum:
214	A101

ATHENS
Acropolis Museum:
446	A6
553	A5
590	A12
606	A30
(now National Museum)	
Δα498	A78

Agora Museum:
P4885	**10**
P4990	**18**
P24946	A11

Ceramicus Museum:
–	A107
HS227	A47
HS583	A56

National Museum:
184	**21**
330	C10
341	C2
531	A9
532	A25
802	**2**
806	**9**
810	**41**
894	**16**
990	**6**
3820-2	**44**
14763	**12**
15116	A30
(= Acropolis 606)	
15261	A15
15995	A1
17935	**27**

Stathatou Collection:
St222	**15**

BALTIMORE
Robinson Collection:
see Oxford, Mississippi.
Walters Art Gallery:
48.2231	**19**

BERKELEY
University of California:
8/60	A40
8/361	C20

BERLIN
Staatliche Museen:
A41	A3
F56	A4
1720	A100
1797	A53
3203	**28**
4823	A13
31006	A2
Borowski amphora	**40**
(on loan in 1960)	

BOLOGNA
Museo Civico:
(PU = Palagi and Universitaria)
C254	A69
DL58	A88
PU1432	A75
PU1436	A81
PU1437	A99

BOSTON (Massachusetts)
Museum of Fine Arts:
63.473	**48**

INDEX OF COLLECTIONS

BRUNSWICK
Herzog Anton Ulrich-Museum:
235   C14
239   A62

BRUSSELS
Musées Royaux d'Art et d'Histoire:
–   C9
–   C11
A710   C19
A1011   C28
A1035   C38
A2135   A71
A2295   A82
R300   A95

BUCHAREST
Kalinderu Museum:
18801   C40

BUFFALO
Museum of Science:
C12847   **38**

CAMBRIDGE
Fitzwilliam Museum:
G50   A79
N132   A58
GR.13.1937   A103

CAPUA
Museo Campano:
144   A105
145   A70

CLEVELAND
Museum of Art:
1927.27.6   **20**

COPENHAGEN
National Museum:
3259   C15
13536   A34

CRACOW
Czartoryski Museum:
1245   **47**

ELEUSIS
Museum:
454   **11**

ERLANGEN
University:
I.458   **26**

ESSEN
Folkwangmuseum:
Borowski amphora   **40**

FLORENCE
Museo Archeologico Etrusco:
3776   X14
3799   A39
4210   X3

GENEVA
Vandoeuvres:
–   A46

GOLUCHOW
Prince Czartoryski: see Warsaw

GOTHA
Museum:
ZV2477   A8

HAVANA
Conde de Lagunillas:
–   A78

HEIDELBERG
University:
84   C41

HONOLULU
Academy of Arts:
3594   A93

KARLSRUHE
Badisches Landesmuseum:
B25   A84

LAON
Musée:
37910   A73
37972   A90
371015   A28
371017   A38

LEIDEN
Rijksmuseum:
I.1909/1.1   **23**

LEIPZIG
University:
–   C46
T314   A32
T4849   C24

LENINGRAD
Museum of the Hermitage:
1312   X8

LONDON
Baring Collection:
–   **34**
British Museum:
B38   C32
B39   C12
B49   A43
B75   X6
B76   A36
B155   X5

INDEX OF COLLECTIONS

B158	A91	10.210.8	**33**
B191	A48	12.2299	C39
B213	A63	14.130.14	**7**
B249	A80	21.88.18	**37**
B304	**46**	25.78.4	A49
B375	A64	41.85	A108
B379	A14	41.162.116	A65
B380	A37	(formerly Gallatin)	
B381	A21	Gallatin (now in *MMA*):	
B400	A44	–	A65
E136	A85	–	A68
1814.7-4.491	C13		
(= OC421)		ORVIETO	
1899.2-19.1	**13**	*Museo Claudio Faiana:*	
99.7-21.3	A92	–	A31
1914.4-13.1	**25**	192	X13
1927.4-11.1	**39**	2599	A102
1933.10-26.1	C44	2604	A86
1936.10-17.1	**36**	2727	C21
1949.2-17.1	A87		
1969.12-15.1	C1	OXFORD	
		Ashmolean Museum:	
MADRID		1916.55	**17**
Museo Arqueologico:		1935.18	**35**
10840	C35	1935.19	**30**
MAINZ		OXFORD (Mississippi)	
University:		*Robinson Collection*	X10
89	A26		
		PARIS	
MANNHEIM		*Cabinet des Médailles:*	
Schlossmuseum:		203	X15
43	A67	*Musée du Louvre:*	
		A437	C27
MARSEILLES		A481 (MNC672)	A94
Musée Borély:		A517	**1**
3000	A24	A522	**4**
		A523	**3**
MUNICH		A541	**43**
Mus. antiker Kleinkunst:		A547	**5**
592	X20	E621	C43
1351	**31**	E628	C16
1502a	A77	E629	C17
2234 (443)	**45**	E630	C18
2242	A60	E633	C45
86000	A29	E636	C33
		E637	C26
NAPLES		E638	C34
Museo Nazionale:		E639	C42
–	A7	E646	C29
H683	C23	E647	C31
H2770	A45	E796	X7
(= 81292)		E802	X17
81144	A83	E804	A51
Naples Market:		E857	A20
–	X9	(= inv. Camp. 285)	
		E870	A18
NEW YORK		E876	A42
Metropolitan Museum of Art:		F65	A27
GR521	A41	F72	A52
(= 01.8.6)		F75	A57
10.210.7	**14**	F206	A97

INDEX OF COLLECTIONS

F211	A96
F217	A61
F306	A55
L49	C36
inv. Campana 256	A33
inv. Campana 259	A19
inv. Campana 285	A20
(=E857)	
inv. Campana 11290	A66
C10354	A74
Musée Rodin:	
TC152	A89
Petit Palais:	
–	**24**
311	A98

PHILADELPHIA
University Museum:
MS5464	**29**

ROME
Capitol Museum:
28	C37

Vatican:
369	A16

Villa Giulia:
1212	**32**
22679	C4

Rome Market (Basseggio):
–	A59

SYDNEY
Nicholson Museum:
46.41	**42**

SYRACUSE
Museo Nazionale:
–	C30

TARANTO
Museo Nazionale:
–	A17

TARQUINIA
Museo Civico:
617	A22
1550	A23
RC1886	A54
RC3454	A104
RC5652	A106
RC5655	X12

TORONTO
Royal Ontario Museum:
929.22.10	**22**
(=C951)	

VIENNA
Kunsthistorisches Museum:
1041	X23

WARSAW
National Museum:
138536	A35
142320	A50
(formerly Goluchów 20)	

WÜRZBURG
University, Martin von Wagner-Museum:
L.162	X16
160	X18
(= 315 + 457)	
206	A76
451	A10

BIBLIOGRAPHY

Adcock, F. E. *The Greek and Macedonian Art of War* (Berkeley and Los Angeles, 1957).
Adkins, A. W. H. *Merit and Responsibility* (Oxford, 1960).
Ahlberg, G. 'Fighting on Land and Sea in Greek Geometric Art', *Acta Instituti Atheniensis Regni Sueciae*, Series in 4°, 16 (1971).
Akurgal, E. 'The Early Period and Golden Age of Ionia', *AJA*, 66 (1962), 369ff.
Albizzati, C. *Vasi antichi dipinti del Vaticano* (Rome, 1926).   Albizzati
Alföldi, A. 'Die Herrschaft der Reiterei in Griechenland und Rom nach   Alföldi
dem Sturz der Könige', *Gestalt und Geschichte: Festschrift K. Schefold* (Berne, 1967).
Amadasi, M.G. *L'iconografia del carro da guerra in Siria e Palestina* (Studi Semitici 17, Rome, 1965).
Anderson, J. K. *Ancient Greek Horsemanship* (Berkeley and Los Angeles,   *AGH*
1961).
—— 'Homeric, British and Cyrenaic Chariots', *AJA*, 69 (1965), 349–52.
Andrewes, A. *The Greek Tyrants* (London, 1962).
Andronikos, M. 'Totenkult', *Archaeologica Homerica* (Göttingen, 1968),   *Arch. Hom.*
vol. 3, ch. W.
Artemis Orthia 'The Sanctuary of Artemis Orthia at Sparta', *JHS*, Suppl. 5   *Artemis Orthia*
(London, 1929).
Asine see Frödin, C.   *Asine*
Beazley, J. D. *Attic Black-Figure, A Sketch* (London, 1928).
—— *Attic Black-Figure Vase-Painters* (Oxford, 1956).   *ABV*
—— 'Amasea', *JHS*, 51 (1931), 256–84.
—— *Attic Red-Figure Vase-Painters* (Oxford, 1963).   *ARV*
—— *The Development of Attic Black-Figure* (Berkeley, 1951).
—— *Etruscan Vase-Painting* (Oxford, 1947).   *EVP*
—— 'Little Master Cups', *JHS*, 52 (1932), 167ff.
—— 'The Troilus Cup', *MMS*, 5 (1934), 102–15.
Benton, S. 'Excavations in Ithaca III' and 'The Evolution of the Tripod-Lebes', *BSA*, 35 (1934–5), 45–73, 74–130.
Blegen, C. W. *Prosymna: the Helladic Settlement Preceding the Argive Heraeum*   *Prosymna*
(Cambridge, 1937).
Boardman, J. 'Early Euboean Pottery and History', *BSA*, 52 (1957), 1–29.
—— *The Greeks Overseas* (Penguin, Harmondsworth, 1964).

BIBLIOGRAPHY

Bothmer, D. von *Amazons in Greek Art* (Oxford, 1957).   Bothmer
Bowra, C. M. *Early Greek Elegists* (London, 1938).
Brommer, F. *Vasenlisten zur griechischen Heldensage* (Marburg, 1960).   *Vasenlisten*
Bronson, R. C. 'Chariot Racing in Etruria', *Studi in onore di L. Banti* (Rome, 1965), 89–106.
—— 'A Re-examination of the Late Attic Geometric Hydria no. 1212 in the Villa Giulia', *AJA*, 68 (1964), 174–8.
Budge, E. A. W. *Assyrian Sculptures in the British Museum in the reign of Ashur-nasir-pal, 885–860 B.C.* (London, 1914).
Burn, A. R. *The Lyric Age of Greece* (London, 1960).
Burr, D. 'A Geometric House and a Proto-Attic Votive Deposit', *Hesperia*, 2 (1933), 542–640.
Callipolitis-Feytmans, D. 'Dinos corinthien de Vari', *AE* (1970), 86–113.
Caskey, J. L. 'The Trojan War', *JHS*, 84 (1964), 1–20. (Part author)
Cassin, E. 'A propos du char de guerre en Mésopotamie', see Vernant, J-P.   *Problèmes*
Charbonneaux, J. 'Deux Grandes Fibules Géométriques', *Préhistoire*, 1 (1932), 191ff.
Coldstream, J. N. *Greek Geometric Pottery* (London, 1968).   GGP
Cook, J. M. 'The Agamemnoneion', *BSA*, 48 (1953), 30–68.
—— *The Greeks in Ionia and the East* (London, 1962).
—— 'Old Smyrna', *BSA*, 53–4 (1958–9).
—— 'Protoattic Pottery', *BSA*, 35 (1934–5), 165–219.
Cook, R. M. 'Dogs in Battle', *Festschrift Andreas Rumpf* (Cologne, 1950), pp. 38–42.
—— *Greek Painted Pottery* (London, 1960; 2nd edn. 1972).   GPP
—— 'Ionia and Greece: 800–600 B.C.', *JHS*, 66 (1946), 67–98.
Corpus Vasorum Antiquorum   CVA
Courbin, P. 'La Guerre en Grèce à haute époque d'après les documents archéologiques', see Vernant, J-P.   *Problèmes*
Davison, J. M. *Attic Geometric Workshops* (Yale Classical Studies 16, New Haven, 1961).   Davison
Dawkins, R. M. see *Artemis Orthia*.
Delebecque, E. *Le Cheval dans l'Iliade* (Paris, 1951).
Desborough, V. R. d'A. *The Last Mycenaeans and their Successors* (Oxford, 1964).
—— *Protogeometric Pottery* (Oxford, 1952).   PGP
Detienne, M. 'La Phalange: Problèmes et Controverses', see Vernant, J-P.   *Problèmes*
—— 'Remarques sur le char en Grèce', see Vernant, J-P.   *Problèmes*
Diehl, E. *Anthologia Lyrica Graeca* (Teubner text, Leipzig, 1925).   Diehl
Dohrn, T. *Die Schwarzfigurigen Etrusk. Vasen* (Berlin, 1937).   Dohrn
Ducati, P. *Pontische Vasen* (Berlin, 1932).
Dunbabin, T. J. *The Greeks and their Eastern Neighbours* (London, 1957).
—— *The Western Greeks* (Oxford, 1948).
—— see *Perachora*, vol. 1.
Elderkin, G. W. 'The Dioscuri on an Early Protocorinthian Aryballos', *AJA*, 38 (1934), 543–6.
Evans, A. J. 'A Mykenaean Treasure from Aegina', *JHS*, 13 (1892–3), 195–226.
—— *The Palace of Minos* (4 vols., London, 1921–36).   *P of M*
Fairbanks, A. *Athenian White Lecythoi* (New York, 1907).

BIBLIOGRAPHY

—— *Catalogue of Greek and Etruscan Vases I: Early Vases* (Boston Museum of Fine Arts).
Finley, M. I. *Early Greece: The Bronze and Archaic Ages* (London, 1970).
—— 'Homer and Mycenae: Property and Tenure', *Historia*, 6 (1957),   *HMPT*
133–59, and reprinted in *The Language and Background of Homer*, ed. G. S. Kirk (Cambridge, 1964), pp. 191–217. (In the notes, the bracketed numerals refer to the pages in *Historia*.)
—— 'Sparta', see Vernant, J-P.   *Problèmes*
—— 'The Trojan War', *JHS*, 84 (1964), 1–20. (Part author)
—— *The World of Odysseus* (Pelican, Harmondsworth, 1962).
Forrest, W. G. 'Colonization and the Rise of Delphi', *Historia*, 6 (1957), 160–75.
—— *The Emergence of Greek Democracy* (London, 1966).
—— 'The First Sacred War', *BCH*, 80 (1956), 33–52.
Frederiksen, M. W. 'The Campanian Cavalry', *Dialoghi di Archeologia*, 2 (1968), 3–31.
Frödin, C. and Persson, A. W. *Asine: Results of the Swedish Excavations,*   *Asine*
1922–30.
Furtwängler, A. *Sammlung Somzée* (Munich, 1897).
Furtwängler, A. and Loeschcke, G. *Mykenische Vasen* (Berlin, 1886).
Furumark, A. 'Mycenaean IIIc Pottery and its Relation to Cypriote Fabrics', *Opuscula Archaeologica*, 3 (1944), 194–265.
Garbini, G. *The Ancient World* (London, 1966).
Gerhard, E. *Auserlesene Griechische Vasenbilder* (Berlin, 1840–7).   *AV*
Graef, B. *Die antiken Vasen von der Akropolis zu Athen* (Berlin, 1909).   *AcrV.*
Gray, D. H. F. 'Houses in the Odyssey', *CQ*, New Series, 5 (1955), 1–12.
—— 'Metal Working in Homer', *JHS*, 74 (1954), 1–15.
Greenhalgh, P. A. L. 'Patriotism in the Homeric World', *Historia*, 21 (1972) 528–37.
Hall, E. H. *Excavations in Eastern Crete: Vrokastro* (University of   *Vrokastro*
Pennsylvania Museum, Anthropological Publications 3, Philadelphia, 1914).
Hampe, R. *Frühe Griechische Sagenbilder in Böotien* (Athens, 1936).
Hanfmann, G. M. A. 'Archaeology in Homeric Asia Minor', *AJA*, 52 (1948), 135–55.
Helbig, W. 'Les Ἱππεῖς Athéniens', *Mémoires de l'Institut National de*   *Helbig*
France, 37/1 (1904), 157ff.
Higgins, R. A. *Greek Terracottas* (London, 1967).
Hignett, C. *A History of the Athenian Constitution* (Oxford, 1952).
Hood, M. S. F. 'A Mycenaean Cavalryman', *BSA*, 48 (1953), 84ff.
Jacoby, F. *Die Fragmente der griechischen Historiker*.   *Jacoby*
—— 'The Date of Archilochus', *CQ*, 35 (1941), 97–109.
Jamot, P. 'Terres cuites archaïques de Tanagre', *BCH*, 14 (1890), 204–23.
Johansen, K. F. 'Clazomenian Sarcophagus Studies', *Acta Archaeologica*, 13 (1942), 1–64.
—— *The Iliad in Early Greek Art* (English translation, Copenhagen, 1967).
—— *Les Vases Sicyoniens* (Copenhagen, 1923).   *VS*
Karageorghis, V. 'A Mycenaean Horse Rider', *Bulletin van de Vereeniging tot bevordering der Kennis van de antieke beschaving*, 33 (1958), 38–42.

BIBLIOGRAPHY

Karo, G. *Die Schachtgräber von Mykenai* (Munich, 1930).
Karouzou, S. *The Amasis Painter* (Oxford, 1956).
Kerameikos: Ergebnisse der Ausgrabungen (6 vols., Berlin, 1939-70). *Kerameikos*
Kirk, G. S. 'The Homeric Poems as History', *Cambridge Ancient History* HPH
  (Cambridge, 1964), vol. 2, ch. 39(b).
—— 'Objective Dating Criteria in Homer', *Museum Helveticum*, 17 (1960), ODC
  189–205, and reprinted in *The Language and Background of Homer*, ed.
  G. S. Kirk, (Cambridge, 1964), pp. 174–90. (In the notes, the bracketed
  numerals refer to the pages in *Museum Helveticum*.)
—— 'Ships on Attic Geometric Vases', *BSA*, 44 (1949), 93–153.
—— *The Songs of Homer* (Cambridge, 1962). SH
—— 'The Trojan War', *JHS*, 84 (1964), 1–20. (Part author)
—— 'War and the Warrior in the Homeric Poems', see Vernant, J-P. *Problèmes*
Kourouniotes, K. 'Αγγεῖα 'Ερετρίας, *AE* (1903), 1–38.
Kübler, K. *Altattische Malerei* (Tübingen, 1950).
—— see *Kerameikos*
Langlotz, E. *Griechische Vasen in Würzburg* (Munich, 1932). G.V. in Würz.
—— *The Art of Magna Graecia* (London, 1965).
Leaf, W. 'The Homeric Chariot', *JHS*, 5 (1884), 185–94.
Lejeune, M. 'La Civilisation Mycénienne et la Guerre', see Vernant, J-P. *Problèmes*
Lobel, E. and Page, D. L. *Poetarum Lesbiorum Fragmenta* (Oxford, 1955). Lobel-Page
Lorimer, H. L. *Homer and the Monuments* (London, 1950). HM
—— 'The Hoplite Phalanx', *BSA*, 42 (1947), 76ff.
Lücken, G. von 'Archaische griechische Vasenmalerei und Plastik', *AM*, 44
  (1919), 47–174.
MacQuitty, W. *Abu Simbel* (London, 1965).
Marangou, E. L. I. *Lakonische Elfenbein- und Beinschnitzereien* (Tübingen,
  1969).
Markman, S. D. *The Horse in Greek Art* (Baltimore, 1943).
Martha, J. *Figurines en Terre Cuite du Musée de la Soc. Arch. d'Athènes* (Paris,
  1880).
Mercklin, E. von *Der Rennwagen in Griechenland* (Leipzig, 1909).
Metzger, H. and Berchem, D. van 'Hippeis', *Gestalt und Geschichte:* Metzger-
  Festschrift K. Schefold (Berne, 1967), pp. 155–8. Berchem
Momigliano, A. D. 'An Interim Report on the Origins of Rome', *JRS*, 53
  (1963), 95–121.
Müller, W. and Oelmann, F. *Tiryns* (1912). *Tiryns*
Murray, A. S. *Terracotta Sarcophagi in the British Museum* (London, 1898).
Mylonas, G. E. 'Burial Customs', *A Companion to Homer*, ed. A. J. B. Wace
  and F. H. Stubbings (London, 1962), pp. 478–88.
Newhall, A. E. 'The Corinthian Kerameikos', *AJA*, 35 (1931), 1–30.
Nierhaus, R. 'Eine frühgriechische Kampfform', *JdI*, 53 (1938), 90ff.
Olympiabericht: Bericht über die Ausgrabungen in Olympia (1936–62).
Oppenheim, M. von *Tell Halaf: A New Culture in Oldest Mesopotamia*
  (London, 1931).
Page, D. L. *History and the Homeric Iliad* (Berkeley, 1959). HHI
—— *Sappho and Alcaeus* (Oxford, 1955).
—— 'The Trojan War', *JHS*, 84 (1964), 1–20 (Part author)
Parry, M. *L'Epithète traditionnelle dans Homère* (Paris, 1928).

BIBLIOGRAPHY

Payne, H. G. G. *Necrocorinthia* (Oxford, 1931).   *NC*
—— see *Perachora*, vol. 2.
—— *Protokorinthische Vasenmalerei* (Berlin, 1933).   *PV*
Pellegrini, G. *Museo Civico di Bologna, Catalogo dei vasi antichi dipinti delle collezioni Palagi e Universitaria* (Bologna, 1900).   Pellegrini
Perachora: The Sanctuaries of Hera Akraia and Limenia (2 vols., Oxford, 1940, 1962).   *Perachora*
Perrot, G. and Chipiez, C. *Histoire de l'Art dans l'Antiquité* (Paris, 1890–1914).
Pfuhl, E. *Malerei und Zeichnung der Griechen* (Munich, 1923).   Pfuhl
—— 'Der archaische Friedhof am Stadtberge von Thera', *AM*, 28 (1903), 1–290.
Pottier, E. *Vases Antiques du Louvre* (Paris, 1897).   Pottier
Powell, T. G. E. *The Celts* (London, 1958).
—— 'Some Implications of Chariotry', *Culture and Environment, Essays in honour of Sir Cyril Fox*, ed. I. Ll. Foster and L. Alcock (London, 1963), pp. 153–69.
Prosymna see Blegen, C. W.   *Prosymna*
Reichel, W. *Homerische Waffen* (Vienna, 1901).
Richter, G. M. A. *The Archaic Gravestones of Attica* (London, 1961).
—— *Archaic Greek Art* (New York and Oxford, 1949).
—— 'Two Colossal Athenian Geometric Vases in the Metropolitan Museum of Art', *AJA*, 19 (1915), 385ff.
Robinson, D. M. and Harcum, C. G. *Greek Vases in Toronto* (Toronto, 1930).
Roebuck, C. A. *Ionian Trade and Colonization* (New York, 1959).
Rumpf, A. *Chalkidische Vasen* (Berlin and Leipzig, 1927).   Rumpf
—— *Sakonides* (Leipzig, 1937).
Santerre, H. G. de *Délos Primitive et Archaique* (Paris, 1958).
Schaeffer, C. F. A. *Ugaritica* (3 vols., 1939–56).
Schede, M. *Meisterwerke der Turkischen Museen zu Konstantinopel* (Berlin and Leipzig, 1928).
Schefold, K. *Frühgriechische Sagenbilder* (Munich, 1964).
Schliemann, H. *Tiryns* (London, 1886).
Sealey, R. 'Regionalism in Archaic Athens', *Historia*, 9 (1960), 155–80.
Snodgrass, A. M. 'Barbarian Europe and Early Iron Age Greece', *Prehistoric Society Proceedings*, 31 (1965), 231.
—— *Early Greek Armour and Weapons* (Edinburgh, 1964).   *EGAW*
—— 'The Hoplite Reform and History', *JHS*, 85 (1965), 110–22.
Stevenson Smith, W. *Interconnections in the Ancient Near East* (New Haven and London, 1965).
Strasburger, H. 'Der Soziologische Aspekt der homerischen Epen', *Gymnasium*, 60 (1953), 97–114.
Strong, D. E. *The Classical World* (London, 1965).
Studniczka, F. 'Der Rennwagen im syrisch-phönikischen Gebiet', *JdI*, 22 (1907), 147–96.
Tarn, W. W. *Hellenistic Military and Naval Developments* (Cambridge, 1930).
Technau, W. *Exekias* (Leipzig, 1936).

BIBLIOGRAPHY

Tiryns see Müller, W.   *Tiryns*
Ventris, M. and Chadwick, J. *Documents in Mycenaean Greek* (Cambridge, 1956).
Vernant, J-P. *Problèmes de la Guerre en Grèce Ancienne* (Paris, 1968). Details of the relevant contributions will be found under the names of the separate authors: P. Courbin, M. Detienne, M. I. Finley, G. S. Kirk, and M. Lejeune.   *Problèmes*
Vos, M. F. *Scythian Archers in Archaic Attic Vase-Painting* (Archaeologica Traiectina 6, Gröningen, 1963).   Vos
Wace, A. J. B. and Stubbings, F. H. *A Companion to Homer* (London, 1962). Details of the relevant contributions will be found under the names of the separate authors: C. Mylonas and T. B. L. Webster.   *CH*
Waldstein, C. *The Argive Heraeum* (Boston, 1902–5).   *Argive Heraeum*

Walters, H. B. *Select Bronzes in the British Museum* (London, 1915).
Webster, T. B. L. 'Homer and Attic Geometric Vases', *BSA*, 50 (1955), 38–50.
—— 'Polity and Society', *A Companion to Homer*, ed. A. J. B. Wace and F. H. Stubbings (London, 1962), pp. 452–62.
Wiesner, J. 'Fahren und Reiten', *Archaeologica Homerica* (Göttingen, 1968), vol. 1, ch. F.   *Arch. Hom.*
Willemsen, F. *Olympische Forschungen* (Berlin, 1957), vol. 3.
Winter, F. *Die Typen der figürlichen Terrakotten* (Berlin, 1903).
Wreszinski, W. *Atlas zur altaegyptischen Kulturgeschichte* (3 vols., Leipzig, 1914–40).
Young, R. S. 'Late Geometric Graves and a Seventh Century Well in the Agora', *Hesperia*, Supp. 2 (1939).

GENERAL INDEX

(*A list of Greek words follows on p. 212*)

Abantes, in the *Iliad*, 91
Abu Simbel, battle-reliefs, 9, 10, 31, 176 n. 11
Acamas, named on Attic vase, 133
Achilles, in Homer, 161-4, 168-9; in vase-paintings, 98, 118-19, 129
Acropolis, of Athens, 111, 113, 115
Adcock, F. E., 74, 179 n. 37
Aeneas, in Homer, 55, 173 n. 18; named on Corinthian vase, 98
Aeneas Tacticus, 16
Agamemnon, in Homer, 7, 161, 169, (relationship to other kings) 167-8, 185 n. 62
Agora, Athenian, 36, 113
Agricola, of Tacitus, 15
Ahhijawa, 11
Ahlberg, G., 66-7
Ajax, in the *Iliad*, 53, 157-8, 169, 178 n. 6; in vase-paintings, 36, 98, 124; name possibly on Linear B tablet, 158
Albertinum Group, Clazomenian sarcophagi, 145
Alcaeus, 93-4, 151, 153-4, 167
Alcinous, in the *Odyssey*, 164-5, 169
Alcmaeonidae, of Athens, 152
Alexander the Great, cavalry of, 79
Alföldi, A., 5, 75-6, 96-8, 103-6, 117, 135
Amasis painter, 124
Amazons, 124, 128-33, 181 nn. 17, 25
Amphidamas, Chalcidian nobleman, 36
anax, Homeric and Mycenaean meanings, 160-1, 167-8
Anchimolius, Spartan invasion of Attica under, 80-1, 92, 149, 181 n. 24
Anderson, J. K., 2, 14-17, 108, 115
Andrewes, A., 72
Andromache, named on 'Chalcidian' vase-painting, 138
Anticleia, in the *Odyssey*, 162
antilabe, 137; *see also* shields (post-Geometric types, hoplite)
Antilochus, in the *Iliad*, 28, 177 n. 59
Antinous, in the *Odyssey*, 160
Arabia, chariotry, 16

archaizing and heroizing: by Homeric bards, 1-3, 6, 18, 38-9, 41-2, 53-8, 61, 156-7, 159-60, 163-70; by vase-painters, 1, 3-5, 18, 35-6, 38, 50, 60-1, 63-5, 70, 82-3, 90, 98, 110-12, 124, 126, 133-4, 136-8
archers, chariot-borne, 2, 9-13, **16-17**, 59, 173 n. 18; foot, 78, 90-2, 94-**5**, **124**, 180 nn. 25-7, (Scythian) 92, 120, 124, 134, 149; mounted, 91, 115, 122, 137-43, 148, 176 n. 11, 180 n. 18
Archilochus, of Paros, 5, 73, 90-3
Argive vase-painting, Geometric, 46, 49, 68-9
Argos, finds from, 46, 48, 51, 158; hoplite army of, 153; relations with Mycenae, 167
Aristarchus, editor of Homer, 53, 175 n. 33
Aristodemus, of Cumae, 153
Aristotle, 3, 42, 44, 53, 74-5, 91, 93, 136, 146, 150, 167, 171
Arrian, *Tactica*, 181 n. 10
Artemis Amarynthia, sanctuary near Eretria, 91
Artemis Orthia, sanctuary at Sparta, 94-5
'ashen-speared', Homeric epithet, 158
Ashur-nasir-pal, King of Assyria, 28
Asia, chariotry, 3, 9-12, 16-17, 19, 28-31, 40, 43-4
Asine, finds from, 51
Assyrians, cavalry, 44; chariotry, 9, 12, 28-9, 44, 173 n. 18
Athens; *see under separate headings*, e.g. Alcmaeonidae, cavalry, mounted infantry, Sicily (Athenian expedition to)
Attic vase-painting, Black Figure, 5, 21, 25, 29, 70, 77, 90, 96, 101-3, 105, 108, 110-36, 147-9; Geometric, 2-3, 13, 19-39, 47-52, 63-70, 76, 88-9, 146; Protoattic, 73, 89-90, 147, 175 n. 29; Red Figure, 130, 144
axe-heads, Protogeometric finds of, 41
axle, of chariot: central, 19-21; rear, 38; shown in Geometric art, 35

Babes, squire of Hippaemon, 145
Babylon, chariots and horses, 43
Bacchiadae, of Corinth, 153

206

GENERAL INDEX

Barca, troop-transports, 16
basileus, Homeric and Mycenaean meanings, 160-1, 168
Bellerophon, depicted in Archaic art, 84, 137, 142
Beowulf, 160
bier; *see* hearse
Black Figure; *see* Attic, Etruscan
boar's tusk helmet, Mycenaean survival in Homer, 157
Boeotia, army 136; coins, 70; emphasis of in Homeric Catalogue, 158; fibulae 18, 20, 32, 50, 173 n. 22; vase-painting, 13, 136, 174 n. 8; *see also* shield (post-Geometric types, 'Boeotian')
Boghaz-Keui, 11
Borelli painter, Clazomenian sarcophagi, 143-5
bosses, on shields, 89, 138, 180 n. 37
bow; *see* archers
British, chariotry, 2, 14-15
Bronson, R. C., 26, 28, 36
bronze, as Homeric metal, 41, 53, 159, 170; representations in, 29, 51, 143
Bronze Age; *see under separate headings*, e.g. chariots, shields etc
'bronze-corsleted', '-helmeted', Homeric epithets, 158, 168
burial customs, 37, 162-3; *see also* cremation, funeral games

Caesar, war-chariotry in, 14-15
Callinus, of Ephesus, 93
Callipolitis-Feytmans, D., 86
Calydon, in Homer, 162, 169
Camarina, Athenian march to, 81
Cannae, battle of, 61
Cassin, E., 12
Catalogue, in the *Iliad*, 91, 158
cataphract cavalry, Parthian, 78
cauldrons, as valuables, 37, 161; bronze from Olympia, 51
cavalry
  development and roles in Archaic Greece, 4-5, 76, 78-81, 99, 135-6, 147-50
  'identified' in Homer, 54-6
  seventh-century: Athenian, 88-9; Corinthian, 84, 88; East Greek, 93; Euboean, 92-3; Spartan, 94-5
  sixth-century: Athenian (armoured) 111, 113, 116-18, 122-3, 125-6, 128-34, 148-9, (unarmoured) 110-12, 114-15, 117-18, 122-9, 131, 135, 148; 'Chalcidian', 139-43, 148; Corinthian (armoured) 99-100, 102-3, 108-9, 143, 148, (unarmoured) 109-11, 148; East Greek, 144-5
  For cavalry of other states, see under separate headings, e.g. Assyrians, Etruria, Macedon, Thessaly; *see also* archers (mounted), horsemen, mounted infantry, spears (used by cavalry)

Cebriones, named squire on 'Chalcidian' vase, 138
Celts, chariotry and horsemen, 9, 14-15, 61
Ceramicus, finds from, 47, 49, 89
'Chalcidian' vase-painting, 5, 82, 92, 136-43, 147-8
Chalcis, 36, 42, 75, 91-3, 136, 148
chariot
  Bronze Age Greek: classification of Mycenaean types, 19, 30-3, 37; military roles, 1-3, 7-12, 40; racing, 36-7, 185 n. 56; technology and connexion with palace-type society, 2, 12, 17, 40, 43-4, 58
  Geometric Age Greek: classification of representations, 19-25, 35; heroic property in battle-scenes, 3, 13-14, 17, 38, 46, 52, 63; identification as contemporary racing-chariots, 2, 21, 25-9, 33, 35-7; supposed influences on, 2, 18, 21, 30-7
  in Homer: essential aristocratic possession, 3, 7, 12, 15, 40, 42-3, 53; generally unrealistic use of, 1-3, 7-17, 28-9, 38-40, 54, 58-9, 61-3; military roles belong to Geometric Age mounted horse, 3, 41-2, 53-63, 119, 146, 156, 159, 168, 170; racing, 3, 28, 35-8, 170-1; technical vocabulary, 36, 39, 53-4
  non-Greek chariot-powers: 2, 9-10, 12, 14-17, 19, 28-9, 31, 40, 43-4; *see further under separate headings*, e.g. Assyrians, Hittites, etc
  post-Geometric Greek: Cyrenaic, 2, 14-17; racing-chariots 2, 19, 21, 25, 36, 86, 89; used as heroic property in Archaic battle-scenes, 25, 29, 90, 115, 119, 143-4
  For parts and construction, see under separate headings, e.g. axle, pole, rails, teams
charioteers, robed as racing-drivers, 22-3, 26-7, 36, 89-90, 176 n. 51; role as squire in Homer, 60-1, 177 n. 59
Chigi vase, 85-6
Chryse, in the *Iliad*, 164
Chryseis, in the *Iliad*, 161
Cicones, in the *Odyssey*, 56
Cimmerians, 144
Clazomenian sarcophagi, 5, 82, 93, 143-5, 147, 180 n. 18
Cleomachus, of Thessaly, 92
Cleomenes, of Sparta, 149
Cnossos, finds from, 10-11, 31, 45
coins, Boeotian, 70
Coldstream, J. N., 52
Colophon, 42, 93, 162, 164
contraction, in Homeric language, 170
Cook, J. M., 164
Cook, R. M., 145
Corinth; *see under separate headings*, e.g. cavalry, Cypselus, mounted infantry

207

GENERAL INDEX

Corinthian vase-painting, Protocorinthian, 26, 59–60, 69, 74, 84–6, 147; Ripe Corinthian, 5, 59–60, 84–8, 96–111, 113, 142, 147–8
corslet, on Linear B tablets, 10, 45; from Argos, 46, 158; worn by horsemen, 47, 103, 116, 129, 131, 140, 148, 181 n. 7
cremation, 162–3, 170, 184 n. 28
Cremera, battle of, 151
cuirass; *see* corslet
Cumae, 153
cutlass, Persian cavalry weapon, 144
Cylon, of Athens, 152–4
Cyprus, 17–18, 39, 63
Cypselus, of Corinth, 153
Cyrene, chariotry, 2, 14–17
Cyrus, chariotry of, 16–17

daggers, Protogeometric finds of, 41
Dawkins, R. M., 95
Delebecque, E., 38, 53–7
Demodocus, named on 'Chalcidian' vase, 141–2
Demophon, named on Attic vase, 133
Desultortechnik, 105, 117
Detienne, M., 8, 70, 75
digamma, ignored in Homer, 170
Diodorus, 14–15
Diomedes, in the *Iliad*, 8, 38, 54–7, 173 n. 18
Dionysius, of Syracuse, 154
Dioscuri, depicted as riders, 47
Dipylon, cemetery, 52; *see also* shields (Geometric Age types: 'Dipylon')
dove-cup, Nestor's, 157
Dorylaeum, grave stele from, 145
'dual-chariot', Bronze Age Greek type, 30–1

East Greece and 'East Greek' vase-painting, 5, 82, 93–4, 143–5
Egypt, cavalry, 44; chariotry and horses, 9–10, 17, 31, 43
'Egyptian' type of chariot in Geometric art, 19–20
Eion, siege of, 150
Elpenor, in the *Odyssey*, 163
Eniopeus, in the *Iliad*, 8
Ephesus, 93
Eretria, 42, 75, 82, 90–1, 93
ethos, heroic in Homer, 165–6, 168–9
Etruria, 28, 82, 136, 141–2, 150–1, 179 n. 7, 180 n. 18
Etruscan Black Figure vase-painting, 82, 141, 179 n. 7, 180 n. 18
Euboea, 5, 73, 90–4, 141, 145, 147–8
Eumaeus, in the *Odyssey*, 76, 160
Eumenes, of Cardia, 61
Euphorbus, in the *Iliad*, 8
Evans, A. J., 30, 45

Fabii, Roman *gens*, 151
feudal system, 3, 40, 160, 168
fibulae, 18, 20, 32, 50, 94–5, 173 n. 22

'figure-of-eight' shield, 65, 158
Finley, M. I., 37, 160, 167–8
'flaps', of Mycenaean chariots, 31–2, 37, 175 n. 21
formulae, as Homeric dating criteria, 163, 170
Forrest, W. G., 72, 91
Frederiksen, M. W., 80
Frödin, C., 51
funeral games, 28, 35–6, 64, 163, 171

Gaul, chariotry, 14–15
genealogies, in Homer, 156
'glittering-helmeted', Homeric epithet, 158
gold relief, 51
Gorgon painter, 90
greaves, worn by horsemen, 100–2, 108, 129, 131, 141
Grumentum, bronze horseman from, 85, 143

Hannibal, cavalry of, 61
Hattusas, 11, 43
hearse, in Geometric art, 21, 34–5
Hector, in Archaic art, 98, 124, 138; in the *Iliad*, 7–8, 53–4, 158, 168–9
hektemoroi, at Athens, 154
Helbig, W., 4–5, 60, 75–6, 85, 94, 96, 110, 117, 135
Helen, of Troy, 168
'Helladic', type of chariot, 32; *see also* chariot (Bronze Age Greek)
Hellespont, Athenian involvement in, 115, 148
Hera, chariot of in the *Iliad*, 37–8
Hermus, plain of, 93
Herodotus, 80–1, 91
heroizing; *see* archaizing and heroizing
Hesiod, 36, 39, 163, 171
Hippaemon, Archaic epitaph of, 145
Hippeis, of Athens, 82; of Eretria, 82, 90–3, 147; of Sparta, 94, 147
hippobatas-hippostrophos combination, 59–60, 84, 96–7, 113, 119
Hippobotae, of Chalcis, 91–3, 136, 147
Hippocles, on Corinthian vase-painting, 98
Hippolyte, on 'Chalcidian' vase-painting, 142
hippostrophos; see *hippobatas*
Hirschfeld crater, 34
Hittites, cavalry, 44, 176 n. 11; chariotry, 9–11, 31, 43
Hood, M. S. F., 45, 51
hoplites, and development of cavalry, 4, 78–81, 99, 147; effect on war-horse as transport animal, 4, 75–8, 99, 146–7; items of panoply, 74; phalanx formation, 71–4, 78–81, 146; possible allusions in Homer, 55, 170; sociology and political role, 4–5, 74–8, 150–5; *for mounted hoplites, see* mounted infantry
horse-guard, on Mycenaean vase, 45

208

GENERAL INDEX

horsemen, aristocratic and military dominance of, 3–5, 40, 42–3, 53, 59–60, 75–6, 91, 93, 136, 146, 150–1; Bronze Age representations, 43–6; criteria for assessing roles of non-combatants in Archaic art, (greaves) 100–2, 108, (second horse) 100, 103–8, 135–6, (shield) 89, 100, 102, 107–8, 113, 116, 118, 130–4, (number of spears) 89, 100, 108–9, 113, 134, 139; Geometric representations, 46–52, 63, 88; in Homer, 3, 40–2, 45, 53–4, 56–62; *see further* cavalry, mounted infantry *and place-names*, e.g. Egypt, Macedon, Thessaly etc
horseshoes, 81

inscriptions, heroic on vases, 60, 83, 98, 110, 112, 124, 136–8
Iolcos, finds from, 65
Ionia, colonies and colonization, 40, 163–4; cremation, 162; racing-chariots, 38
Iran, cavalry, 79
iron, in Homer, 161–2, 170
Iron Age, Protogeometric period in, 41
Italy, 136; *see also* Etruria
Ithaca, civil strife at, 166
ivories, from Artemis Orthia, 94–5

javelin; *see* spears (throwing)
javelin-container, of war-chariots, 9–10
javelineers, on foot in hoplite warfare, 78, 94, 124, 180 nn. 25, 27; *for mounted javelineers, see* cavalry *and* spears (throwing, used by cavalry)

Kadesh, battle of, 9, 176 n. 11
Karo, G., 11
Kavousi, figurine from, 45
kingship, 3, 42, 160–1, 166, 171
Kirk, G. S., 12, 14, 17, 157–9, 165, 167, 170
knives, Protogeometric finds of, 41

lance; *see* spears (thrusting)
land, Homeric and Mycenaean tenure, 160
Langlotz, E., 143
Laodocus, squire of Antilochus, 177 n. 59
Leaf, W., 55
Lechaeum aryballos, 69–70
Lejeune, M., 10, 12
Lelantine Plain, war of, 91–2
Lesbos, 93–4, 151; *see also* Mytilene
Lethargos, dog of Hippaemon, 145
Linear B tablets, 10–12, 31, 45, 158, 160–1, 170
Livy, 104
Lorimer, H. L., 11, 19–20, 31–2, 38, 45, 55, 65–7, 70–1, 161, 163
Lücken, G. von, 143
Luxor, battle-reliefs, 176 n. 11
Lycaon, in the *Iliad*, 37
Lycurgus, of Athens, 154
Lydia, horsemen, 93
Lydos, Attic vases, 119

Lysippides, Attic vases, 122

Macedon, cavalry, 59, 79, 177 n. 58
Maeander, river, 42
Magnesia, 42, 93, 145
Marangou, E. L. I., 94
Marathon, plain, 154
Media, chariotry, 16
Mediaeval cavalry, 78–9
Megacles, of Athens, 154
Megara, 152
Meleager, Homeric anecdote of, 169
Menelaus, in the *Iliad*, 167
Menestheus, in the *Iliad*, 56
Meno, of Pharsalus, 150–1
Mercklin, E. von, 31–2
metal inlay, technique known in Homer, 183 n. 11
Middle East, Bronze Age powers, 43
Midea, relations with Mycenae, 167
migrations, past event in Homer, 166
Molione, depicted in vase-paintings, 13, 34, 36, 52, 175 n. 29
Mouliana crater, 46, 176 n. 21
mounted infantry, advantages in hoplite warfare, 4, 75–8, 147; Athenian, (seventh-century) 88–90, (sixth century) 60, 77, 105–6, 111–14, 117–21, 130–5, 147; 'Chalcidian' (sixth-century), 60, 137–9, 142–3, 147–8; Corinthian, (seventh-century) 59–60, 84–8, (sixth-century) 60, 96–8, 101–9, 147; East Greek, (seventh-century) 93, (sixth-century) 144–5, 147; Etruscan, 179 n. 7, 180 n. 18; Euboean (seventh-century) 90–3, 147; Geometric Age, 3, 42–4, 52, 59–63, 75–6, 146; heroized by Homeric bards, 3, 41–2, 53–63; Spartan, 94–5, 147; theses of Helbig and Alföldi, 60, 75–6, 85, 96–8, 103–6, 110, 117, 135; *see also* archers (mounted), cavalry, horsemen
mule-car, Priam's in the *Iliad*, 38
Mycenae, finds from, 11–12, 30–2, 45–6, 51, 157; possible suzerainty 167–8
Mycenaeans, nature of Mycenaean states, 2–3, 12, 17, 37, 40, 43–4, 160–1, 164, 167–8; possible survivals in Homer, 8, 10, 12, 18, 157–9, 165–6, 170; vase-painting, 30–3, 44–6; *see also under separate headings*, e.g. burial customs, chariot (Bronze Age Greek), horsemen (Bronze Age representations), palace-states, shields, spears
Mylonas, G. E., 162–3
Mytilene, 151, 153–4, 167; *see also* Lesbos

Nabis, of Sparta, 104
Naples lekanis-lid, 110–11
naucraries, 76
Nausicaa, in the *Odyssey*, 165
Nausithous, in the *Odyssey*, 163
Naxos, Lygdamis of, 153; war with Paros, 90
Neleids, 52
Neoptolemus, 61

209

GENERAL INDEX

Nessos amphora, 90
Nestor, in the *Iliad*, 7–10, 12, 28, 157, 166
Nicias, of Athens, 81
Nierhaus, R., 71

Odysseus, in the *Iliad*, 3, 54–7, 169; in the *Odyssey*, 53, 76, 160, 163, 165, 167, 169; palace of, 183 n. 11 (Appendix)
Olympia, finds from, 32–3, 38, 51; four-horse chariot-race at, 27
Orestes, of Thessaly, 150

Page, D. L., 94, 157–8
palace-states, 2–3, 12, 17, 40, 43–4, 58, 160–1, 164, 168
Palatine Anthology, epigram, 145
Pallene, battle of, 153
Panachaean theme, in Homer, 167–9
Pandarus, in the *Iliad*, 7, 173 n. 18
Paros, war with Naxos, 90
Parthia, cavalry, 78, 101
pa₂-si-re-u, on Linear B tablets, 161
patriotism, in Homer, 168–9
Patroclus, in the *Iliad*, 8, 54, (funeral) 28, 35, 163
Pausanias, 27, 61
Peloponnesian War, 150
pelta, 131–2
Peneus, plains of, 149
Pentacosiomedimnoi, at Athens, 82
Penthesilea, shield 51, 68; on Attic vase, 129
Perachora, finds from, 51
Periphetes, in the *Iliad*, 158
Persia, cavalry, 143–5, 179 n. 37
Persson, A. W., 51
Phaeacia, in the *Odyssey*, 163, 166, 169; see also Scheria
phalanx: see hoplites, mounted infantry
Phalerum, battle of, 80–1, 92
Phegeus, in the *Iliad*, 8
Pheidon, of Argos, 153
Philopoemen, 104
Phoenix, on Corinthian vase, 98; in the *Iliad*, 169
Pisistratidae, of Athens, 81, 92, 149, 152–3
Pisistratus, of Athens, 152–4
Pittacus, of Mytilene, 153–4
Plutarch, 61, 92
Podargos, horse of Hippaemon, 145
pole, of chariots, 14, 37–8; 'pole-end support', 19, 37–8, 175 n. 44
polemarch, at Corinth, 153–4
Pollux, 76, 104, 179 n. 33
Polybius, 61
Polyphemus, in the *Odyssey*, 162
'Pontic' vase-painting; see Etruscan Black Figure
porpax, 131, 137; see also shields (post-Geometric types, hoplite)
Poseidon, temple of in Scheria, 164
Powell, T. G. E., 9
Priam's mule-car, in the *Iliad*, 38

Prosymna, finds from, 45
Pylos, chariot-wheels at, 10; Neleids of, 52; royal household of, 160
pyxis-lids, horses on Attic LG, 27, 36

quadriga, 28–9, 53; see also chariot, teams
quivers, attached to war-chariots, 10; of mounted archers, 141–3, 180 n. 18

rails, of chariot, 20–5, 32, 35–8
Rhesus, in the *Iliad*, 38, 54–7
rhipsaspia, in Alcaeus, 94
Richter, G. M. A., 132
riders (unarmed), figurines of, 51; on Geometric vases, 46–7, 88; on Protoattic vases, 90; on Protocorinthian vases, 47, 84; see also cavalry, horsemen, mounted infantry
riding, art known in Bronze Age Greece, 45–6; in Homer, 3, 40–1, 53–6
Roland, Song of, 160
Rome, cavalry, 61
'Rosellini' chariot, 20, 31–2, 35

Sacred War, First, 148
'saddle-cloths', 181 n. 8
sarcophagi, Clazomenian, 5, 82, 93, 143–5, 147, 180 n. 18
Sarpedon, on Corinthian vase, 98
Schaeffer, C. F. A., 44
Schede, M., 145
Scheria, in the *Odyssey*, 42, 163–6, 169–70; see also Phaeacia
scythe-chariots, 17
Scythians, cavalry, 118, 120, 127, 129, 131, 144, 149, 178 n. 23; foot-archers, 92, 120, 124, 134, 149
sea-battles and raids, in Geometric art, 53, 76
shaft-graves, Mycenaean, 11–12, 30, 157, 175 n. 35
shields
  Bronze Age types: body-shields, 65, 73, 157–8, 170; Hittite incurved-edge type, 178 n. 5; small round shields, 65
  Geometric Age types: 'Dipylon' incurved-edge type, 4, 34, 46–7, 63–70; pre-hoplite round, 64–8, 178 n. 9; rectangular, 64–7
  post-Geometric types: 'Boeotian', 50, 64, 70, 83, 98, 110–11, 124, 126, 133–4, 137; hoplite, properties of, 69–74, 79, (as cavalry shield) 88, 102–3, 107–8, 117–18, 122, 130–2, 134, (oval type on 'Chalcidian' vases) 137–8, (slung on back) 108, 130, 181 nn. 17, 25; pelta, 131–2
'Siana' cups, 105, 112–13, 115
Sicily, Athenian expedition to, 4, 80–1, 180 n. 26
siege-warfare, in Homer, 166
similes in Homer, 'horse's cheek-piece', 54–5; riding revealed in, 53–6
slingers, 78, 90–4, 180 nn. 25–7

210

GENERAL INDEX

Smyrna, Old, 42, 164, 166
Snodgrass, A. M., 2, 8, 13, 18–20, 29, 32–4, 41, 45, 51, 55, 63–4, 70–1, 75, 93, 150
Solon, of Athens, 82, 154
Sparta, 73–4, 80, 94–5, 147, 151–2, 168
Spartolus, battle of, 136
spears
    throwing-spears (javelins): as chariot-weapon, 2–3, 8–10, 13–15, 40, 59, 173 n. 18; Bronze Age, 11–12; Geometric, 2, 13–14, 41, 59, 63; Homeric, 2, 8–9, 40–2, 59, 170, (archaizing bronze of) 41–2, 159, 168; used by cavalry, 59, 78–9, 91, 100, 104, 112, 114–15, 122–3, 126, 148, 177 n. 58; used with 'Dipylon' and pre-hoplite shields, 68–9; used with hoplite shield, 71, 73, 91–2, 94, 178 n. 20
    thrusting-spear (lance): as chariot-weapon, 7–13, 59, 173 n. 15; Bronze Age, 8–12, 41; Geometric, 13; Homeric, 7–9; used by cavalry, 78–9, 91, 100, 107–8, 116, 122, 126, 128–9, 148; used by hoplites, 59, 71–4, 91, 94, 97, 119, 178 n. 20
spearheads, Protogeometric finds of, 41
spoke-wheels, invention of, 2, 9
squires, possibly indicated by second horse, 47, 87–8, 106, 117; roles, 3, 55, 59–63, 77, 109, 112, 118, 135, 146, 177 n. 59; shown with second horse, 59, 77, 84–6, 88, 96–8, 105–6, 112–13, 120–1, 135, 142; with single horse, 60, 84–5, 110, 114, 143, 179 n. 6
Sthenelus, squire of Diomedes, 55
stirrups, value of, 78–9
Strabo, 91
Strasburger, H., 161, 165
sword, as cavalry weapon, 91, 144, 180 n. 18; as hoplite weapon, 71, 73–4, 91, 147, 179 n. 7, 180 n. 18; as pre-hoplite weapon, 63; Chalcidian (Euboean), 73, 90–4; Protogeometric finds of, 41; used by Celtic chariot-borne warriors, 15
Syracuse, cavalry, 80–1; under Dionysius, 154
Syria, cavalry, 44; chariotry, 12, 16

Tacitus, *Agricola*, 15
Tanagra, finds from, 29, 51
'Tarentine' cavalry, 104
Tawagalawas, 11
teams, of chariot-horses: four, 16–17, 27–9, 35–6, 52–3, 174 n. 15, 175 n. 33; single (impossible in practice), 34, 174 n. 4, 175 n. 25; three, 27–9, 35–6, 52, 175 nn. 27, 33
technical vocabulary, for the chariot in Homer, 38–9, 53–4
Tegea, finds from, 51
telamon, mentioned in the *Iliad*, 178 n. 6, 183 n. 3 (Appendix); of Dipylon shield, 67; of hoplite shield, 73; of Mycenaean body-shield, 158
Telemachus, in the *Odyssey*, 58, 160, 164

Tell Halaf, battle-reliefs, 44
temples, in Homer, 170; development of separate temples, 184 n. 45
Thasos, revetment at, 132
Theagenes, of Megara, 152
Thebes, Egyptian, 164, 183 n. 11 (Appendix)
Theophrastus, 78
Thera, Attic LG bowl from, 47; cremation in, 163
Thessaly, cavalry, 80, 82, 92, 135, 148–51, 181 n. 24
Thracians, 131, 134
throwing-loop, used by mounted javelineer, 122
Thucydides, 4, 72, 80–1, 91, 94, 136
Tiryns, finds from, 32–3, 49, 51, 173 n. 15; relations with Mycenae, 167
'tower-shield', 158
trace-horses, 28
'trainers of horses', on Attic LG vases, 47
triga, 27–9; *see also* chariot, teams
trimarcisia, 61
tripods, 35–7, 51, 161, 170–1, 175 n. 32, 184 n. 20
Troilus, as mounted squire in Archaic art, 118–19, 182 n. 39
Trojan War, as subject in Archaic art, 98, 111, 116, 124, 138; Greek involvement in, 167
Troy, burial customs at, 162
terracottas, chariots, 27, 38, 174 nn. 10, 15; horses, 49–50; racing-driver, 27, 36; riders, 45, 51; shields, 67–9, 105; Thasos revetment, 132; *see also* pyxis-lids, sarcophagi
tyranny, 5, 151–5
Tyrtaeus, 94, 168

Ugarit, 44

Vapheio, sardonyx from, 11, 30
Veientes, at battle of Cremera, 151
Vix, bronze crater from, 29
Vrokastro, Geometric sherd from, 46

waggons, on LG vases, 18, 21, 33–5; as troop-transports, 9, 16
Waldstein, C., 51
wanax, on Linear B tablets, 161, 167
Warrior Stele and Vase, from Mycenae, 11
Webster, T. B. L., 64, 70, 160
'well-greaved', Homeric epithet, 158, 168
wheels, of chariots in Geometric art: single wheel profiles, 20, 22, 34, 175 n. 26, 176 n. 51; two-wheel profiles, 20, 33–4, 176 n. 51; two wheels shown as concentric circles, 22; *see also* spoke-wheels
Willemsen, F., 51

Xenophon, 16, 59, 79, 179 nn. 37, 50
xyston, cavalry weapon, 59, 91, 177 n. 58

zygodesmon, 19, 37–8, 175 n. 44; *see also* pole

211

LIST OF GREEK WORDS

ἄγαπτον, implies 'uncremated' in the Odyssey (11.72), 163
Αἴαντε, dual form in Homer, 158
ἀκροβολισταί, Cyrenaic chariot-borne warriors, 17
ἄμιπποι, 135–6
ἀμφιπποι, 104
γενναῖοι, hoplites classed as by the Old Oligarch, 178 n. 27
δῆμος, hoplites contrasted with by the Old Oligarch, 178 n 27
δίφρος, of Homeric chariot, 37
ἐλατήρ, in Homer, 54–5
ἐπιδιφριάδος, of Homeric chariot (Iliad 10.475), 37
εὐκνήμιδες, Homeric epithet, 158
εὐμμελίης, Homeric epithet, 158
ἡνίοχοι, in Homer, 54
θάπτειν, implies cremation in Homer, 163
ἱππεῖς, unusual Homeric plural, 55
ἱππεύς, ἱππῆες, meaning in Homer, 53–5
ἵπποι, meaning and phrases with in Homer, 55–6, 177 nn. 55, 59
ἱππομάχοι, Mimnermus' description of Lydians, 93
κέλης (ἵππος), κελητίζειν, 53, 177 n. 49
κορυθαίολος, Homeric epithet, 158
μεταβάται, Alföldi's theory of, 105, 117
Μολίονε, dual form in Homer, 158
ὅπλα παρεχόμενοι (οἱ), Greek concept of, 151
ὁπλῖται, social classification in the Old Oligarch, 178 n. 27
παραιβάτης, in Homer, 38, 54, 61
πολιός, Homeric epithet, 161
πολύκμητος, Homeric epithet, 161
πύργον (φέρων σάκος ἠΰτε), 183 n. 3 (Appendix)
τηλεβόλα, banned in Euboea, 91–2, 180 n. 27
φάσγανον ἀργυρόηλον, 158
χαλκοκορυστής, Homeric epithet, 158
χαλκοχιτώνων, Homeric epithet, 158
ψιλοί, acting with cavalry at Spartolus, 136; on Corinthian vase (C9), 97

Printed in Great Britain
by Amazon.co.uk, Ltd.,
Marston Gate.